THE TYRANTS

CLIVE FOSS

Quercus

Quercus Publishing plc
21 Bloomsbury Square
London
WC1A 2NS

First published 2006
Reprinted 2007

A catalogue record for this book is available from the British Library.

ISBN   Cloth case edition 1 905204 79 5
       Printed case edition 1 905204 35 3
       Paperback edition 1 905204 96 5

Printed in Hong Kong

Project management, editing and picture research by the Cambridge Editorial Partnership, Michael Young Centre, Purbeck Road, Cambridge CB2 2PF. Designed by Zoe Naylor.

Acknowledgements

The publisher would like to thank the following for permission to reproduce photographs:

AFP/Getty Images p. 171; Archivo Iconografico, S.A./Corbis p. 75; The Art Archive/Corbis p. 71; Bettmann/Corbis pp. 7, 19, 31, 55, 87, 115, 135, 143, 151, 155, 159; The Bridgeman Art Gallery pp. 11, 23, 51, 107; The British Library p. 59; Corbis p. 139; Courtesy of the Cresswell Archive, Ashmolean Museum and Fine Arts Library, Harvard University p. 47; Alain DeJean/Sygma/Corbis p. 195; Khaled El-Fiqi/EPA/epa/Corbis p. 179; Kevin Fleming/Corbis p. 83; Christel Gerstenberg/Corbis p. 39; Getty Images pp. 63, 67, 91, 95, 111, 119, 175, 183; Handout/Reuters/Corbis p. 147; Hulton-Deutsch Collection/Corbis pp. 123, 127,131; INA/Handout/Reuters/Corbis p. 199; Araldo de Luca/Corbis p. 35; Mary Evans Picture Library p. 103; Alberto Pereira, Embassy of Paraguay, London p. 99; Reuters/Corbis p. 203; Roehnertt/dpa/Corbis p. 27; Keren Su/Corbis p. 15; Sygma/Corbis p. 167; Time Life Pictures/Getty Images pp. 43, 79,163, 191; Horacio Villalobos/Corbis p. 187.

Contents

Dates indicate period of rule.

Introduction

The word 'tyrant' was first used by a Greek poet in the seventh century BC to describe the king of Lydia, the first foreign power to bring Greece under its control. He was referring to something unknown in his own country – an enormously rich ruler who exercised unlimited power. The word he used probably came from the Lydian language. At that time, 'tyrant' was merely descriptive, without any negative connotation. But as Greece fell under the rule of a series of powerful men, the word came to mean something like the modern 'dictator' – a ruler who breaks the rules, and who goes beyond the limits imposed by laws and traditions to take arbitrary power, very often with cruelty or oppression. These are the tyrants described in this volume – rulers who go too far, who exercise more violence and brutality than society normally accepts. Rulers routinely tax, conscript, arrest or even execute their subjects, but hacking off their limbs or burning them alive is not normally part of the job description. The tyrants described here may not all commit such horrendous acts (although a lot of them do), but they all oppress their subjects. Alexander the Great, who killed his best friend and burnt the Persian capital, is not included in this book. Nor is Louis XIV, who herded his courtiers into the garrets of Versailles and sent a minister whose own palace was too grand to prison for life. Alexander was only occasionally a tyrant and Louis's behaviour was not unusual for a monarch in an age of absolutism. Nor does this volume lend space to minor figures – Elisabeth Bathory, who bathed in the blood of virgins, controlled (fortunately) only one castle – or to those without independent power of their own, like Heinrich Himmler, who organized the systematic murder of millions.

Tyrants have played a role since organized states and governments were first formed. There have always been ambitious or aggressive rulers willing to break the rules for their own benefit. The ancient world had its share. The kings of Assyria delighted in portraying themselves slaughtering and enslaving the peoples they defeated, the Egyptian pharaohs forced people into service building pyramids, and tyrants oppressed the states of ancient Greece – some of them, like Periander of Corinth or Pisistratus of Athens, renowned in their day – but information about them is scarce or unreliable. Phalaris of Acragas, for example, supposedly roasted his victims in a bronze bull, but that alone provides no basis for discussion. Aztec rulers, who sent thousands of captives to have their hearts torn out in sacrifice to the sun, would richly deserve a place here if their history could be reliably reconstructed. With a few exceptions, substantial knowledge about tyrants begins with the Romans and continues to the present day. The 50 presented here have been chosen to illustrate a variety of origins, careers, oddities, successes and failures, and ultimate fates. They appear in chronological order, according to the time they were in power, which is indicated on the opening page of each chapter.

People from all backgrounds have become tyrants. Julius Caesar traced his family back to the goddess Venus but Mussolini's father was a blacksmith. Education is not a qualification. Lenin and 'Papa Doc' had university degrees, but Genghis Khan never attended school and Kim Il Sung never finished it. Much more significant is the intelligence, determination and ambition that illuminate every career. Intrigue, treachery and ruthlessness have also played their part.

Until modern times, royal birth was the easiest route to tyranny, but after the French Revolution the field became much more open. Among earlier tyrants, Caesar, Genghis Khan, Tamerlane and Shaka had to fight their way to the top. Herod and Cesare Borgia had an easier time, being installed by the Romans and the Pope respectively. From her roots as a lowly concubine, Wu Zetian manoeuvred her way to dominance. The rest more or less legitimately succeeded to power. Modern tyrants, however, usually rise through the military or politics. Napoleon, like most of the Latin Americans and Africans, commanded armies before he became dictator. The politicians campaigned for votes and won elections, like Hitler or Mussolini, or manoeuvred through the apparatus of an already ruling party, like Stalin or Saddam. Perón, anomalously, was a military man who was freely elected, while Solano López, not especially skilled at war or politics, had the advantage of being the son of a dictator. Revolution and civil war also help: Robespierre, Lenin and Khomeini led or exploited vast popular movements; Caesar, Franco and Mao conquered their countries. A lucky few (Kim Il Sung, Trujillo, Sukarno) were helped into office by powerful foreign backers.

Once in power, tyrants behave in many different ways. They often start wars – some even try to conquer the world. Genghis Khan was remarkably successful; Xerxes much less so; Hitler and Solano López left their countries in ruin. Francia, on the other hand, sealed his country off completely to avoid war and the Latin Americans and Africans generally used their considerable military apparatus to stay in power or to fight their own people rather than foreign enemies.

Robespierre is inevitably associated with a Reign of Terror, but the term could apply equally well to the regimes of Ivan the Terrible, Stalin, 'Papa Doc', Ceausescu, Saddam or Idi Amin, who instituted secret police systems that cowed the population into fearful submission. Mao, Stalin, Hitler and Pol Pot were responsible for the deaths of millions of their own subjects, Abdul Hamid II for hundreds of thousands – but Mussolini killed very few and Perón hardly anyone. Most tyrants fall somewhere in between, as they do in terms of cruelty. Few could approach the sadism of Vlad 'The Impaler' or Idi Amin, who enjoyed seeing people suffer. Most distanced themselves from the horrors their regimes inflicted. Genghis Khan, Tamerlane and Leopold II form a special category: they killed only foreigners. They were not tyrants towards their own people.

Some tyrants made positive contributions. Shi Huangdi, Sukarno and Mobutu unified their countries; Herod, Stalin and Kim Il Sung were enthusiastic builders;

Justinian and Napoleon produced lasting codes of law; King John, albeit unwillingly, laid the foundation of English liberties. On the other hand, many thought only of themselves, their glory or their pockets. Caesar, Trujillo, Mobutu and 'Papa Doc' wound up enormously rich. But in virtually every case the picture is ambiguous: for even the mildest tyrants were still tyrannical, and some of the most bloodthirsty did a great deal for their countries.

Tyrants usually have large egos. A few even believed they were gods: Caligula demanded worship; al-Hakim still receives it. Bokassa claimed that he was the Thirteenth Apostle. Cromwell, Franco, Pinochet and most emphatically Khomeini were convinced that they had God on their side. Many more, like Stalin, Mao or Kim Il Sung built extravagant personality cults that raised them to a superhuman level, and Trujillo, Bokassa and Saddam encouraged something similar. Caesar and Cesare Borgia were fearless, but Abdul Hamid cowered in his palace frightened of almost everyone.

Some tyrants displayed extremely peculiar behaviour. Xerxes whipped the Hellespont; Caligula carried on conversation with a statue of Jupiter; Commodus, dressed as Hercules, fought in the arena. Dionysius would strip all his visitors naked to make sure they were not concealing weapons; Francia ordered all doors and windows along the roads he used to be kept shut, in order to thwart would-be assassins; Ceausescu washed his hands with alcohol after any physical contact. Ivan the Terrible killed his own son; Herod had three of his executed. Shi Huangdi buried scholars alive; Tamerlane built the heads of defeated peoples into pyramids. Dionysius died of overindulgence at a banquet celebrating his own literary success; Hitler was a vegetarian and teetotaller. In other words, most tyrants would not make very appealing or comfortable company, with some exceptions: Caesar was undoubtedly extremely interesting, Perón was genteel, and Stalin was convivial, at least with his inner circle, although Hitler's tea parties were excruciatingly boring. Few, however, would enjoy spending time with tyrants like Caligula, 'Papa Doc' or Ceausescu.

Considering their characters and actions, most tyrants would be expected to come to a violent end but this is far from being the case. Of the 50 presented here, seven were assassinated, three were executed and two committed suicide. Three were killed in battle and eight others died after losing office, one of them in jail. Almost half of them, however, including some of the most monstrous, died peacefully in their beds.

This book would not have existed without the determination and encouragement of Wayne Davies at every stage; and I wouldn't have been writing it had not Peter Furtado suggested my name. My thanks to both.

Clive Foss
Washington, May 2006

Xerxes

(485–465 BC)

'If we crush the Athenians and their neighbours, we shall extend the Empire of Persia so that its boundaries will be God's own sky.'

In Greek terms, most of the kings of the ancient Near East would have qualified as tyrants. The Assyrians, in particular, were proud of the violence with which they ruled, capturing cities, slaughtering their enemies and transplanting whole populations. Babylonians like Nebuchadnezzar, who conquered Jerusalem and displaced the Jews, were not much better. But information about these figures is scarce, inadequate to support even short biographical sketches. Real personalities only emerge with the Achaemenid kings of the Persian Empire, whose careers are known in some detail. The founders of the Persian Empire, Cyrus and Darius, were moderate and reasonable – powerful men, but not tyrants. Darius's successor Xerxes, however, stands out among them from the vivid portrayal by the Greek historian Herodotus, who wrote from a victor's viewpoint. His story portrays Xerxes as a sacrilegious monster and vastly exaggerates the power of the nation the Greeks defeated. Other sources provide only minor supplements to this hostile view of the Persian ruler.

Xerxes is the Greek form of the Persian name Khshayarsha, meaning 'king of heroes'. He was born around 518 BC. His father Darius was the ruling Persian king, and his mother was the daughter of Cyrus, the founding ruler of the Empire. This impeccable pedigree gave Xerxes precedence over Darius's oldest son, who had been born before his father came to the throne and whose mother was a commoner. Xerxes claimed, 'Darius had other sons but, by the will of God, my father made me greatest after himself.' It is more likely, however, that an intrigue led by his mother enabled Xerxes to become heir apparent by 498 BC. In carvings decorating the palace in Persepolis, Xerxes appears standing by his father's throne, subordinate only to the Great King.

When Darius died in 485 BC, Xerxes inherited serious problems: revenge on the Greeks, who had defeated his father's forces at Marathon five years earlier, revolt in Egypt, and the efforts of his younger brother Ariamenes to claim the crown. Xerxes placated his brother with gifts, promised to make him next in succession, and set out for Egypt. Since Egypt was of great economic importance to the Empire, Xerxes led his army in person and suppressed the revolt in 484 BC. He imposed a harsher regime and confiscated wealth from the temples. He was on his way home when news of a serious revolt in Babylon reached him. A pretender who called himself the King of Babylon had seized power and killed the Persian Governor. Xerxes sent his most competent general to attack the city, which soon fell. Persian vengeance was severe. Babylon's massive fortifications were demolished along with its greatest temple, and the gold statue of its chief god was carried off so that no future rebel could claim legitimacy by the tradition of grasping its hands. The estates of the rich were turned over to Persians, harsh taxation was imposed and the country reduced to such subservience that nothing was heard of it for decades afterwards. The name Babylonia was abolished. Xerxes was now free to move against the Greeks.

Preparations began in 483 BC, when the king sent a corps of engineers ahead to cut a canal through the promontory of Mount Athos in northern Greece, whose stormy seas made passage around it extremely dangerous. The workers were driven to the task by whips. At the same time, Xerxes' men brought papyrus from Egypt to make cables for suspending bridges that would allow the army to cross the Hellespont from Asia into Europe. The army assembled in central Asia Minor. It was made up of contingents from the 20 provinces of the vast Persian Empire, which stretched from India and central Asia to Libya and the shores of the Aegean. At its core was the elite royal corps of Immortals, so called because their number was permanently maintained at 1000, with wounded and killed soldiers immediately replaced by others. Persians, Armenians, Indians, Arabs, Ethiopians, Greeks and many others fought beside them, with their varied native dress and weapons. Herodotus's account magnifies the army's size to an impossible 1,700,000 (not including the fleet). It reality it probably numbered in the tens of thousands.

In the spring of 480 BC, this host mustered at Sardis, the Persian capital of western Asia Minor. On the way there, a rich Lydian named Pythius had met the King and offered his whole fortune to help finance the expedition. Xerxes was delighted. He refused the man's offer and made him his friend. Xerxes had just set out from Sardis when he learnt that the bridges over the Hellespont had been destroyed by a storm. In a rage, he ordered the engineers to be beheaded, then had the water whipped in punishment. Chains were thrown into the Hellespont to symbolize its subjection as Xerxes addressed it insultingly:

> 'You salt and bitter stream, your master lays this punishment upon you for injuring him, who never injured you. But Xerxes the King will cross you with or without your permission. No man sacrifices to you and you deserve the neglect by your acid and muddy waters.'

This was considered serious sacrilege by the Greeks, who believed that any moving body of water was home to a divine spirit.

The army had not gone far when Pythius the Lydian approached Xerxes with a request. Because he was old and had five sons in the army, Pythius asked the King to release his oldest son from duty to take care of him and his property. Xerxes, who was exposing himself to danger by leading the expedition, lost his temper. He ordered Pythias's son to be cut in half and then marched his troops on between the two body parts. The army was so huge that it took seven days and nights to cross into Europe. Xerxes watched as his men were driven across the reconstructed bridges by whips.

At first the King's confidence in the size of his army was justified. All the Greeks north of Athens submitted, his fleet won a major battle, and his men finally forced their way through the bottleneck of Thermopylae where the King of Sparta and 300 warriors died fighting. Xerxes occupied Athens and burnt its temples, but he became over-confident. Advised not to engage the Greeks at Salamis, he nevertheless ordered the battle to go ahead, sitting on a golden throne to watch the fighting. The Greeks trapped the Persian fleet in the narrow waters off the island

and crushed it completely. Xerxes returned home, leaving his general, Mardonius, to direct the war. The following year, Mardonius was beaten at Plataea in central Greece by the Greek infantry, superior in skill to the Persians, although smaller in number. This defeat and the loss of a further naval battle marked the end of Persian ambitions to expand into Europe. The Greeks, now organized into a confederacy, pursued the war into the eastern Aegean and the Mediterranean, where they destroyed another Persian fleet in 466 BC.

Little is known of Xerxes' last years. He enlarged the palace at Persepolis, but seems to have spent much of his time there embroiled in intrigues within the court and harem. When he returned to Sardis after the failure in Greece, he attempted to seduce his brother's wife, who rejected him. Not prepared to abandon his quest, Xerxes instead seduced her daughter when they returned to the Persian capital. When Xerxes' wife discovered the intrigue, she blamed the girl's mother, and had her horribly mutilated. Xerxes' brother fled to join frontier tribes whom he hoped to stir to revolt, but Xerxes captured and killed him, together with his whole family.

Xerxes appears in the Book of Esther in the Old Testament under the name of Ahasuerus. According to this account, which appears nowhere else, the Persian King held a lavish week-long banquet in the city of Susa. On the last day, he invited his wife to attend but she refused. Ahasuerus was so angered by this that he divorced her and decided to choose a new wife from the most beautiful virgins in the Empire. His choice fell on Esther, who did not reveal that she was a Jew. Some years later, under the influence of his Jew-hating advisor Haman, Ahasuerus issued an edict to all his provinces, ordering the massacre of every Jew in the Persian Empire. Esther persuaded Ahasuerus to relent, and saved her people. They in turn were allowed to rise against their oppressors. The Book of Esther recounts that 'the other Jews that were in the King's provinces gathered themselves together, and stood for their lives, and had rest from their enemies, and slew of their foes seventy and five thousand'.

Whatever the truth of the biblical story, the capricious changes and violent orders of King Ahasuerus would fit Xerxes very well. He was eventually murdered in his bed in a conspiracy led by his eunuch chamberlain and the commander of the palace guard, in 465 BC.

Dionysius of Sicily

(405–367 BC)

'I would like somebody to be hated more than I am.'

Ancient Greece, famous for democracy, gave the world its first tyrants, in the sense of people who exercised arbitrary one-man rule, in violation of law and tradition, rather like modern dictators. The earliest known is Cypselus who seized power in Corinth in the mid-seventh century BC. He was followed by many others, notably Periander in Corinth and Pisistratus in Athens, but most of them are shadowy figures, portrayed in stories that passed through an oral tradition. Among the Greek kingdoms, Sicily was renowned for its tyrannical regimes. Its rulers exercised habitual violence against their populations and each other. Best known is Dionysius of Syracuse. He rose from humble origins, deposed the local democracy, established firm control and used it to create the most powerful empire in the Greek world. Since he thought more in terms of a nation than a city-state, and acted like a monarch, he is a forerunner of Alexander the Great.

Dionysius, whose origins are obscure, was a follower of Hermocrates, who had saved Syracuse from the Athenians in 415 BC, during the Peloponnesian War. When Hermocrates later appeared to favour oligarchy, the radical faction banished him from the city because Syracuse had been a democracy since 466 BC. Sicily was divided between a zone controlled by Carthage and another consisting of independent Greek city-states, of which Syracuse was the largest, richest and most powerful. Rivalry between Greeks and Carthaginians often led to war. In 409 BC, a huge Carthaginian army advanced on the Greek territories. Hermocrates joined the fray, hoping to return to power. He advanced into Syracuse, but was killed. Dionysius, fighting with him, was left for dead, but recovered and defended Syracuse in the war that began again in 406 BC. When the Carthaginians captured the Greek city of Acragas, panic struck Syracuse. Dionysius spoke in the Syracusan Assembly, accusing the city's leaders of treachery and expressing himself so violently that he was fined. He continued to agitate against the ruling class, however, and eventually he and his democratic allies were elected to the Board of Generals who ran the city. The neighbouring city of Gela now came under enemy threat as well. Dionysius mobilized forces in Gela's defence and accomplished a social revolution that removed the rich from power and confiscated their goods. He then returned to Syracuse with further accusations of treason against the city's rulers. When he claimed that his life was in danger, Dionysius was assigned a personal security force, which he promptly used to overturn the government. He took over as sole general, married Hermocrates' daughter, executed his rivals and assumed full power.

The Carthaginians now turned their attention to Gela, which the Greeks were forced to evacuate. The Syracusan cavalry, provided by rich citizens and appointed to protect the city, blamed Dionysius and rushed back to Syracuse, where they wrecked his house and killed his wife. Dionysius pursued them with a mercenary force that took them by surprise and massacred them. With that, he removed his last powerful body of opponents. At this point, plague broke out in the Carthaginian camp and peace was made. The respite allowed Dionysius to consolidate his own position and reinforce Syracuse against renewal of the war. His own security was paramount. He fortified the island of Ortygia, on which the city of Syracuse had been founded, turning it into a palatial residence and impregnable citadel, staffed by slaves. He surrounded himself with armed guards and appointed relatives and close friends to all positions of authority. He searched the houses of citizens and removed all their weapons, and raised money through high taxation and confiscation of property. Ingeniously, he made himself guardian of all Syracusan orphans so he could use the income from their estates until they came of age.

Dionysius then extended his domain by conquering the Greek cities of Catania and Naxos and massacring their inhabitants. Leontini prudently surrendered and its population was deported to Syracuse. A massive military buildup followed. Dionysius constructed walls to enclose a greater area for Syracuse. Taking 60,000 workers from city and country, he organized them in teams, worked beside them and saw the walls rise in two weeks. Here, as elsewhere, he showed himself a man of the people, a major reason why he stayed in power so long. He consistently favoured the poor: he distributed land confiscated from the rich to his own followers and even liberated slaves to join the ranks of citizens who supported him. He also brought in foreign workers to manufacture 200 ships and 140,000 sets of weapons and armour. Dionysius was ready to move against the Carthaginians.

Despite his tyranny and contempt for conventional mores (he once married two women and consummated both marriages on the same day), Dionysius nominally respected the Greek political system. He maintained the Syracusan administration and even went before the Assembly to ask for support for his war policy. They agreed, of course, because the government was little more than a façade. The campaign began in 398 BC with looting and expulsion of all Carthaginians residing in Greek cities. Syracusan forces advanced far to the west where they lay siege to the enemy base of Motya, using stone-throwing catapults that Dionysius had invented. When they captured the city, they massacred the population – men, women and children – and crucified any Greeks who had fought on the Carthaginian side. The Carthaginians fought back, massing a huge army that drove Dionysius back to the walls of Syracuse. Fortune favoured Dionysius when plague once again struck the enemy, ending the war, but the island of Sicily was still left divided.

Dionysius aimed to dominate the seas of Sicily and Italy. To that end he conquered Rhegium, at the extreme south of Italy, in 387 BC, took over the ports of northwest Greece and struck against the Etruscans of western Italy. He made money at Rhegium, allowing the citizens first to buy their freedom, then selling them into slavery anyway. By now the most powerful ruler in the Greek world, Dionysius uprooted whole populations, created colonies and looted places he did not control. He showed none of the traditional reverence for the temples of the gods and even planned to attack the great shrine of Apollo at Delphi. He was determined to control trade, gain access to recruiting grounds for soldiers, and raise money for his mercenary troops.

His great plan was to drive out the Carthaginians and rule all Sicily but he never succeeded, despite two more wars. In the first (383–378 BC), although he won a major land battle, he actually had to cede territory in the peace settlement. The final war began in 368 BC. Dionysius took over northwest Sicily, but the Carthaginians destroyed his fleet. The inconclusive struggle dragged on and ended only with his death.

Like many rich tyrants, Dionysius patronized arts and letters, inviting poets and philosophers to his court. His most famous visitor was Plato, who believed that the problems of universally bad government could only be solved if philosophers ruled, or rulers embraced philosophy. Plato had despaired of ever seeing his ideas put into practice until he came to Syracuse in 388 BC. Although he was disgusted by the extravagance and luxury of the city, Plato saw hope in the tyrant's brother-in-law, Dion, who became his pupil. Plato taught Dion philosophy but had less success with Dionysius, who was not moved by his criticism. The exasperated tyrant finally asked Plato what he was doing in Syracuse: 'I'm looking for a virtuous man,' the philosopher replied. Dionysius told him he was wasting his time and sent him away. Although Plato wrote little about his stay in Syracuse, Dionysius obviously made an impression, for he provided the image of the tyrant – 'by far the most miserable of all men', leading 'the most miserable of states' – that appears in Plato's *Republic* and *Politics*.

Dionysius lived in luxury in his fortified island, but never relaxed. Everyone who entered his presence, even members of his family, was stripped naked by guards, then dressed in different clothes. He would not allow barbers to cut his hair or beard with knives, trusting only his daughters to groom him – and they had to use live coals. He shut his son up in the palace, to keep him from subversive or corrupting influence. A famous story illustrates the atmosphere of fear and suspicion in the court. When Damocles, one of his courtiers, told Dionysius how much he envied his luxurious life, Dionysius offered to change places with him. Damocles sat in the throne, feasted and drank, then noticed a sword suspended over his head by a fine thread. Dionysius explained that the sword represented the reality of power. Damocles was quite content to return to his old life.

Dionysius was an educated man who wrote bad poetry. The audience hissed when it was performed at the Olympic Games. A story is told about the philosopher Philoxenes, who was arrested, brought to Dionysius and forced to listen to some of his verse. When Dionysius asked Philoxenes what he thought, he is said to have replied, 'Take me back to the prison.' In the end, literature was the death of Dionysius. When news arrived that a play he had written had won first prize in Athens, he drank so much in a celebratory debauch that he died.

Qin Shi Huang

(247–210 BC)

'I collected all the writings of the Empire and
burnt those which were of no use.'

Qin Shi Huang, also called Shi Huangdi ('First Emperor') unified China, laying the foundations for what became a vast and enduring state. He founded the short-lived Qin (pronounced 'chin') Dynasty whose name is the origin of 'China'. He created a centrally-controlled, efficient administration, bound his realm together with new road and canal systems, and defended it with long walls. Yet he ruled with extraordinary brutality.

The future Emperor was initially called Zheng, after the first month in the Chinese calendar in which he was born. He grew up in the Warring States Period, when several kingdoms fought for supremacy. As the result of a war between Zheng's state (Qin), and their enemy (Zhou), Zheng's father was taken to the Zhou capital as a hostage, and Zheng was born there. His father managed to escape and became King of Qin. When he died in 247 BC, 12-year-old Zheng succeeded to the throne ruling under a regent until 238 BC, when Zheng assumed full power. Qin was the most well-organized state in China, having developed a centralized bureaucratic system that reduced the power of the aristocracy. Peasants were allowed to own their land, free from the control of the aristocracy but under direct supervision of the state. Legalism prevailed, a doctrine that relied on punishments and rewards to maintain the supremacy of the ruler and treated all equally. Strictly enforced laws that made groups of families responsible for the misdeeds of individuals produced a system of informers and reduced the independence of family units. Legalism differed sharply from the widespread Confucian doctrine that advocated the harmony of ruler and ruled and considered the well-ordered family as the basic unit of society. The Qin regime strengthened the internal structure of the state, which was geographically vulnerable. Its location in western China meant constant exposure to attack from nomad tribes. Long generations of frontier warfare had produced a formidable Qin fighting force.

Zheng was barely in power before he was threatened by a plot implicating his mother and the most powerful man in the kingdom, Lu Buwei. The facts are obscured in dubious stories but it seems that Lu, a wealthy merchant who had helped Zheng's father escape captivity and gain the throne, had virtually run the state during Zheng's minority. There were suggestions that Zheng was Lu's son, and not his father's. In 237 BC, Lu fell from power and went into exile where he committed suicide. The Queen Mother was kept under house arrest. Distrust stirred by this plot was exacerbated ten years later when the Prince of Yen sent as ambassador to Qin a famous swordsman who almost succeeded in assassinating Zheng.

One by one, Zheng conquered his rival states. The most bitter struggle was with Zhou, where his father had been held hostage. After its capital was taken in 223 BC, Zheng ordered all his family's enemies there to be buried alive. Yen fell soon after and with the conquest of the last independent state, Qi, in 221 BC, Zheng became supreme ruler of all China and assumed a new title, Shi Huangdi – First Emperor.

A vast empire presented vast problems. Each region had an ancient tradition of independence, local aristocracies were used to dominance within the feudal system, communications were poor and systems of administration differed widely. Externally, the Xiongnu nomads (Huns) posed a constant threat. Shi Huangdi's answer was standardization under a unified military rule that extended Qin's practices throughout China, unifying the country firmly against any threat.

He began by crushing feudalism. Peasant farmers were given ownership of their land and made subject to taxes, conscription and forced labour. Former royal families were forced to move to the capital Xianyang (near Xian in what is now Shaanxi province) where they could be closely supervised, while the old nobility and their families were moved away from their natural bases of support. At least 120,000 families were relocated in the first year of Shi Huangdi's reign. To reduce the danger of revolt, all subjects were required to turn in their weapons, which were melted down and turned into bells and statues erected in the imperial palace. Only the Emperor's troops could bear arms.

China was divided into 36 provinces called commanderies, ruled by an effective system of checks and balances. In each commandery, there were civil and military governors. The civilian governor took precedence, with the aim of keeping the army under government control. Yet to avoid the civilian governor gaining too much power, he was moved to a different province every few years. In addition, an inspector in each commandery reported back to the Emperor on how his decrees were being enforced, what local problems were arising, and how well the two governors were carrying out their duties. This system, which destroyed the last elements of feudalism and imposed the supremacy of imperial and civil power, remained the base of the Chinese political system for the next 2000 years.

Improved trade and communications were necessary for the unity and prosperity of China. Before, each region had had its own legal and economic system. Shi Huangdi ordered standardization. Qin laws were to apply everywhere, along with a common system of weights and measures and a new round bronze coinage. All carts were to be built with axles of a standard length so they could negotiate the new road network. Because the capital was in the far west, good roads were essential for fast communication. Highways spread out from Xianyang to the most remote parts of the Empire. Some 7500 kilometres were built, with the longest running to Yunnan in the far southwest. Canals also crossed the country, the most important uniting the river Yangtze with the river system of south China. Most enduring, though, was the reform of the writing system. Shi Huangdi's grand counsellor, Li Si, imposed the use of a standard simplified script everywhere and abolished redundant or incorrect characters. Thanks to this, all Chinese, however different their spoken dialects, could read and write in a universal language.

New conquests had pushed enemy nomadic tribes north of the Yellow River and increased the need for improved defences along the frontier. Shi Huangdi began the construction of a system of fortifications along the Yellow River and reconstructed and extended an older rampart that ran above the river's great loop. As well as keeping the Emperor's enemies out, the wall was designed to keep his subjects in. They were encouraged to move south into the newly conquered but unassimilated regions that stretched as far as Canton. Forced labourers and convicts built the walls and fortifications; thousands of them died in the process. To meet the costs of the expanding Empire, the Chinese people were subject to ever-increasing taxes and requisitions that left most of the rural population impoverished. The new roads also imposed a burden, for communities had to maintain those in their vicinity and pay for the horses of the imperial postal system. The detested road police enforced the obligations and collected customs. Suppressed peasant resentment was to have devastating results in the years after Shi Huangdi's death.

The Emperor's policy naturally stirred the hatred of the former ruling classes and the intellectuals closely associated with them. Shi Huangdi's attacks on them won him perpetual infamy. In 213 BC, he ordered all 'useless' books – those published under previous regimes or in rival states, except volumes of practical use – to be burnt. Old books contained insidious ideas that might lead to opposition. The Emperor aimed to prohibit 'use of the past to discredit the present'. The success of his suppression of old values inspired a much later leader, Mao Zedong, and the Cultural Revolution of the 1960s.

As Shi Huangdi's suspicion and paranoia increased, he began to move constantly between his numerous residences so that no one would ever know where he was. He became obsessed with the search for an elixir of immortality. When his scholars and scientists failed to find one, he rounded up 480 leading Confucians and buried them alive. As protests spread, he tore down city walls so that their populations could not resist his troops. War and conquest continued.

Shi Huangdi died in eastern China in 210 BC while on a vain search for the mythical Islands of the Immortals. He was interred in an extraordinary tomb that contained one of the world's most remarkable sights, a terracotta army of 7500 life-size figures that were buried with him. This pottery assembly of soldiers, horses and riders, which has been described as the eighth wonder of the world, was used instead of living slaves and servants to accompany Shi Huangdi to the next world – a rare example of imperial compassion.

Julius Caesar

(49–44 BC)

*'Veni, vidi, vici – I came, I saw,
I conquered.'*

Julius Caesar, a radical aristocrat of unbounded ambition, and a successful commander and politician, gained wealth and glory by conquering Gaul, then won supreme power in a civil war. He destroyed the Roman Republic and seemed to be moving toward monarchy, but was assassinated before he could complete his plans. Most of the world still uses the Julian calendar he introduced.

Caius Julius Caesar, born about 100 BC, descended from an ancient patrician family closely connected with radicals who wanted to undermine the Senatorial ruling class. Roman aristocrats believed that power naturally belonged to them, but they had to compete for it. That meant establishing powerful connections, raising money to bribe voters, and building a body of support. Success in both military and civic life, especially the law, was essential.

At the age of 20 Caesar was appointed to the staff of the governor of Roman Asia. He won military distinction and became known as a successful prosecutor and speaker. He married a rich wife and had a well-connected mistress. In 69 BC, Caesar took the first step to power when he was elected *quaestor*, an office that guaranteed admission to the Senate. His patron was Crassus, a prominent politician and general and the richest man in Rome. Caesar's post took him to Spain, then to Cisalpine Gaul (northern Italy), where he gained popularity by agitating for Roman citizenship for the region. In the Senate, he supported the famous general and war hero Pompey, as well as Crassus, whose funds helped his further election as *aedile*. That post involved organizing games in the public arena, a sure route to popularity. In 63 BC, Caesar became *pontifex maximus*, head of the state religion, which gave him a residence in the centre of Rome and great prestige.

Suspicious of his increasing influence, the Senate refused Caesar a triumph – a procession and celebration in his honour – when he returned victorious from war in Spain in 60 BC. Undaunted, Caesar joined forces with Pompey and Crassus to form the First Triumvirate, which took over the government. Under this arrangement, Caesar took the republic's highest office, the Consulate, in 59 BC. He passed legislation favourable to Pompey and the army, but was bitterly opposed by the aristocracy. He also became rich by accepting a bribe from Ptolemy XII of Egypt who wanted Roman recognition. Normally, consuls became governors for a year after their term in office. Caesar overturned precedent by taking the governorship of Cisalpine Gaul for five years, adding unconquered Transalpine Gaul (France). He raised an army and set off on campaigns that conquered territory and gained masses of loot. Caesar used the money to maintain his supporters in Rome, organized around one of the tribunes of the people who had the power of proposing or vetoing legislation. When the triumvirs met in 56 BC, Caesar was granted governorship of Gaul for another five years. This was an essential appointment, for as long as he remained in office, Caesar was immune from prosecution by his enemies or rivals. Pompey took Spain, but governed it from Rome by proxy, while Crassus took Syria, where he mistakenly thought he could defeat the Parthians, who destroyed his whole army in 54 BC.

With his conquest of Gaul, Caesar added a huge province to Rome's Empire. He used the enormous personal wealth the campaign brought him to increase his public standing and to benefit the people, funding the construction of a new law court, a voting precinct and a large forum around a temple to his supposed ancestress, the goddess Venus. Rome, meanwhile, was sinking into chaos as Pompey, the enemy of the Senate, joined with conservatives to undermine Caesar. Partisan gangs brawled and rioted in the streets, and burnt down the Senate House. Pompey was determined to thwart Caesar's plan to run for Consul in 49 BC. He persuaded the Senate to pass an emergency decree to declare Caesar an outlaw.

When the news was brought to Caesar he reflected in silence, then said, 'The die is cast.' Caesar led his forces across the river Rubicon into Italy, an act of open treason. Civil war had begun. Pompey and the government fled Rome, which Caesar's forces occupied. Caesar then set off to subdue Spain and southern Gaul. On his return, the *praetor* Lepidus had Caesar appointed Dictator, a special office that gave supreme power during an emergency. Caesar, ever concerned to maintain the image of republican government, then conducted elections that made him Consul. He crossed into Greece, where he crushed Pompey's much larger forces in 48 BC. Caesar then sailed to Egypt to collect money still owed him by Ptolemy, but his high-handedness so offended the Egyptians that he was blockaded in Alexandria for the winter. Caesar overcame his enemies, killed the King and made the acquaintance of his daughter, Cleopatra. The two disappeared on a long Nile cruise, after which Caesar left for Judaea and Syria, where he restored order, then Asia Minor to finish off Pompeian loyalists, the occasion for his famous three-word pronouncement, '*Veni, vidi, vici*' ('I came, I saw, I conquered').

On his return to Rome in 46 BC, Caesar took the dictatorship for ten years. He had conquered the Roman world and was free to remodel it as he liked. His plans were unclear, perhaps even to himself. He concentrated power in his own hands and those of some trusted followers, but maintained at least a façade of republican government and assumed no office that did not already exist in the constitution. He had no use for the old ruling aristocracy but relied on the knights (the non-aristocratic rich), the Italians, especially those from Cisalpine Gaul, and the people of Rome. The army, however, was his most important body of support. Caesar's long and invariably successful campaigns had built a solid core of loyal troops and veterans. The soldiers looked to him, not the Senate, for their rewards, and had shown they would follow him anywhere. They received large bonuses and land in the new colonies that Caesar was establishing outside Italy, rising to positions formerly monopolized by the aristocracy. Caesar maintained his popularity in Rome by staging lavish triumphs and gladiatorial combats, giving generous gifts and public banquets, and starting an extensive building programme that provided people with work. All this was accompanied by a personality cult that he actively encouraged: images of Caesar were everywhere, and skilled propaganda publicized his achievements, including his writings – his deceptively simple account of the *Gallic*

Wars has remained in print for over 2000 years. Unusually for a dictator, Caesar never suppressed free speech. He allowed the people to meet and even to lampoon him. He had no fear of a public that was devoted to him.

As Dictator, Caesar had unlimited power. The docile Senate, packed with his supporters, granted him supervision of public morals, allowed him to sit between the Consuls at meetings and gave him the right to name candidates for high offices. As sole Consul in 45 BC, he passed laws restricting the senators' use of public funds, restraining the extravagance of the rich and limiting terms in office so that no one else could emulate his own progress to power. He organized Rome's food supply, obliged landowners to employ free labour instead of slaves and founded colonies that provided land for the poor. His most long-lasting reforms were associated with Cleopatra, who took up residence in Rome with an entourage that included scientists. Under her influence, Caesar opened Rome's first public library and reformed the Roman calendar, synchronizing it with the seasons. The Julian calendar, as it became known, fixed years of 365 days (with an additional day every four years) and determined the number of days in each month.

Caesar ruled through a clique of supporters, of whom the most important were Lepidus and Mark Antony. The Senate, although nominally retaining voting powers, did what Caesar told it to do. Since Caesar named high officials two or three years in advance of their appointment, and selected provincial governors, elections were merely a formality. Although he appeared to be establishing a monarchy, when he was offered the title of King, Caesar refused.

However, he soon began to cast aside even the semblance of a republic. In 45 BC, he began a ten-year term as Consul while remaining Dictator. Ominously, he started to wear a gold crown and to sit on a golden throne that was exhibited in the circus – a symbol of his power – when he was absent. Caesar stamped the coinage with his image and allowed himself to be worshipped as a god, acceptable behaviour in the east but alien to Roman tradition. Early in 44 BC, he declared his birthday a public holiday and named a month in the calendar (July) after himself. In February that year, he took the title Dictator in Perpetuity: his intention to retain supreme power became plain. At the same time he announced that, on 16 March, he would set out on a great expedition to conquer the Parthians. His great-nephew Caius Octavius, whom he adopted and named his heir, was sent on ahead as his right-hand man.

Caesar was obviously establishing a monarchy that would be run by his faction. Those who believed in the Republic formed a conspiracy with a number of disgruntled aristocrats and aspiring office holders. When Caesar attended the Senate meeting on the eve of his departure on the Parthian campaign – the Ides of March – the conspirators assassinated him with their daggers. He fell dead at the feet of Pompey's statue.

Herod the Great

(37–4 BC)

'Since some evil genius makes my dearest ones rise against me, I shall lament my cruel fate, but I will let no one escape who thirsts for my blood.'

In popular memory, Herod is inevitably associated with the Massacre of the Innocents. He also killed his wife, three sons and numerous opponents. Yet, he was the successful ruler of a kingdom that provided stability in a turbulent region and one of the greatest builders of the age, erecting fortresses, palaces and entire cities. He lived in the shadow of the Romans, who installed and maintained him in power.

Herod, born in 73 BC, was the son of Antipater, ruler of the Idumaeans, who lived in southern Palestine and had been converted to Judaism. His mother was an Arab. Problems of identity plagued Herod all his life: he considered himself a Jew, but according to Jewish law he was not one. Antipater had backed the Jewish prince Hyrcanus in his struggle to become King of Judaea. When the Romans installed Hyrcanus, Antipater's fortunes rose. In the Roman civil wars, both took the side of Caesar who confirmed Hyrcanus in power, with Antipater as his Chief Minister. Antipater in turn named the 16-year-old Herod Governor of Galilee in 47 BC. Herod made himself popular by suppressing banditry, but attracted the hostility of conservative Jews who resented the rise of Idumaeans. When Caesar was killed in 44 BC, the Roman East supported his assassins, for whom Antipater and Herod raised money. After Antipater was murdered in 43 BC, Hyrcanus's old rival for the Judaean throne, Antigonus, reappeared. Herod defeated him and was rewarded with the hand of Hyrcanus's granddaughter Mariamne. The next year, when Mark Antony was supreme in the region, Herod ingratiated himself with him, receiving official Roman appointment as ruler of Galilee. Soon after, the Parthians swept through Asia Minor and Syria. The Jews took their side, installed Antigonus and mutilated Hyrcanus. Herod took refuge in Rome, where Antony and Caesar's heir Caius Octavius (Octavian, later Augustus) agreed that he could be a stabilizing force in a country rent by faction. Since Herod was not really Jewish, he would always have to depend on Rome for support. The Romans drove out the Parthians, defeated Antigonus and installed Herod as King of Judaea in 37 BC.

Herod faced serious opposition from the Jewish religious establishment. He responded by executing 45 prominent supporters of Antigonus, and appointing his own men to the supreme religious council, the Sanhedrin. Dealing with the High Priesthood was a greater problem, since the office had been hereditary in Hyrcanus's Hasmonean family, and priests served for life, uniting religious and temporal power. Herod made a concession to the Hasmoneans by naming his brother-in-law Aristobulus, even though he was under age, but soon had him drowned so that he could be replaced by one of his own men. Herod had a powerful enemy in Cleopatra, Queen of Egypt, who wanted to rule Palestine and Syria. Her intrigues were more dangerous since she had the backing of Antony, to whom Herod remained loyal. When Antony and Cleopatra were defeated by Octavian, Herod murdered Hyrcanus to prevent the new Roman ruler installing him in power. He then made his peace with the conqueror. Rather than denying his loyalty to Antony, he promised Augustus the same, and made him a huge cash present. Augustus confirmed him in office. Herod was finally secure.

Because Herod had killed his wife's brother and grandfather, Mariamne grew to hate him. To forestall her opposition, he fabricated a charge of adultery against her and had her executed, killing her mother soon after. The Hasmoneans now had no adult males who could serve as a focus for rebellion, but Herod never lost his fear of his own Jewish population. With this in mind, he embarked on a remarkable construction programme. He first built a new citadel for Jerusalem, in close proximity to the Temple, giving him as much control over the sacred space as any Gentile could have. He then rebuilt the walls of the city on a massive scale, using perfectly squared blocks of limestone 12 metres long. He also undertook the reconstruction of Jerusalem, which had been devastated by an earthquake, building a market, a theatre, a hall for the Sanhedrin and a palace, and initiating reconstruction of the badly-damaged Temple. The city's walls were part of a network of fortresses designed to control Herod's territory and give him suitable places of refuge, notably Herodion south of Bethlehem and Masada above the Dead Sea. Masada contained a lavishly decorated palace and extensive facilities for storing water and food in case of a siege.

Herod was also a great builder of cities. In 27 BC, he refounded Samaria as Sebaste, renamed in honour of his patron the Emperor Augustus (*Sebastos* in Greek). Its walls stretched two miles (3 km) around a hilltop crowned by a temple of the imperial cult. On the coast he created Caesarea, a Greek city with a vast artificial harbour, a theatre, stadium, and a grand temple of Rome and Augustus, dedicated in 9 BC. Herod also erected buildings or paid for public works in cities with a Jewish population throughout the Greek world. He promulgated Greco-Roman culture, which he hoped to implant in Judea, where the Jewish religion was supreme. Herod was fluent in Greek, studied Greek philosophy and rhetoric, and employed Greek tutors for his children. But he himself was neither one thing nor another: to the Greeks and Romans he was a foreigner, and the Jews considered him a Gentile. Although he hoped to Hellenize the Jews, he was careful to respect their traditions. None of his pagan temples trespassed on established Jewish cities, least of all Jerusalem, where his new Jewish Temple rose on a magnificent scale. He followed the model of Solomon, and trained priests to work as masons and carpenters to avoid violation of the inner reaches of the complex. The outer colonnades, however, were in the Greek style. Herod followed the Jewish proscription of images, allowing no statues of himself (though he was not a modest man), nor did he put his image on the coinage. With completion of the Temple in 10 BC, Jerusalem became one of the greatest cities of the Roman East.

Since Romans had installed him and could depose him, Herod had a policy of scrupulous loyalty. He paid a regular tribute to Rome and contributed military force whenever required. Augustus rewarded his protégé by adding to his territory, so that it stretched from Gaza to the Golan Heights, the largest Jewish state since the days of David and Solomon. Herod remained on friendly terms with Augustus and his right-hand man Agrippa. He sent his sons to Rome to be educated and, when they finished their schooling, travelled personally to Rome to bring them home: Augustus received him graciously. For the Romans he was a bulwark of stability on the dangerous eastern frontier, a buffer against the Parthians.

Herod's fortunes began to wane in 12 BC when he quarrelled with his two sons by Mariamne. He took them to Italy to stand trial (problems within a subjected royal family directly concerned the Emperor), but Augustus managed to reconcile them. While Herod was away, tribes in southern Syria revolted. Herod's troops suppressed them easily, but then went further, moving against the Nabataeans of Transjordan. By extending the war outside his own domains, Herod angered the Emperor who was at that moment proclaiming universal peace. Although the quarrel was eventually resolved, Herod never regained full favour. His family problems continued and in 8 BC he finally received permission to bring charges against his sons. They were tried before a Roman court the next year and executed, leading Augustus to remark that he would rather be Herod's pig than his son (Herod followed Jewish dietary restrictions and ate no pork). He then faced problems with the conservative Pharisees, who opposed any Hellenization. They objected to Herod's insistence on swearing an oath to him and Augustus jointly. Six thousand who refused to do so were only fined – but in 5 BC, when Pharisees rioted to destroy a golden eagle that Herod had placed above the Temple entrance (which they saw as an intrusive symbol of Roman power), he had several rabbis and their students burnt alive and deposed the High Priest.

Herod's next and most famous atrocity is recorded in only one source, the Gospel of Saint Matthew in the New Testament. The Bible story recounts that wise men from the East told Herod that they had come to worship the King of the Jews, who had been born in Bethlehem. Herod asked them to return and tell him where they had found the baby, claiming he wanted to worship the child as well, but the wise men were warned that Herod planned treachery and returned by a different route. After making enquiries about the date when the mysterious child had been born, Herod took no chances but ordered the slaughter of all male children under two years old in Bethlehem and the whole region.

The apparent date for this atrocity was 4 BC, the year Herod had his oldest son executed on justified charges of treason, since he had been lobbying for support in Rome for his plan to supplant his father. Four days later, Herod himself died. Mourned by few, he was buried in his hilltop fortress of Herodion.

Caligula
(AD 37–41)

Virtually everything known about Caligula comes from hostile sources that portray him as a bloodthirsty maniac. Even allowing for exaggeration, there is no doubt that he never hesitated to torment or kill the common people, the ruling elite, or even his own family. His destructive reign was ended by assassination.

Caius Caesar's ancestors were emperors. His father Germanicus was nephew and adopted son of Emperor Tiberius, while his mother Agrippina was granddaughter of Augustus, who was still in power when Caius was born at Antium in AD 12. Germanicus was a popular hero and Rome's greatest general. He won important victories on the German frontier, then moved east to defeat the Armenians, but on his return died suddenly in AD 19. Germanicus had taken his family with him to the Rhine. The miniature soldier's uniform that Caius wore attracted the attention of the troops who nicknamed him affectionately Caligula, or 'little boot'.

Caligula grew up in the atmosphere of suspicion and treachery that surrounded Tiberius. After Germanicus's death, Caligula's mother broke with Tiberius (whom she suspected of poisoning her husband) and Caligula went to live first with his great-grandmother, then his grandmother. In AD 31 Tiberius summoned him to Capri, where he absorbed the perversion and depravity of the Emperor's court for the next six years. During this time, Caligula's mother was exiled and starved to death, and his two older brothers met similar fates as the Emperor's suspicion raged against members of his family. Caligula was servile, passive and indifferent to intrigue – assumed attitudes that kept him alive. He had an extremely nervous temperament and enjoyed singing, dancing, and watching tortures and executions. He supposedly had incestuous relationships with his sisters, whose images were put on his coinage when he became Emperor. He made himself useful to Tiberius by carrying out many of the duties of state, but he was never promoted to high office. In AD 37, as Tiberius lay dying, Caligula smothered him with a pillow and took his signet ring.

Tiberius's will specified that imperial power should be shared between Caius Caesar and his grandson Tiberius Gemellus. Thanks to the support of Macro, commander of the imperial Praetorian Guard, Caligula had Tiberius's will set aside on the grounds that the Emperor had been insane, and assumed sole power. After the grim years under Tiberius, the Senate and people welcomed him with unbounded enthusiasm. He paid a large bonus to the Praetorians – the first case of a practice that later became insidious – and showed his piety by conducting Tiberius's funeral and giving a speech in his honour, afterwards sailing to the prison islands where his relatives had perished to bring back and bury their remains. Caligula won immediate popularity by recalling exiles, cancelling outstanding criminal charges, ending the treason trials that had terrorized the population, and burning evidence written by informers. He reduced taxes, reformed the administration and restored power to the elected state officials. Omens were good for a peaceful and happy reign.

The people appreciated Caligula's public entertainments. He staged chariot races, gladiatorial contests, boxing matches and theatrical performances, and showered gifts on the public. He built temples, theatres, aqueducts and other public works in Rome and abroad, but his most spectacular construction was the least useful of all. This was a bridge of boats three Roman miles (4.8 km) long from the resort of Baiae to the port of Puteoli. Caligula rode across it in the dress of a triumphant general. He may have done it to impress, or in response to a remark of Tiberius that Caius had no more chance of becoming Emperor than riding a horse across the Bay of Baiae. It was the first in a series of extravagances that soon took on the aspect of madness.

Late in AD 37, Caligula, who was epileptic, suffered a serious medical problem described as 'brain fever'. From this time, his behaviour became increasingly erratic and he seemed to be completely insane. One manifestation was a growing megalomania that appeared in his religious practices. Augustus had not allowed himself to be worshipped as a god in Italy, though the Greeks were free to set up his cult in conjunction with the goddess of Rome. After his death, however, Augustus, like Julius Caesar, was worshipped as a god. Tiberius had shown no interest in the imperial cult, but when Caligula's sister Drusilla died in AD 38, he demanded that she be worshipped as a goddess. Whenever he took a solemn oath, he swore by Drusilla and in an unprecedented extension of normal practice, he demanded divine honours for himself. He had the imperial palace extended so that the temple of Castor and Pollux would serve as its entrance. Caligula would stand between the statues of the gods and demand to be worshipped as Jupiter. He eventually built a shrine to himself with a golden statue and regular sacrifices. People competed to become its priests to gain imperial favour. Caligula felt so close to Jupiter that he would carry on conversations with the god's statue, and eventually had a bridge built across the Forum to connect his palace with Jupiter's temple on the Capitoline Hill. In Rome and the provinces, he ordered the heads to be cut off statues of the gods and replaced with his own. These activities almost brought disaster when he demanded that a statue of himself as Jupiter be erected in the Jewish Temple in Jerusalem, an act that would have provoked a major revolt. The local Governor and the Jewish prince delayed the project beyond the Emperor's lifetime.

Caligula soon exceeded Tiberius in murder and cruelty, where he introduced his own perverted sense of humour. He executed Macro, the Prefect who had brought him to power, and forced his father-in-law to commit suicide. He sent an officer to kill Tiberius Gemellus when he heard that he was taking antidotes against poison, asking, 'Is there an antidote against Caesar?' He enjoyed observing tortures, made parents watch the execution of their sons, and preferred to inflict slow lingering deaths. Threats and humiliation were directed at the ruling class. When dining with the two Consuls, he burst out laughing at the thought he could have their throats cut at a moment's notice. When a Governor asked for extended sick leave, Caligula ordered him to be killed, saying that if medicine did not work, he needed bleeding. He made officials run beside his chariot or wait on him while he ate. Nor did he spare the common people. When a crowd rushed into the theatre early to take free seats, he had them driven away with clubs. Many were killed in the crush. When

Caligula decided that meat was too expensive for feeding to the wild animals he had gathered for a spectacle, he fed prisoners to them instead. Once, when the people were cheering the opposing team at the races, he burst out, 'I wish all you Romans had only one neck!' People might be imprisoned, tortured or killed for failing to cheer his performances or to swear by his name.

Caligula was a devotee of chariot races where he lavished a fortune on his favourite team. He took special care of his horse, Incitatus, who had an ivory stall in a marble stable, a staff of servants and a detachment of soldiers to ensure the horse had silence the night before a race. Making his horse Consul is one of the few lunacies Caligula did not commit, however. He only threatened to do so.

Extravagant villas, galleys and useless building projects eventually exhausted the vast treasure Tiberius had left. Caligula resorted to novel means to fill his coffers. Confiscation of condemned people's property was an established practice, but Caligula extended it to officers who had failed to name him in their wills, and executed some who made him their heir but had not obligingly died. An additional novelty was auctioning his own or confiscated property. Caligula would drive the prices to ridiculous heights: on one occasion, a Senator who had dozed off and started nodding woke to find that he had bid a fortune for a few gladiators. Caligula introduced new taxes and sent out troops to collect them. Even prostitutes were taxed, having to pay the equivalent of a single act even if they had retired from work.

Augustus, Tiberius and Germanicus had made great conquests. Caligula too longed for military glory. He mustered his legions and marched rapidly to the German frontier where he made a few feeble forays across the Rhine that he called victories. Then, he led them to the English Channel, after sending a fast messenger to tell the Senate that the whole island had surrendered to him. He lined up the artillery, then ordered the troops to take off their helmets and fill them with seashells, later building a lighthouse to celebrate his triumph. The hostile sources that report this incident may conceal a conspiracy that forced Caligula to abandon his planned conquests.

After three years of this, the Romans had had enough. In January AD 41, Senators and army officers planned Caligula's assassination, which the Praetorian Guard carried out in a corridor of the imperial palace. Caligula's wife and baby daughter were killed soon after. He was 28 years old.

Nero

(AD 54–68)

'What an artist is perishing with me!'

Nero came to power when his mother poisoned her husband, the Emperor. As Emperor himself, Nero indulged his tendencies to debauchery and cruelty. No one was safe from him, especially those who failed to appreciate his self-proclaimed skill as a musician and actor. His extravagances bankrupted the Empire, provoking the revolts that finally deposed him. An admirer of Greek culture, he effectively rebuilt Rome after a devastating fire.

Nero Claudius Caesar was born at Antium in AD 37. His mother Agrippina was descended from both Augustus and Mark Antony. When Nero was three, his father died and Agrippina was exiled by her brother, the Emperor Caligula. For a time, Nero was raised by his aunt, but when Claudius became Emperor in AD 41, he recalled Agrippina, who made a good marriage with a rich senator. In AD 48, Claudius had his wife executed and subsequently married his niece Agrippina, who was by then a widow, having, it was rumoured, poisoned her husband. Agrippina's ambitions brought Nero advancement. She secured his engagement to Claudius's daughter Octavia in AD 49 and his adoption by the Emperor the following year. Nero began to enter public life, giving speeches and gifts to the people and troops, addressing the Senate and pleading legal cases in both Greek and Latin before the Emperor. He was making a good impression when Agrippina fed Claudius a dish of poisoned mushrooms, with fatal effect, in AD 54. Nero succeeded through his mother's influence; Claudius's young son Britannicus was pushed aside.

Nero began well. He immediately visited the imperial guard and the Senate, gave Claudius a splendid funeral and announced that he would try to rule like Augustus. He gave generously to the people, Senate and troops, and presented spectacular games, races, mock sea battles and gladiatorial combats. He ordered that no gladiator should be killed and deeply regretted ever having to sentence a criminal to death. Moderation seemed to guide the 17-year-old Emperor, who was influenced by his tutor, the distinguished philosopher Seneca. Nero reduced taxes, judged cases carefully and cracked down on a variety of abuses. Like several of his predecessors, he faced a serious threat from the Parthians who overran Armenia, but his general Corbulo drove them out in AD 58. A triumphal arch celebrated the victory, part of a building programme that featured a huge wooden amphitheatre and an imposing public market. Only one murder marred Nero's first year as Emperor when he had Britannicus poisoned to remove a potential rival to the throne.

For five years Agrippina played a dominant role in the Empire. She and her son were so close that they fed rumours of incest, but she was gradually eclipsed by Nero's mistresses. The most prominent of these was Poppaea Sabina, one of the Emperor's growing entourage of degenerate but amusing favourites. Nero finally tired of his mother's nagging, expelled her from the palace, harassed her constantly and resolved to be rid of her altogether. When poison failed (she had taken all the antidotes), he presented her with a conciliatory gift, a yacht designed to sink when she was at sea. It did, but Agrippina swam to safety. He then arranged her murder. Although everyone congratulated him on escaping Agrippina's plots, the murder haunted him for the rest of his life. It also inspired popular songs and lampoons, as his prestige plummeted.

Now free of all restraint, Nero could indulge his artistic and other passions. He had long loved music and strenuously practised singing and playing the lyre. When he felt he was a master of both, he started to give public performances. These coincided with the inauguration in AD 60 of a new festival, the Neronia, an artistic competition modelled on the Olympic Games. Nero would sing all day long, performing parts from tragedies. The doors were locked so that no one could leave. Women feigned childbirth and men jumped out of windows or pretended to be dead in order to escape the tedium. Nero even had himself represented as the lyre-playing god Apollo on his coinage. His behaviour grew worse after AD 62, when Tigellinus, a friend of Poppaea's, became Prefect of the Guard and the Emperor's closest adviser. Nero dismissed Seneca, who was ordered to commit suicide, then divorced and killed Octavia, leaving him free to marry Poppaea, who was pregnant with Nero's daughter.

Nero made such a spectacle of himself and gained such a reputation for debauchery of every kind (his favourite partner was a young boy he had castrated to make more like a girl), that when disaster struck, he was held responsible. In July AD 64, a devastating fire consumed a large part of Rome, which was crowded with old wooden buildings. The fire lasted a week, destroying temples, trophies, villas and monuments. Rumours raged almost as fiercely as the fire. One claimed that Nero had started it because he wanted vacant land to build a palace. According to another he put on tragedian's garb, mounted a tower, and performed a song about the burning of Troy, hence the saying that Nero fiddled while Rome burnt. In fact, Nero went to work as soon as the fire stopped. He paid for the removal of rubble and set up a fund to compensate the victims. He brought in architects and town planners from the Greek East and redesigned the city on modern lines with broad boulevards. New buildings were set apart from each other, with porches for fighting fires, and used fireproof materials. Yet he spoiled the impression by taking the opportunity to erect an enormous palace with a mile of colonnades, a huge pool, pavilions set in landscaped gardens and decorations of ivory, gold and mother-of-pearl. The entrance hall contained a statue of Nero, 120 Roman feet (35.4 m) high. When Nero dedicated his Golden House, he exclaimed that at last he could live like a human being. He blamed the fire on the Christians, an unpopular but growing sect, and used this as an excuse to persecute them. Saints Peter and Paul are both supposed to have been his victims. Many others were thrown to the wild beasts, crucified, or dipped in pitch to serve as human torches to illuminate his Games.

Nero's sense of the theatrical showed in AD 65 when he solemnly closed the doors of the small temple of Janus in the Forum, a sign that the Empire was at peace – the first time this had been done since the reign of Augustus. A serious revolt had been suppressed in Britain, and the Parthians had been beaten. Corbulo, Nero's most successful general, was forced to commit suicide, an act that stirred resentment in the army. Not long after, Nero quarrelled with Poppaea when she complained that he came home late from the Games. Although she was pregnant once more, he kicked her to death.

Peace meant that the Emperor was free to travel. True to his artistic inclinations, he went to Greece. He was actually a serious and well-informed philhellene, deeply imbued with classical culture. He ordered all the Games, normally held at four-year intervals, to take place while he was there and introduced an unprecedented musical contest to the agenda. He not only sang, played the lyre, and acted in tragedies but joined in the four-horse chariot race. Unsurprisingly, he won all the contests, even when his chariot broke down. He gave lavish prizes and granted freedom to all the Greeks. His return to Rome was the occasion for a grand parade in which Nero, wearing an Olympic wreath, stood in the chariot Augustus had used for his triumphs.

Nero's projects drove the Empire to the edge of bankruptcy. His faithful aide Tigellinus used every means to raise money. Rich Senators were executed so that Nero could confiscate their fortunes, people were forced to change their wills in his favour and temples were robbed of their gold and silver images, which were melted down. People with money had little chance of escaping Nero's agents. Nevertheless, there was not enough to pay the army and discontent soon led to conspiracy.

Nero's first warning came in AD 68 when Vindex, Governor of Gaul, revolted, declaring he would free the human race from the tyrant. The news reached Nero in Naples, but he was too engrossed in the Games to pay attention. Vindex then sent a message that struck home: he accused Nero of being a bad lyre player. The Emperor rushed to the Senate to deny the charge. Fortunately for Nero, the army of Germany suppressed the revolt, but then the Governors of Africa and Spain threw off their allegiance, and Spanish legions started marching on Rome. Nero panicked: it was obvious the people loathed him and would offer no support. Nor would the Praetorian Guard, who had been bribed away. Deserted by his bodyguards and friends, Nero took refuge in a country house where he learnt that the Senate had deposed him and was preparing an especially horrible form of execution for him. With great reluctance, he committed suicide, lamenting that such a great artist should die. He was the last of the Augustan dynasty.

Commodus

(180–92)

'*Pacifier of the Whole Earth, Invincible, the Roman Hercules, to the fortunate Commodian Senate, greetings.*'

History has recorded little that is good about Commodus, whose reign marks the beginning of the decline and fall of Rome. Most sources were written by the ruling elite who especially despised him and did all they could to blacken his memory. Even allowing for exaggeration, however, Commodus was a monster. Not only did he have many of his real or imagined opponents murdered (other Emperors did that), but he debased his office by fighting in the arena as a gladiator, and became such a monomaniac that he identified himself with the god Hercules, and renamed everything in sight Commodian.

The second century AD marked the height of the Roman Empire. The Romans brought stability and prosperity to the vast area they ruled – all the Mediterranean with Western Europe and half the Near East – and generally maintained peace. Rome won its wars and successfully defended its borders. A major reason for the Empire's stability was the system of appointing emperors. Instead of relying on the blood relationship that had produced such horrors as Caligula or Nero, the rulers of this period chose as their successor someone they considered especially qualified, adopted him as a son and trained him for imperial power. Nerva (AD 96–8) adopted Trajan (AD 98–117), Trajan adopted Hadrian (117–38), Hadrian adopted Antoninus (138–61) and Antoninus adopted Marcus Aurelius (161–80). The last of this line was one of the great emperors: he crushed the Persians, fought successful campaigns against invading German tribes and was a practising Stoic philosopher whose volume of *Meditations* is still in print. Unfortunately, Marcus Aurelius ended the practice of adopting a successor. Although his wife was especially fecund, giving birth to 13 children, only one boy, Lucius Aurelius Commodus, survived his father, who decided to groom him for rule. He was to become one of the worst of all Roman emperors.

Commodus had the best tutors, considerable military experience and held high offices of state. Made Caesar (junior Emperor) at the age of five, he was presented to the army when he was ten, and accompanied his father during his eastern campaigns. He returned to Rome to share Aurelius's triumph, and was given the title *imperator* (victorious general). Commodus became Tribune, a major post in the government, and Consul, the highest honour in the state, all before his 16th birthday. In 177, he was formally made co-Emperor and married the aristocratic Bruttia Crispina. Soon after, he joined his father in wars against German tribes north of the imperial frontiers, and was present when Aurelius died there in 180. Commodus brought the war to a successful conclusion, imposing a harsh treaty that guaranteed Roman security on this front, but abandoned any plans to annex more territory.

He returned to Rome, celebrating his German victories with a triumph. The people received him with tremendous enthusiasm: with blond curls that glowed like the sun, and his imperial descent, Commodus seemed to offer the promise of a new age. But trouble soon started. Nineteen-year-old Commodus, although fond of the military, had no patience for routine administration and became lazy and self-indulgent once he held supreme power. The first to profit from this was his chamberlain Saoterus, who rode behind him in the triumphal chariot. The Romans were scandalized to see their Emperor constantly turn and kiss his servant in the most public manner possible. Rumours circulated that the Emperor spent more time in taverns and brothels than attending to affairs of state. It was said, implausibly, that he had a harem of 300 women and an equal number of boys. For the time being, however, Commodus surrounded himself with the advisers who had worked for Aurelius – until the first attempt was made on his life.

In 182, as Commodus was entering the Amphitheatre, one of his close friends rushed at him with a sword, exclaiming 'The Senate sends you this!' His words cost him his life, Commodus survived, and from that moment bitterly hated the Senate. The assassination attempt was part of a conspiracy organized by Commodus's sister and two of her high-placed lovers. They reflected an increasing disgust with Commodus's behaviour, but they were all rapidly wiped out. In the aftermath, Perennis, the Praetorian Prefect (commander of the imperial guard and head of the civil service) who had crushed the conspirators, became the Emperor's closest adviser. He brought out the worst in Commodus, playing on his fears, jealousies and general hatred of the Senate. As Commodus's paranoia increased, a real reign of terror began. Leading Senators, rich or learned men, and anyone distinguished enough to attract suspicion were executed. Their fortunes usually wound up in the pockets of Perennis who used the money to build up a faction of his own within the army. In 185, however, when members of Commodus's entourage convinced the Emperor that Perennis was plotting against him, he and his sons were executed.

The succeeding administration was even worse. Cleander, a former slave who had succeeded Saoterus as chamberlain, now began to assert himself. He turned the imperial court into a marketplace for seats in the Senate or high civil or military posts. Through intrigue and murder he also gained control of the Praetorian Guard. His actions provoked more plots against Commodus's regime, which were suppressed with more and more bloodshed. Blatant murder and secret poisoning eventually wiped out most of Aurelius's old associates and most current potential leaders. Eventually, Cleander went too far. In 190, when Rome was struck by plague and threatened by famine, he hoarded most of the grain supply, intending to keep the army supplied and perhaps gain popular favour by distributing it later, when people were starving. Outrage at his actions provoked a riot that Commodus finally appeased by having Cleander beheaded and his head passed around on a pole.

By the time of Cleander's downfall, the Emperor had delegated many of his duties to his servants while his own behaviour became increasingly irresponsible. Completely neglecting affairs of state, he spent his time with charioteers and gladiators, pausing long enough to order the execution of more prominent Senators. For a time, he raced chariots and slaughtered wild animals in his own private grounds, but soon turned to more dramatic exhibitionism. An eyewitness records how the Emperor, dressed as the god Mercury, would appear in the Colosseum, shooting down at wild birds and beasts (he had an unfailing aim with the javelin), then change into the uniform of a gladiator, descend into the arena and fight sparring contests that he always won. The degradation of their Emperor, who was also High Priest of the state religion, was more than most educated and civilized Romans could bear, although the common people apparently loved it. This particular spectacle was mounted for two weeks and forcibly attended by the Senate who, attempting to conceal their terror, shouted in unison, 'You are the lord, the first, the most fortunate of all. You conquer, you will conquer; Amazonian, you will conquer for ever.' On another occasion, Commodus brandished his bloody sword and the head of an ostrich he had just killed, grinning menacingly toward the Senators. Death and confiscation of personal wealth were real dangers to the Roman elite, but so was humiliation. Commodus once pushed his heavily-robed new Prefect into a pool, then forced him to dance naked before his concubines.

Commodus's last years were an epic of megalomania. He changed the names of the months to correspond to his names and titles: Amazonius (Amazonian, suitable for a gladiator), Invictus (unconquered), Felix (fortunate), Pius (dutiful), Lucius Aelius Aurelius Commodus (his name), Augustus (venerable), Herculeus Romanus (Herculean Roman) and Exsuperatorius (supreme). He was portrayed on coins and statues as the Roman hero Hercules, wearing a lion's skin and carrying the god's huge club, suitable symbols of his divine strength. He added Commodiana Herculea to the names of Alexandria and Carthage as well as the imperial grain fleet, but reserved the greatest honour for Rome. After a devastating fire and consequent rebuilding, he changed the city's name to Colonia Commodiana on the grounds that he was its new founder. The Romans themselves could not escape his image, as he cut off the head of the 100 foot (30 m) statue of the Sun God next to the Colosseum and substituted his own, adorning it with lion skin and a club and setting up an inscription that praised him as 'Conqueror of a Thousand Gladiators'. Finally he announced that he would assume the office of Consul on 1 January 193 dressed as a gladiator and emerging from the gladiatorial barracks.

That was the last straw. His favourite mistress, Marcia (Crispina had long since been executed) was one of a number of conspirators forced into action when they discovered the suspicious Emperor's order for their execution. Marcia gave Commodus poison but it only made him vomit, so he was strangled by a wrestler before he could bring further disgrace on the city and Empire.

Justinian
(527–65)

'We work night and day in reflecting upon what may be agreeable to God and beneficial to our subjects.'

Justinian was the last of the great Roman Emperors. He reunited the Mediterranean world, issued a code that remained the basis of law for a thousand years and patronized magnificent works of art and architecture. At the same time, he was a revolutionary who wanted to transform society and who tolerated no deviation. His powerful wife, Theodora, mitigated some of his policies but made others more vicious, crushing anyone who might stand in the way of the imperial couple. Although Justinian's Empire did not last, his laws and buildings formed an enduring heritage.

Petrus Sabbatius was born in a Balkan village in 483. His uncle Justin had emigrated to Constantinople, where he joined the imperial guard. He adopted his nephew, who took the name Justinian and received the best possible education as well as military training and experience. After Justin became Emperor, he promoted Justinian to the highest offices of Senator, Consul and army commander. Justinian succeeded to the throne without opposition in 527.

Justinian was a man of enormous energy who hardly ever slept and was constantly planning conquests or reforms. As a native speaker of Latin, he was conscious of his Roman imperial heritage and determined to restore the Empire. Long before his time, the West had fallen to barbarian invasions. His own territories were plagued by religious divisions and a cumbersome and corrupt government. Justinian aimed to organize administration and finance and to reconquer the West. He never hesitated to attack the established aristocracy and to choose his advisers from people of talent, regardless of their origin.

Justinian's closest associates were the general Belisarius, who came from the same background as Justinian himself, John of Cappadocia, who rose from obscurity through the financial bureaucracy, and his wife Theodora. Her origins were notorious. She had been raised in the Hippodrome, the scene of chariot races and public entertainment. She was an actress, famous for a pornographic reenactment of the story of Leda and the Swan, and a well-known and highly talented prostitute. Justinian was only able to marry her after a special law revoked the prohibition of marriage between Senators and actresses. These three advisers had enormous skill and, together with generals, lawyers and architects, led the Empire to glory.

Justinian's ambitions required money. The treasury was full, but wars and construction imposed a demand far beyond the normal revenues. John of Cappadocia sent teams of tax collectors throughout the Empire to extract money from the privileged classes whose rank and influence had previously enabled them to escape taxation. John, like the Emperor, was no respecter of persons. He used threats, beatings and torture in his private dungeons to force even respected Senators to pay. His exactions were a major factor in the first crisis the regime had to face.

The Empire was a despotism in which the people had no power. Their only opportunity for political expression was at the Hippodrome where they could conduct a dialogue with the Emperor, who usually attended the Games and races.

There was a direct entrance from the adjacent imperial palace to his box. The people were ardent partisans of either the Blues or the Greens, the sporting factions – rather like powerful and violent fan clubs – that organized the races. The people conveyed their complaints and desires through the factions' spokesmen, who addressed the Emperor's representative. The Blues and Greens were usually bitter enemies, but in 532 they united in rioting about alleged mistreatment of their members that quickly grew to direct revolt against Justinian's tax collecting. The cathedral and the Senate House were burnt down in the violence. The rioters demanded the dismissal of John of Cappadocia and other officials, then proclaimed a rival Emperor. Justinian was about to flee in desperation, but Theodora dissuaded him. He stayed and called in Belisarius whose Gothic troops slaughtered 30,000 people. The Blues and Greens put up no further resistance. Justinian had mastered his people. In the place of the destroyed cathedral he built the new cathedral of Saint Sophia, which stands as one of the greatest architectural achievements of all time.

Justinian was now ready for war. Belisarius conquered North Africa with incredible speed, then moved against Italy. He took Naples and Rome and finally entered the Gothic capital, Ravenna, in 540. With the addition of the islands and southern Spain, the Roman Empire was restored. At the same time, Justinian had to fight devastating, if inconclusive, wars with the Persians. Victory in the West had been rapid, but Justinian had to spend much of his reign and his revenue keeping the new territories under control in the face of continuing resistance, revolt and attack. Problems were complicated by the bubonic plague that devastated the whole Empire in 542–3, seriously reducing the manpower available for the army.

Justinian, like other despots, did not allow his subordinates to feel secure in their power or popularity. Belisarius, whose victories had been celebrated with magnificence, fell from favour in 542, when Theodora had him removed from command and arrested, ostensibly for embezzlement. Although Belisarius was eventually restored, he never regained imperial confidence. John of Cappadocia was even more unfortunate. In 541, Theodora trapped him in an intrigue that made him appear traitorous. He was sent into exile from which he never returned. In these cases (and there were many others), it seemed as if the malign Empress was using her influence to destroy the highest officers of state. In fact, Justinian was the prime mover, striking down anyone too successful or popular after they had done their job, and using Theodora to front his actions. With her hatred of the aristocracy, she was well suited to carrying out the Emperor's policy of bringing everyone under tight control.

However tyrannical, Justinian's regime was based on the law, where he created his most lasting legacy. By his time, the Roman law was a complex jumble of precedents, decrees and interpretations reaching back a thousand years. As soon as he came to the throne, Justinian appointed a commission of lawyers who purged obsolete laws and organized the rest into one code, the Corpus of Civil Law, issued in 529. This worked so well that it formed the basis for the legal systems in most of Europe until modern times.

The laws were part of an effort to assert control over every aspect of society, and to remove anomalies or deviation. Justinian enforced his ideas of correct behaviour and belief. He especially detested pederasty, for which the punishment was castration. In one notorious case in 528, three bishops and a former Prefect of the Guard were convicted and paraded around the city with their amputated members on display. Christian heretics and followers of other religions also suffered. Manicheans were condemned to death, the Samaritans were persecuted so severely that they rose in revolt, Jews lost civil rights and were forbidden to use Hebrew in their services, and a determined effort was made to root out paganism. People who still believed in the old Greek gods were dismissed from their jobs and tortured or imprisoned. Many were driven to suicide. Pagan books were burnt in public. Philosophers also fell victim to these persecutions. Plato's Academy in Athens lost its funding and its leading teachers emigrated to Persia. A determined campaign also destroyed temples and converted pagans in the countryside.

Justinian was an expert theologian who dictated what his subjects should believe. But he faced one intractable problem. The people of his richest and most strategic provinces, Syria and Egypt, followed the Monophysite doctrine, an interpretation of Christ's nature that was considered heretical in Constantinople and Rome. Justinian first attempted persecution, but that risked alienating a vast population, so he devised a clever solution. He pretended to persecute the Monophysites (to placate the Patriarch of the Orthodox Church and the Pope) but allowed Theodora to protect Monophysite clergy in her palace. Thanks to her patronage, the heretical church survived and even sent out missionaries, while the Emperor appeared as the defender of Orthodoxy. Theodora's religious influence reached its height in 536 when, as a result of her manoeuvring, a Monophysite sympathizer, Vigilius, was named as Pope. After he was installed by Belisarius, he killed his predecessor, then openly espoused Catholicism. In 543, Justinian issued a decree condemning the works of three long-dead theologians in an effort to reach compromise with the Monophysites. When Vigilius rejected it, imperial troops hauled him from Mass and took him to Constantinople, where he was detained for several years. Finally, in 553, Justinian called an ecumenical council and ordered it to follow his theology. He never solved the religious problems.

After Theodora died of cancer in 548 the later years of Justinian's reign were dismal. Wars dragged on, devastating Italy and Africa, and merely maintaining the *status quo* with the Persians. The Huns invaded near Constantinople, forcing the Emperor to recall Belisarius from retirement, and many of his reforms failed. Justinian devoted greater attention to religion. He died in 565, after a reign that saw glorious achievements but ultimate failure. His laws and buildings survived him.

Wu Zetian

(690–705)

'My name was a symbol that would make all men submit to Us and facilitate good government.'

imaginary enemies, but in 695, when she was well established in power, she closed it down and executed its leaders. Investigations revealed they had condemned at least 850 innocent people.

Wu and her family now began to aim for open acknowledgement of her power. In 688, a massive temple of the Wu clan was built in the capital and a mysterious stone was discovered in the river, inscribed 'The Holy Mother has come among men to rule with perpetual prosperity.' Wu took the title Holy Divine Imperial Mother and wiped out most of the legitimate imperial family, including two of the late Emperor's sons. In 690, she finally announced a change of dynasty, becoming Emperor in her own name, with Ruizhong demoted to Imperial Heir. This was unprecedented in Chinese history.

During her sole rule, Wu's favourites accrued tremendous power. The foremost was Xue Huaiyi, a strong, vigorous, itinerant pedlar whom she made a monk, since monks were the only uncastrated men who could enter the imperial palace. He ran a large monastery with gangs of monks who occupied houses and land with impunity and generally oppressed the people. Xue was additionally a gifted architect who erected some of the most magnificent buildings in the capital. It did him no good. He became so generally loathed that Wu had him strangled. Her family caused greater problems. Since the legitimate Emperor stood in their way to supremacy, they accused his wife and favourite concubine of using sorcery against Wu. Both were executed. To isolate Ruizong further, she had officials who visited him too often cut in half. Intrigues and denunciations made court life extremely dangerous.

China faced serious trouble from the Turks in 697, when forces led by incompetent Wu princes suffered massive defeats. The Empress brought Zhongzong back from exile and he raised an army that convincingly turned the tide. His reward was to replace his brother as Imperial Heir, but it became clear to Wu that her family was useless and that the Tang would eventually have to be restored.

The last chapter of Wu's life is bound up with the Zhang brothers, musicians widely reputed to be her lovers, although they actually preferred young boys, and she herself was over 70. She showered such favour on them and they flaunted their newly-acquired wealth and offices so blatantly that they became widely hated, tarnishing the reputation of the Empress and her whole regime. By 700, Wu's health had started to deteriorate, but she still had the energy to arrange for her grandson and the leading statesman to be exiled for criticizing the Zhangs. By 704, she was confined to bed, seeing only the Zhangs. Courtiers, fearing that she would die and that her favourites would fabricate decrees giving them permanent power, conspired to kill the Zhangs and depose Wu in February 705. She retired to a monastery in the mountains where she died at the end of the year.

Al-Hakim

(996–1021)

'In the name of al-Hakim Allah, the Compassionate, the Merciful.'

Blasphemous words proclaiming al-Hakim God

The Egyptian Caliph al-Hakim is probably the only tyrant to be worshipped as a god. He inherited a powerful state that he maintained despite ever-increasing eccentricities. He murdered his tutor and virtually everyone who came into close contact with him. He persecuted Christians and Sunni Moslems and imposed outlandish restrictions on the population. His destruction of Jerusalem's holiest shrine helped provoke the Crusades. His nocturnal peregrinations through the streets of Cairo became part of folklore in the Arabian Nights, but he tried to destroy the city. He allowed himself to be proclaimed and worshipped as a god. He disappeared mysteriously, leading his followers to expect his miraculous return at the end of days.

Al-Hakim bi-Amr became Caliph of Fatimid Egypt at the age of 11 when his father al-Aziz died. He inherited a rich, well-organized state where Ismaili Shiites ruled a majority Sunni and Christian population. It stretched over much of North Africa and into Syria. The Fatimids were the greatest power in the Near East, matched only by their rivals, the Byzantines. Al-Hakim's first years were disturbed by conflict between the Berbers and Turks in his army, but order was restored and the state was run by the Caliph's tutor, the eunuch Barjuwan, who profited immensely from his position. In 1000, when he was 15, the Caliph decided to free himself from tutelage by personally murdering Barjuwan. He calmed the crowd who came to protest and started his reign well by appointing competent officials to run the state. In 1003, however, he had his secretary executed, beginning the series of purges and bizarre orders that displayed his absolute power. So many government officers fell from favour to be tortured or mutilated that al-Hakim created a special department to look after the property he confiscated from them.

Al-Hakim was an enthusiastic Shiite, determined to ensure the domination of his sect by persecuting Christians, Jews and Sunnis. Beginning in 1003 and continuing for ten years he directed a series of laws against non-Moslems. Churches were demolished and replaced by mosques, land and fortunes belonging to monasteries were confiscated, Palm Sunday and Epiphany processions were forbidden, Christians and Jews were required to wear distinctive dress (and in the baths, where people removed their clothes, to wear crosses and bells, respectively). The most notorious result of this campaign was the destruction of the most sacred site in Christendom, the Church of the Holy Sepulchre in Jerusalem, in 1009, part of a general persecution of Christians in Palestine. This act had long-lasting repercussions. Even though the Byzantine Emperor had the church rebuilt in 1048, its destruction made a deep impression on the Christian world and was a contributory factor to the Crusades that began later in the century. Persecution and demolition reached their peak in 1012, when only the monastery of Mount Sinai survived. So many Christians converted to Islam out of fear that the office for recording conversions was overwhelmed. Many who remained Christian left the country. Those who stayed were subject to constant reminders of their humiliated state.

The majority Sunni population also felt the Caliph's wrath, although less consistently. He arrested people who prayed incorrectly (not according to the Shiite rite), and publicly cursed the first four Caliphs, a Shiite practice the Sunnis always bitterly resented. At the same time, however, he demonstrated his piety by building grandiose mosques. The largest mosque in Egypt, shown in ruins in the photograph on page 47 but now restored, is named after Al-Hakim. He also established the House of Science, Islam's first real university. It had a well-stocked library, scientific implements and everything necessary for teaching a great range of disciplines. The core was theology, for the university's mission was to spread Shiism, but it attracted scholars from the entire Islamic world.

Al-Hakim was a puritan, determined to enforce his particular morality on everyone. Drinking wine was forbidden, even to infidels who were normally allowed to make and consume it. Beer followed, as did grapes and honey: vines were chopped down and honey poured into the Nile, for both of these could be fermented. Various vegetables and fish were also prohibited, for reasons that were unclear. In his early years, the Caliph used to ride or walk around the streets of Cairo at night, ordering merchants to keep their shops open and the streets illuminated for him. When he began to suspect that the population were enjoying themselves too much, or practising immorality, he cracked down on public and private entertainment. Gambling, musical instruments and even chess were forbidden. Singers, musicians and singing girls could no longer perform and for modesty men had to wear a towel round their waist in the baths. Violation of even the most trivial regulation could result in death. Women, whom al-Hakim seems to have considered founts of debauchery, were his special victims. They were forbidden to wear jewellery, to attend the baths, to sit in windows where they could be seen, and finally to leave home at all. To ensure that, he forbade cobblers to make womens' shoes so they could not walk outside. If, in spite of everything, a woman was found in the bath, she was walled up inside. Dogs fared even worse: since the Caliph disliked their barking, all the dogs in Cairo were slaughtered.

These lunatic laws, which were enforced throughout the realm, naturally stirred opposition. They added to the misery of a population suffering from a prolonged drought and gave support to a serious revolt in 1005 led by a member of the ancient Umayyad family who proclaimed himself Caliph. He attracted the support of many Berbers, occupied Libya and approached Cairo before al-Hakim's loyal general al-Fadl defeated him. When he was finally captured, his head and those of thousands of his followers were put on the backs of a camel train, paraded around Syria, then thrown into the Euphrates. The general was too successful, and made the mistake of finding the Caliph busy cutting up the body of a boy he had just killed. Wisely, he returned home and made his will before al-Hakim's executioners arrived.

Al-Hakim killed his officials, however much he had favoured them, members of his family and a group of his concubines whom he had drowned. Even though no holder of high office could be sure of staying alive, the reign was relatively peaceful. There was only one other major revolt, in 1012, when a Palestinian tribal leader broke away and established the ruler of Mecca as a rival caliph. He also called in Bedouin tribes who helped him gain control of most of Palestine, but they devastated settled communities. Although the Anti-Caliph conciliated the Christians by promising to rebuild the Holy Sepulchre, al-Hakim's bribes and armies put an end to the rebellion.

The reign reached its extreme point when al-Hakim decided he was God. In a sense, this was an extension of the Ismaili doctrine, which held that their leader was divinely appointed, although not himself divine. In 1017, a mystic from Central Asia started to preach the divinity of al-Hakim but he was soon murdered by the outraged population. Another, from Persia, had better luck and attracted a following, proclaiming that the Caliph was God and that the religious law, the *sharia*, was abolished. Al-Hakim supported him. Some of the adherents of the new doctrine rode into Cairo's oldest mosque with a letter that they handed to the *qadi*. It began 'In the name of al-Hakim Allah, the Compassionate, the Merciful', phrasing blasphemous to any Moslem because it gave the Caliph attributes appropriate only to God. Many were killed in the ensuing riot, but the Persian mystic escaped to Syria where his teaching took root as the Druze religion, which still survives.

The Caliph became more and more eccentric. He wandered around Cairo day and night, with unkempt hair and in pauper's robes, riding on a donkey. He enjoyed watching street brawls (some stirred by his guards). On one occasion, as he passed a butcher's shop, he seized a carving knife and killed one of his men on the spot. People were too terrified to react, but he was nevertheless exposed to satire and insults. Al-Hakim's claim of divine power led him to abandon the basic Islamic practices of prayer, fasting and pilgrimage. He also began favouring Sunnis and Christians to such an extent that Christians who had converted to Islam were allowed to return to their old religion, an apostasy universally condemned in Islam. The population was close to revolution. In 1020, enraged by the people's hostility and jeers, he sent his African slave troops in to loot and burn Cairo. Many perished in devastation that lasted an entire week and destroyed much of the old city. Al-Hakim finally called back his men after Turkish and Berber troops started to side with the people.

Al-Hakim's end was as mysterious as his behaviour. In February 1021, he set out on one of his habitual rides into the hills south of Cairo, an area he had long frequented and where he had built the observatory he used for practising the astrology forbidden to his subjects. He was never seen again. Five days later, his bloodstained clothes were found, but not his body. It appears that he was murdered in a conspiracy organized by his sister, but the Druze believe that he never died, and will reappear to bring a reign of truth and justice at the end of the world.

King John
(1199–1216)

'Since I became reconciled with God and
submitted my self and my kingdom to the
church, nothing has gone well with me, and
everything unlucky has happened to me'

The foundation of English civil liberties ironically derives from the actions of its most tyrannical king. After behaving badly as a prince, and even worse as a king, John managed to lose most English possessions in France, became involved in a disastrous quarrel with the Pope, and antagonized virtually everyone in his kingdom. His rebellious barons finally forced him to sign Magna Carta, an unprecedented concession by a ruler to his people and a key document in human rights.

John was born in 1166, the youngest of the four sons of King Henry II and the formidable Eleanor of Aquitaine. He grew up overshadowed by his father's oldest and favourite son Henry (who died young) and by his heroic brother Richard. At the age of ten, he was made Lord of Ireland, but damaged his reputation irrevocably when he went there to establish his authority in 1185. Attempting to replace established local lords with his own men, and looting churches, he provoked a hostile uprising that led to his defeat and he returned to England in humiliation. By then, his brothers had raised a serious rebellion against their father. John remained loyal to the King until 1189 when he joined a conspiracy against Henry, who was weak and ageing and died soon afterwards, saddened by John's treachery.

Richard then became King, but almost immediately set off on the Third Crusade, draining the wealth of the country to meet the costs involved. During his absence, a regency council, from which John was deliberately excluded, ruled England. Although the Crusade failed to capture Jerusalem, Richard became a hero. However, on his return from the Holy Land he was captured and held for ransom for two years by the German Emperor. During this time, John conspired with King Philip of France to seize the English crown and turn Normandy over to the French. Hubert Walter, the Archbishop of Canterbury, thwarted the plot and denounced John's treachery. After he was released and returned to England in 1194, Richard accepted John's submission and restored him to favour. These years were marked by greatly increased taxation to pay for Richard's crusading debts and ransom, but the King's heroic reputation saved him from the hatred that would later descend on his brother.

When Richard died in 1199, John succeeded, but not without opposition. Although the dowager Eleanor ensured John's recognition in England, an important party formed around his nephew Arthur of Brittany, who by strict primogeniture (he was the son of John's older brother Geoffrey) had the right to the crown. Philip of France backed him, and invaded Normandy. During the war, Arthur fell into John's hands. Sources variously report that John planned to have him blinded or castrated. Arthur's fate is uncertain, but he was never seen alive after 1203. His presumed murder further blackened John's reputation, and led Brittany into revolt. The war with France was a disaster for England. After capturing Richard's new fortress on the Seine, Philip gained control of Normandy. John was left only with his territories in the southwest, while the crucial Channel ports remained in Philip's hands.

Before the war, John had made a procession through his French territories during which he caught sight of the striking 16 year old Isabella of Angoulême. He fell for her immediately, arranged the annulment of his existing marriage and married the Princess, acquiring a reputation for uxoriousness, as the pair spent so long in bed. When Eleanor of Aquitaine died in 1204, John annulled her will and transferred her estate to his young wife. Nevertheless, despite his attachment to Isabella, John produced numerous illegitimate children. His appetite for women was notorious. He would seduce the wives of his barons and even boast publicly of his conquests in front of his victims. On one occasion, however, the offended husband managed to insinuate a prostitute in the King's bed instead of his wife. His ruse was successful, and he wisely fled the country.

In spite of his reputation, John was a hard-working and effective king. He administered justice, set up an orderly system of record-keeping and financed the basis for England's navy, which would later be world-renowned. At the same time, he made himself unpopular by raising taxes to pay for the wars, especially by doubling, then tripling the charge of scutage, which a knight could pay in lieu of personal service.

When Archbishop Walter died in 1205, John naturally wanted to appoint his successor, but the monks of Westminster preempted him by naming one of their own. Both sides appealed to Pope Innocent III, who had considerable power and had already had dealings with John. Since 1200, Innocent had been demanding that John respect Richard's will and pay a dowry to his widow. In the event, Innocent rejected both candidates and named his old schoolfellow, Stephen Langton, as Archbishop. John refused to accept Langton, and sent officers to take over Canterbury Cathedral. He was within his rights and was backed by many of his barons, who resented the Pope's interference. When Innocent threatened England with the interdict – the closing of all churches and end of sacraments and services – John flew into a rage, seized church property and promised to expel clergy from the country. In 1208, the Pope carried out his threat. Church doors closed, there were no marriages or burials – none of the functions of the church in a deeply religious age were available. Many priests and monks left the country, but religion survived, as the church made concessions that allowed children to be christened and some services to be held. The people, however, did not rise against John. They benefited from not paying the tithe and by confiscating church property.

Innocent then took the next step of excommunicating the King in 1209 and later, when attempts at compromise failed, absolved the population from their allegiance to John and excommunicated anyone who served him. The final blow came in 1213 when the frustrated Innocent officially deposed John and turned his throne over to Philip of France. Philip raised a huge army and fleet for an invasion, only to learn that John had not only capitulated, but made himself a feudal vassal of the Pope – in theory, Innocent ruled England. John had surrendered completely. He agreed to accept Langton and to repay all the church's losses. Innocent, who had no desire to see his new realm ruined by exorbitant demands, settled for a moderate sum, and told the infuriated Philip to call off his invasion. The interdict was finally lifted after more than six years. Nothing like this had ever happened before, but both monarchy and church survived.

Relations with France remained hostile. John formed a coalition with continental rulers, entered into another war with Philip, and was soundly beaten. When he returned to England in 1214, he was once again in need of money. The loathed scutage and other taxes were raised, essentially on the feudal barons who had borne the brunt of fiscal oppression since the reign of Henry II. Now their anger was increased by John's use of the money. Not trusting his barons, who had lost patience with the long and unsuccessful wars (although most had stood by him in the conflict with Rome), he diverted the taxes to pay an army of mercenaries, who rapidly gained a reputation for violence. They formed a force independent of any baron, loyal only to John.

Archbishop Langton felt no gratitude to John, on whom he had been imposed. A student of canon law, he was convinced of the evils of feudalism and the need for reform. In 1214, he began meeting leading barons, revealing to them a forgotten charter of Henry I that had granted basic rights to the people. The barons, who formed an affiliation against John, swore to uphold the charter. They met at Christmas and submitted their demands to the King. He promised to give them an answer by Easter and proceeded immediately to look for a way out. He announced that he was going on a new crusade, swore his fealty again to Innocent, fortified his castles, and brought in more mercenaries for the coming struggle.

His precautions were redundant. His supporters fell away, and by the time he met the barons at Runnymede near Windsor on 15 June 1215, he had no choice but to capitulate. With tremendous reluctance he signed Magna Carta, which guaranteed some fundamental civil rights: that no one could be arrested or imprisoned without the judgement of his peers, and that scutage could not be levied without agreement. These and other clauses protected the barons against the King and even granted some rights to the common people. For the first time, the King was forced to recognize the right of his subjects to make demands and his own obligation to obey the law.

Although John signed, he had no intention of obeying. He called on Innocent, who annulled the charter, suspended Langton from office and excommunicated the barons. John raised an army and had some success until the barons called on Philip of France, whose son Louis arrived with an invading army. John was retreating from them when he crossed the tidal Wash on England's east coast, only to see his entire treasure swept away by the sea. Now destitute, he fell into a rage exacerbated by illness and died two days later in 1216. The barons then switched sides, proclaimed John's nine-year-old son Henry, King, and sent Louis home. Magna Carta was restored and its principles have prevailed ever since.

Genghis Khan

(1206–27)

'In the space of seven years I have succeeded in accomplishing a great work and uniting the whole world in one Empire.'

Genghis Khan is infamous as a merciless and bloodthirsty conqueror – outside Mongolia, where he is a national hero. One of the greatest organizers in history, he forged mutually hostile and disunited tribes into a Mongolian nation that extended its power over an unprecedentedly vast Empire. He patronized learning and founded dynasties that dominated Asia, Eastern Europe and the Near East for centuries after his death. Although he slaughtered huge numbers of his enemies, he brought peace to lands he ruled and prosperity to his homeland.

Temujin, as Genghis was known until he achieved power, was born in 1162 in a distant mountain region of Mongolia. His father, a minor tribal chief, was poisoned by Tartar enemies when Temujin was nine. The family, deserted by the rest of the tribe, was left weak and destitute, owing their survival to the determination and skills of Temujin's mother Hoelun. They lived in a world where tribe preyed on tribe, often descending suddenly to snatch away women and animals and never hesitating to kill the men. Temujin drew his first blood when he was 13, killing his older stepbrother after an argument over game they had shot. That left him in a very vulnerable position, as head of one tent with only nine horses in a society where strength and wealth were determined by the number of men and horses that could be mustered.

In 1183, Temujin's wife was captured by the rival Merkit tribe. They had only recently married, although they had been betrothed since childhood. Temujin and his brothers, outnumbered by the hostage takers, rode to safety, knowing that a young woman would not be killed. With the help of his childhood friend Jamuka, and Toghrul, powerful leader of the Keraits and blood-brother of Temujin's father, Temujin rescued his wife and slaughtered her captors. Toghrul eventually accepted him as his own son and Temujin and Jamuka allied in forming a joint camp. Temujin now became more of a herdsman and steppe warrior than a low-grade hunter.

By 1185, when his cousins joined him, Temujin was becoming a recognized leader and developing the skills that would bring him to supremacy. He organized his followers in novel style, creating separate heavy and light armed units, and giving everyone a defined responsibility, rather than following the tradition of loosely-allied independent warriors. Temujin's success provoked Jamuka's jealousy and led to a confrontation that Temujin lost. Jamuka behaved so badly, however, that many clans deserted to Temujin, who in 1197 adopted another fundamental innovation: he occupied the land of defeated tribes but incorporated their men into his own tribe as equals. He was building a nation. Five years later, before a great victory over the Tartars, he ordered his warriors to pursue the enemy, loot their camp, and to bring all the booty to him for distribution. Central control was emerging. He was winning more and more battles because his men were fighting as organized units in new and flexible formations that Temujin devised. He frequently improvised his tactics on the battlefield. With the defeat of Jamuka and the Merkits in 1206, Temujin eliminated his last rivals on the plains of Mongolia. An assembly of the Mongol chiefs gave him the title Genghis Khan. He had united the country for the first time and brought peace.

Genghis owed his success to organization and adaptation. He had no formal instruction in the art of war, but learnt as he fought. All males aged between 20 and 60 were given regular military training and specific duties. To break divisive ethnic loyalties, tribesmen were distributed throughout carefully defined units, based on a decimal system, ranging from small groupings of ten warriors to the *tumen* of 10,000. The smaller units elected their own officers, but the Khan named commanders of 1000 or more. Promotion was by merit, and so successful that no general ever deserted Genghis's army.

The Mongol forces were all cavalry, as the men learnt horsemanship and archery from childhood. They carried their own supplies, tools and weapons in a sack that could be inflated for crossing rivers, and rode with several mounts, so they could travel over long distances without a break. They preferred brood mares, whose milk fed them on the way, together with dried meat and yogurt. The Mongols took great care of their horses. Once a horse had served its career it was put out to pasture and no one was allowed to kill it. Since the army had no heavy train of supplies or equipment, it could cover vast distances in a short time and surprise its enemies before they even suspected an attack. In battle, the light armed forces shot arrows from a distance to disorient the enemy, and the heavy armed cavalry charged behind them.

A strict code of law regulated both army and nation. Each tribe had its own grazing grounds and was forbidden to raid others for animals or women, under penalty of death. No Mongol could be enslaved. Lost property had to be turned in or the finder would be punished as a thief. News was spread rapidly by a courier service that could cover 120 miles in a day. Total religious toleration was practised. Regular assemblies explained policies and obtained the personal commitment of every individual warrior.

The Mongols' most powerful neighbours were the Jurchen Manchus whose Jin dynasty based in Zhongdu (now Beijing) dominated the steppe by instigating inter-tribal aggression. In 1210, when the Jin demanded tribute, Genghis refused. He was in a strong position, for the Uighurs to the west had submitted, providing educated manpower for the administration of a growing Empire, while his campaigns against the Western Xia had taught him the techniques of siege warfare. In 1213, Genghis and his sons led three armies into China, where they encountered a peasant society with innumerable people working the land. The Mongols, who wanted land for grazing, herded the Chinese peasants like animals, driving them as refugees into the towns, which they proceeded to attack. Towns that surrendered were looted. Those that resisted saw their populations massacred, although doctors, artisans and skilled workers, who would be useful at home, were spared. Zhongdu, which resisted attack for three years, was burnt to the ground and the corpses of its slaughtered inhabitants piled in huge mounds. Genghis returned to Mongolia with so much looted wealth that the Mongols, who had lived in poverty, became rich and began demanding even more luxuries.

Genghis next took over the territories to the west, bringing him into contact with the imposing Islamic realm of Khwarezm that stretched from the Indus to the Caspian. Bukhara and Samarkand, its greatest cities, were rich and sophisticated seats of trade and learning. Genghis proposed peace, but when the Khwarezmian Sultan Muhammad insulted his envoys, he decided on war. This took his armies to another unfamiliar environment, with enormous stretches of desert between the settled lands. In 1219, Genghis crossed the Tien Shan Mountains, dividing his 200,000 men into four units, to engage the enemy simultaneously from every side. Genghis personally led the force that crossed the supposedly impassable Red Sand Desert to surprise Bukhara. The Sultan's cities fell one by one. The Mongols drove out the local population and systematically looted the city. Leaders, especially aristocrats, were usually killed so they could not organize resistance. Few buildings were left standing in Bukhara but at Samarkand, the people were allowed to ransom themselves, although the garrison was massacred (they were infantry, no use to the Mongols). These campaigns had a permanent effect. The Turks replaced the Persians in much of Central Asia, and the ancestors of the Ottoman Turks were pushed westwards toward Europe.

The worst atrocities took place in eastern Iran and Afghanistan. The whole population of Nishapur, except 400 artisans who were sent to Mongolia, was massacred, with the heads of men, women and children piled in separate mounds. Even the domestic animals were killed. When Herat revolted, the city was destroyed and its population wiped out. These acts were intended as a warning – cities that surrendered would be treated well, those that resisted would be shown no mercy. For the Mongols, settled populations were an inferior kind of being whose lives were of no special account. A fast-moving cavalry force could not accommodate prisoners and captives were usually killed quickly, without cruelty or torture. Genghis Khan's aims were total victory and subjection through striking fear into his enemies. From Iran, Genghis despatched an army that devastated the Caucasian principalities, defeated the Russians and made the entire circuit of the Caspian without a single defeat.

The Khan of the Western Xia, who had refused to participate in the campaign against Khwarezm, allied with the Jin. Genghis crushed them in 1226, but died during the campaign in the following year. His body was transported back to Mongolia. To keep the site of his grave secret, his bearers killed anyone they encountered along the route. Genghis's sons were to bring Eurasia under total Mongol domination.

Muhammad bin Tughlak

(1325–1351)

At the end of the tenth century Turks from Afghanistan began raiding India, a country of enormous wealth, ripe for conquest and incorporation into the Islamic world. In 1206 the Turks established the Sultanate of Delhi, which dominated the subcontinent for the next 300 years. The Sultans reached the height of their power in the reign of Muhammad bin Tughlak. His expansionist policies, which brought most of India under his control, reflected an uncontrollable and erratic ambition that eventually impoverished the country, and provoked a series of devastating revolts. He was famed for his learning, piety – and cruelty.

Fakhr al-Din Muhammad Jauna Khan, also called Ulugh Khan, was the oldest son of the military leader Ghiyath al-Din Tughlak, who had seized supreme power in Delhi in 1320. Tughlak ruled equitably, restoring prosperity and favouring Islam, but needed to suppress a major rebellion in the south. He sent Jauna, who succeeded in quashing the rebellion and then allowed his advisers to spread the rumour that Tughlak had died, in a bid to have himself proclaimed ruler. When news arrived that Tughlak was still alive, Jauna had his advisers killed, rushed back to Delhi, and obtained his father's forgiveness. In 1323 he was sent south again, where he conquered important territory. Meanwhile, Tughlak decided to intervene in a dynastic dispute in Bengal and recalled Jauna to administer the capital in his absence. The Prince took advantage of his position to build his own party and obtained the support of a leading sheikh, who predicted his imminent accession to power. Tughlak, disturbed by rumours of his son's treachery, returned in 1325. Jauna met him outside Delhi in a pavilion specially designed to collapse easily. When the Sultan was comfortably installed, the structure fell. Tughlak was killed and Jauna succeeded, taking the name of Muhammad Sultan.

Muhammad had received an excellent education. He was eloquent and learned in Persian and Arabic, a master of philosophy and science, a skilled writer and calligrapher. He had a superb memory, but his domineering nature demanded instant obedience (he never asked or took advice) and his pride aimed for universal dominion. His grandiose projects led only to disaster.

The Sultan was concerned with justice and organization. He ordered a register of all the land in his kingdom, so he could ensure equitable and efficient taxation. At the same time, he manifested the violence that was to become characteristic by having his popular younger brother murdered. When his cousin, who governed the Deccan, revolted in 1326, Muhammad sent a general who defeated and captured him. The cousin was flayed alive, his flesh given to his family and fed to elephants (they refused to eat it) and his stuffed skin exhibited throughout the kingdom as a warning to others.

To maintain a domain that stretched far to the south, Muhammad decided to build a new capital in a more convenient location than Delhi. In 1327, he chose Deogir in the Deccan which he refounded as Daulatabad, adorning it with palaces, markets and enormously imposing fortifications shown in the photograph on page 59. He moved there with the court and its dependents, as well as essential workers like merchants and artisans, making it his base for successful campaigns in the region. He was hardly settled, however, when he had to suppress a serious revolt west of Delhi then deal with a damaging Mongol raid. Muhammad returned to Delhi in 1329 to find its people resentful at the loss of the court and the commerce it generated. They expressed themselves in anonymous letters that infuriated Muhammad. He ordered the evacuation of the whole population to Daulatabad, some 700 miles (1125 km) away. They were supposedly given three days to pack and any who stayed behind were executed. Since Delhi was seven miles (12 km) across and densely populated, this was a massive undertaking. Even though a good road had been built, with frequent inns and post stations, thousands perished on the way. The Sultan visited the empty city and rejoiced.

At the same time, claiming that the Hindus who inhabited the rich plains of the north had collaborated with the Mongols, he increased the assessments on their land and revived old taxes. The result was not increased revenue but impoverishment, revolt and abandonment of the land, especially when drought set in soon afterwards. When continued wars and building projects made Muhammad more desperate for money, he experimented with a new coinage. Previously, coins had been struck in gold and silver, the value of which was universally recognized. Muhammad decided to issue a token coinage of brass, which he ordered to be accepted as equivalent to silver. To guarantee its value, he took the new currency in payment of taxes. The scheme, which operated for three years, was a complete failure. Merchants would willingly pay with tokens, but refused to accept them as payment and their value in relation to precious metals plummeted. Far worse, though, was the wave of counterfeiting they inspired. Gold and silver were too expensive to be forged, but since brass cost virtually nothing and the coins were easy to copy, there was great incentive to produce quantities of false coins, which undermined the whole project. Finally, Muhammad redeemed the tokens at great loss. Mounds of them could still be seen a century later.

By 1333, the situation in the north was so desperate that most of the population was in revolt. Muhammad marched on the region, treating his own subjects as enemies. Towns were captured, their inhabitants slaughtered, and the heads of the defenders displayed on the battlements. Many fled to the jungle as Muhammad laid waste to a wide region. In 1335, while he was subduing another revolt in the south (his policies led to endemic revolts), he tried a new and even more pernicious financial experiment by introducing tax farming. Starting in the Deccan, tax collection was auctioned to the highest bidder. This naturally led to corruption and overextension as tax farmers frequently bid more than they could collect only to find the Sultan implacable, refusing to take account of circumstances, and forcing them into rebellion. During his southern campaign Muhammad suffered from terrible toothache. When the offending tooth was extracted, he had a monumental tomb built for it, which still exists today.

In 1337, Muhammad allowed the citizens of Delhi to return home if they wished, only to move them to another site a few years later as the whole region was so ravaged by mismanagement and famine that people were turning to cannibalism. Muhammad issued grain to villagers and fed the displaced population of Delhi, but the relief he supplied was often conditional on specific improvements to the land that the recipients were unable or unwilling to perform. Anyone who resisted these obligations was brutally executed.

It was during this period that a famous Arab traveller, Ibn Battuta, arrived in India. The generous Sultan gave him honours, wealth and high office. Ibn Battuta has left an account of the Sultan's palace in Delhi. Guards and musicians manned the outer door, beside the public executioners' platform, where bodies were left exposed for three days. The Sultan's vast audience hall lay deep within the complex. Here he sat surrounded by heavy armed troops, officials and notables. Elephants trained to bow before him would be brought in, their tusks tipped with metal so they could kill criminals more efficiently. Although Muhammad was pious, learned and exceedingly generous, his punishments were frequent and savage. Every day except Friday, chained prisoners were brought to the audience hall for beating, torture or execution. Ibn Battuta enjoyed the Sultan's generosity but his account could not conceal Muhammad's cruelty.

Muhammad saw himself as a world conqueror. His first move outside India was against eastern Iran and failed completely. More ambitiously, in 1338, he decided to conquer China. He amassed an army of 100,000 which he sent into the Himalayas. They had hardly penetrated the foothills before Chinese mountain warriors killed most of them, leaving the surviving 10,000 to limp back to Delhi. The loss of men and money was catastrophic. The revolts that followed impelled Muhammad to seek new ways to raise his prestige and revenue. One solution was to obtain the blessing of the Caliph, the nominal head of Islam. Even better, he found a descendant of the Abbasid Caliphs who moved to India from Central Asia in 1343 to a royal welcome but turned out to be so unpleasant and parsimonious that he was no help to Muhammad at all.

With starvation and revolt rampant, Muhammad embarked on a programme of agricultural reform. All the lands he controlled were to be divided into new units and cultivated regardless of their nature, sown with rotating crops of wheat, barley and sugar-cane. The officials he appointed to supervise the project, which was wholly impractical, stole most of the money allotted to it. Muhammad would have had them all killed had he not been preoccupied with revolts. Districts were constantly breaking away, and the Sultan was ceaselessly rushing from one end of the country to the other in a vain effort to regain control. The Deccan and all the south were permanently lost. Muhammad died on one such expedition in 1351, leaving a diminished state.

Tamerlane

(1370–1405)

'When I rise from the dead the whole world will tremble.'

Tamerlane, who built the last great Empire of the Steppes of Central Asia, seems a worthy heir of Attila the Hun or Genghis Khan. He piled up the skulls of defeated enemies in monstrous pyramids and struck fear wherever he went. Yet he was a patron of learning who created an Empire that brought enormous benefits to his homeland. He made his capital Samarkand one of the greatest and most sophisticated cities of the Islamic world. He was a tyrant whose atrocities were carried out abroad rather than at home.

Tamerlane's name derives from Timur-i Leng, 'Lame Timur', a nickname he received after being wounded as a young man while stealing sheep. He was born in 1336 near Kesh in what is now Uzbekistan, about 50 miles (80 km) from Samarkand. Timur was neither Mongol nor nomad. His father was head of a small Turkic tribe that had settled the land, one of many that accompanied the hordes of Genghis Khan. Despite his later claims, there is no evidence that he was descended from the great Mongol. Genghis had left Central Asia to his son Chagatay, whose successors could no longer maintain unity. Rivalry between the nomad Mongol aristocracy and the settled urban people produced constant instability in Timur's time.

Timur grew up riding, hunting and fighting, and had little formal education. However, his broad interests and retentive memory enabled him to profit so well from the company of learned Moslems (Timur's father was the first of his tribe to convert to Islam) that he acquired a deep knowledge of history, law and theology. He also became a skilled chess player, inventing a variation of the game.

Timur first made his mark in 1360, when the Mongols reconquered his homeland. He submitted to the new ruler and rose in his service, but soon opted for independence by allying himself with Hussein, grandson of a former Emir of Samarkand. They were soldiers of fortune, living by raiding or selling their services, and soon became leaders of resistance to the Mongols, whom they drove out in 1363. Two years later the Mongols returned, crushed the forces of Timur and Hussein, and moved on Samarkand, where the population held them off so effectively that they withdrew from the whole area. In 1366, treachery enabled Timur and Hussein to take over Samarkand. Hussein was domineering, mean and avaricious, but Timur was wise. He realized the need for economic stability and a conciliated population. He gained the crucial support of merchants and local aristocrats who enabled him to defeat and capture Hussein. By 1370, Timur was recognized as the region's ruler, although he never took the title Khan, which was reserved for Genghis's descendants.

Timur was much more than a bloodthirsty conqueror. Unlike the Mongols, he understood the interests of the settled as well as the nomadic population. He followed the organizing principles of Genghis Khan, but created a very different army. Instead of relying only on nomad cavalry, he incorporated troops from settled regions as well as Turkish slaves and even Christians, creating a force bound by personal loyalty to himself. Because they were generously rewarded with treasure looted from their conquests, constant campaigns were required to keep them happy.

Timur was also a great builder who adorned Samarkand with massive fortifications, an elaborate citadel, palaces, markets, baths and gardens. Much of his work survives, still witness to his identification with the urban population and its prosperity, as well as Islam.

In the first stage of the great campaigns that began in the 1370s, Timur subdued all Central Asia. His notoriety derives from his style of warfare in Afghanistan and eastern Iran. In 1383, when Herat revolted after being occupied, its inhabitants were slaughtered and their heads built into a tower, with the faces directed toward the roads, as a warning to anyone who might think of resisting. Western Iran was next, followed by the Christian kingdoms of the Caucasus. During this war, which began in 1386, an uprising in the elegant centre of Persian culture, Isfahan, destroyed Timur's garrison. He responded by slaughtering the whole population of 70,000, including a delegation of small children who were sent to appease his wrath. Pyramids of heads arose around the city.

While Timur was away, the Mongol Khan of the Golden Horde, based on the Volga, attacked Central Asia. Timur returned, drove the Golden Horde out, captured their capital, and struck the region a serious economic blow. He redirected the Silk Road from China to Europe to run south of the Caspian, through his own domains, increasing the prosperity of the cities that submitted to him. Timur hoped that by defeating the Mongols he would establish a monopoly on the valuable silk trade.

In the five-year campaign that began in 1392, Timur's forces reasserted control of Iran, captured Baghdad, devastated Iraq, massacred the Christian population of Kaffa in the Crimea, smashed the Golden Horde once more and advanced to the outskirts of Moscow. The Russian capital was spared, but only because the invading army's supplies were running short. Their withdrawal had an important long-term effect. It weakened the Mongols and allowed the principality of Moscow to take an important step towards independence.

From 1396 to 1398 Timur remained in his capital, where news reached him that the Moslem Sultans of Delhi were being too lax in dealing with their Hindu subjects. Determined to prove himself a defender of Islam, Timur descended on India while it was torn by civil war. His pious protests almost certainly concealed a desire for loot, since the country he attacked was enormously rich. He led his large army of 90,000 through the high Hindu Kush into Afghanistan, where local Moslems complained about harrassment by tribes known as Kafirs (unbelievers), who would attack them, then retreat to their inaccessible mountain homes. Timur rose to the challenge, even though it involved developing new techniques of fighting in high snow-bound cliffs. The Kafirs submitted, then revolted. Uncharacteristically – but showing himself a good Moslem – Timur spared them on condition that they convert to Islam. He took pride in conquering tribes that had defied even Alexander the Great whose example, along with that of Genghis Khan, was always before him.

As they headed towards Delhi, Timur's forces were ambushed by local rulers. Although his losses were not great, his response was extreme. By this stage of the campaign, Timur's army had acquired a huge number of Hindu captives. When he heard reports that they had welcomed the attacks on their captors, Timur ordered his men to kill them all. Some 50,000 perished in an hour. The troops made up for the material loss of so many enforced servants by looting Delhi and leaving it a pile of smoldering ruins. The city took almost 200 years to recover. Timur returned to Samarkand with a train of elephants and extraordinary amounts of looted treasure. The elephants were used to carry huge stones intended for building the biggest mosque in Central Asia. The whole campaign had lasted little more than six months.

Timur's domain was vast, but he had rivals. Among these, the most aggressive and successful was the Ottoman Sultan Beyazit who had conquered much of the Balkans, besieged Constantinople, and extended his control far into Asia Minor. When the rulers of some of the Moslem states Beyazit had annexed sought Timur's support in 1399, he took up their cause, destroying Sivas in eastern Turkey, enslaving its Christian inhabitants and burying its defenders alive. Then he descended into Syria, where Aleppo and Damascus received similar treatment, and on to Baghdad, where he ordered every soldier to bring him a severed head. In total, the harvested heads formed 120 towers. Finally Timur returned to Asia Minor to face Beyazit and his powerful army, famed for fighting infidels. When the Ottoman refused to submit, Timur met him at Ankara in 1402, winning a tremendous victory and dragging the Sultan off in humiliating captivity. Timur's forces proceeded through Anatolia till they reached Smyrna, on the west coast, whose impregnable citadel was held by the Christian Knights of Rhodes. Smyrna, too, fell and its population was slaughtered in what was to be Timur's last campaign.

By 1404, Europe had begun to regard Timur as a potential ally against the Turks. Ambassadors from France, Spain and England arrived at his court, and were encouraged, as Timur was always interested in extending his prosperous trade networks. The ambassadors, who travelled securely along post roads, found a large and sophisticated city with a thriving population of administrators, learned Moslem clerics, artisans and traders, as well as scientists, theologians, poets and historians. They were overwhelmed by the size and magnificence of its palaces and mosques. Timur lingered in his marvellous capital only briefly before setting off to complete his conquests by adding China to his realm. He became ill on the way and died in February 1405, after a long and successful rule over one of the greatest Empires ever assembled.

Vlad 'The Impaler'
(1456–62)

*'These men live off the sweat of others, so
they are useless to humanity. May such men
be eliminated from my land'*

If Vlad III had not been one of history's most monstrous sadists, he would only have earned a footnote as a minor Balkan prince who managed to hold off the onslaught of the Ottoman Turks. He might have been remembered for eliminating the local aristocracy and recruiting a new ruling class from the common people. Instead, his activities earned him the title 'The Impaler', while one of his family names meant that he would forever be associated with the vampire legends of Dracula. When in power, he committed unparalleled atrocities on his own people and their neighbours.

Vlad's family was one of two that contested for control of Walachia (now southern Romania), a principality squeezed between Hungary and the growing Ottoman Empire. When Vlad was born in 1431, the rival Danesti were in power and his father, Vlad II, was governor of Transylvania under the Hungarian King. Since he had joined the secret Order of the Dragon to fight the Turks, the elder Vlad was called Dracul ('dragon' in Romanian), and his son used the surname Draculea, 'son of the Dragon'. In 1436, Vlad II seized Walachia, but was expelled in 1442. The next year, he regained it with Turkish support, making a treaty that he guaranteed by sending his two younger sons as hostages to the Sultan. The boys were interned in a remote fortress of Asia Minor. When his father was murdered in 1447, the Turks sent Vlad with an army and made him Prince of Walachia. After two months, the Hungarians drove him out and installed the Danesti. Finally, in 1456, Vlad regained control, and established his capital at Tirgoviste. After the fall of Constantinople in 1453, Walachia was a bulwark against the Turks, whom Vlad fought. He held them off for six years, but never had the manpower or sufficient support to inflict a major defeat, although he did give the Balkans a respite from the Ottoman onslaught.

Vlad's notoriety comes not from war but from the cruelty made known by widely disseminated printed pamphlets, the immensely popular products of what was then a new technology. Their gruesome narratives and gory illustrations were supplemented by Romanian oral traditions, and Vlad's story was so embellished in folklore that his legitimate name Draculea eventually became associated with one of the few horrors of which he was not guilty. Vlad the Impaler was a sadistic murderer but he was no vampire.

Vlad's first aim was to assert his personal control over an unstable state. Princes rarely lasted long (there had been 12 of them since 1418) and had constantly to contest with the landed aristocrats, or boyars, who provided most of the army. Vlad had a special grudge against the boyars, who had murdered his father and elder brother and supported the Danesti. His first atrocity was directed against them. At Easter in 1459, the prince held a great banquet for his boyars. He asked them how many princes they had seen come and go and discovered that all of them had lived through several reigns. In retribution, and to put an end to their tenacity, he arrested them as they left the banquet and impaled the older men and their wives on large stakes in the courtyard and around the town. The younger boyars and their families, all still in their Easter finery, were marched to the mountains where they were set to work building a remote castle (later called Castle Dracula). They worked till their clothes disintegrated and fell from their bodies. None survived.

Vlad's soubriquet 'The Impaler' (*Tepes* in Romanian) derived from his preferred means of punishment. Victims were lowered onto a stake which penetrated their insides from the buttocks and often came out through the mouth. Alternatively, people would be impaled through the stomach, or women through the breasts. To make death slower and more painful – it could take days – the stakes were often smoothed and oiled. Corpses were left hanging until they rotted away. Vlad derived real pleasure from these scenes. He often had the stakes ranged in concentric circles or geometrical patterns, and held banquets in their midst.

Vlad's treatment decimated the old ruling class. Only those who fled survived. This left Vlad free to choose entirely new associates, courtiers and administrators, whom he raised from the common people while he recruited his soldiers from the free peasantry. They were supplemented by his personal guard and the garrisons of his numerous castles. By terrorizing the church, Vlad established a degree of personal control unprecedented in the region.

Raising supporters from lower ranks of society did not mean that Vlad was a populist or a revolutionary. He was, in a strange way, a moralist whose punishments were so horrendous that crime virtually disappeared from Walachia. He particularly abhorred social parasites and anyone guilty of sexual misdemeanours. Adulteresses and unchaste women were skinned alive (skin and body displayed on separate poles) or had their sexual organs cut off, or were impaled through the vagina. He had no patience with people who did not or could not work. Early in his reign he invited all the old, sick, poor and beggars to his palace for a lavish feast. As it concluded, he asked them if they would like to be completely free from cares, lacking nothing in the world. When they responded positively, he boarded up the room and burnt them all alive. He justified this to his courtiers by claiming he had eliminated people who would be a burden, and that he wanted no one in his realm to be poor.

Hungarian Transylvania felt the Impaler's special wrath. Its leaders were local landed boyars and well-established Saxon merchants, who dominated the province's prosperous cites and the trade between them and Walachia. In 1457, when Hungary was suffering from internal divisions that Vlad could exploit, his forces struck deep into the country, sacking villages and towns and massacring their populations. Men, women and children were burnt alive except for some captives who were taken back to Walachia for impaling. In 1459 he arrested and burnt 400 young Transylvanian apprentices who had come to Walachia to learn the language. The same year, he attacked the prosperous city of Brasov, looting churches, burning the suburbs and impaling thousands of its inhabitants. He celebrated his victory by holding a banquet among the dying victims, the subject of a widely circulated woodcut that made his name notorious in Europe. When one of his boyars objected to the stench of blood and excrement, Vlad allegedly paid him the compliment of impaling him on a much longer stake so he could breathe his last more freely, high above the odours. Whatever the truth of these and other horror stories, the general fact of his sadism is well established.

For the first few years of his reign, Vlad chafed under the Turkish suzerainty that he, like his predecessors, was obliged to recognize. Although the Turks left him a free hand and imposed only a nominal tribute, he had to fend off their demand for slaves for their army, and planned to join a new crusade against them. In 1469, sure of the support of the new Hungarian King, he stopped paying the tribute and drove off the Turks when they attempted to remove him. It was probably at this time that, insulted by Turkish envoys who kept their turbans on in his presence, he reportedly had the turbans nailed to their heads and sent them home. In 1461, Vlad went on the offensive, crossing the Danube to devastate a prosperous Turkish region. He sent lists of those killed (along with their body parts) back to the Hungarian King, and brought numerous captives to Tirgoviste for impalement. The Sultan responded in force, leading a huge army in person into Walachia. When he arrived outside Vlad's capital, he was so revolted by the thousands of impaled bodies around the city, many of them Turkish prisoners of war, that he turned for home. His army remained and captured Tirgoviste, leaving Vlad to continue a guerrilla war. The Turks installed Vlad's brother, Radu, as prince, and Vlad withdrew into Transylvania.

He took refuge with the Hungarian King, who responded by imprisoning him, then relented. Since Radu was a pawn of the Turks, Vlad could still be a useful ally. He converted to Catholicism and married the King's cousin (his first wife had gone mad). In 1476, he descended on Walachia in alliance with the princes of Transylvania and Moldavia. After successfully restoring Vlad to the throne, the allies departed. Vengeance soon followed. The Turks sent a large army against Vlad, by now so detested that he could command little support, and he fell in battle in December 1476. His body was embalmed and sent back to the Sultan who, appropriately, displayed it on a stake for all to see that their loathsome enemy was indeed dead.

Cesare Borgia

(1500–03)

'*My task is not to tyrannize but to
destroy tyrants.*'

The princes of the Italian Renaissance routinely used intrigue, treachery and murder to further their aims. The most notorious among them were the Borgias, whose despotic rule of church and state made a lasting impression. Their leader, Pope Alexander VI, was a greedy and lecherous reprobate. His daughter Lucrezia gained an undeserved reputation for poisoning and incest, and her cold-blooded brother Cesare stopped at nothing to gain and increase power. Together, they terrorized Rome and expanded its domain. Their enterprise collapsed when Alexander VI died, possibly by poisoning.

The Spanish Cardinal Alfonso Borgia arrived in Rome in 1445, followed by his nephew Rodrigo, who became an expert in canon law – and attracting women. When Alfonso became Pope Callixtus III in 1455, he made Rodrigo Cardinal, then Chancellor of the Holy See, an extremely lucrative position. Rodrigo's several children included Cesare, born in 1475, and Lucrezia, five years younger. In 1492, Rodrigo's enormous bribes ensured his own election as Pope Alexander VI. He was determined to control the church and its domains in central Italy. For that, he groomed his elder son Giovanni as a soldier and the younger, Cesare, for the church.

From the age of nine, Cesare held ecclesiastical offices that brought him a large income. He was Archbishop of Valencia at 17 and a Cardinal the following year. He was educated in law, humanities and theology, but the church held little appeal for Cesare, who saw his brother Giovanni winning glory at the head of the papal armies. In 1497, when Giovanni was mysteriously murdered, suspicion fell on Cesare. Often taciturn, Cesare could be charming, but no one could tell from his expression whether he was about to strike or embrace them. His ambition knew no bounds or scruples. In 1498, he resigned as Cardinal and began the military career he had always wanted, in the service of his father.

Alexander's plans included two buffer states for Rome, one in Latium to be run by Lucrezia and her descendants and the other, much larger, in Romagna, the Pope's eastern territories, to be ruled by Cesare and ideally used as a base for further expansion. In 1499, Cesare, who had never commanded forces before, set off against Forli. Here he faced an unusual and formidable enemy, Caterina Sforza, who ruled in place of her murdered husband. The people of Forli, long oppressed by Caterina, were willing to open the gates to Cesare on condition that he kept his French troops out. He agreed, then entered the city followed immediately by the French, who looted it. Caterina held out in the citadel for three weeks until Borgia's artillery broke through her walls, forcing her surrender. Cesare raped her, then claimed that she defended her virtue less well than her castle. He established an effective local government after obliging the citizens to petition the Pope to name Cesare their ruler.

Cesare returned to Rome in 1500 for a triumph worthy of ancient Rome, with wagons full of loot and captives, including Caterina in golden chains, himself standing out in austere black clothes. Since the year 1500 was a Jubilee year, tens of thousands of pilgrims were in Rome. Alexander was busy and handed over control of the city to Cesare, who put on lavish public entertainments and special private ones. The most notorious was a banquet for Alexander and Lucrezia that featured 50 whores dancing clothed, then naked, then coupling with the palace servants to compete for a prize for the best performance. Cesare would also amuse himself by lining up unarmed prisoners in the courtyard to use as target practice.

Alexander's ambitions required money. He sold indulgences, increased tithes and absolved dubious potentates from their sins in return for high fees. A prime source of revenue was the creation of new cardinals. Aspirants needed to consult Cesare, who collected 120,000 ducats from the successful candidates, while the Pope blessed his choice.

In 1500 the Borgias also renewed their alliance with the French King, who insisted on attacking Naples with their help. Under these circumstances, Lucrezia's husband, a Neapolitan aristocrat, was an embarrassment. In July, a gang stabbed him on the steps of the Vatican. He barely survived and was being nursed back to health when Cesare's personal executioner strangled him in his bed. Lucrezia was distraught and even the Pope seemed disturbed. By now he himself was increasingly under Cesare's domination. Alexander packed Lucrezia off to a nearby castle with her infant son, and took the first steps towards war by excommunicating the rulers of the cities he planned to attack.

Cesare set out in October. The Italian cities fell one by one, usually happy to throw out their tyrants in favour of Borgia, who proved a remarkably fair and effective ruler. He collected standard taxes, maintained public order, suppressed banditry and generally ensured justice. He made such an impression that the writer and scholar Machiavelli, who met him, believed that Cesare might save Italy from an age of chaos. Cesare reserved treachery and murder for important opponents like the popular young Prince Astorre Manfredi, who held out in Faenza despite siege and blockade until a renegade revealed a weak spot in the city's defences. Cesare hanged the traitor, then trained his guns on the spot. Faenza surrendered on terms that included safe conduct for Manfredi. Instead, Cesare shipped him to his father's fortress in Rome, where his body was later found floating in the Tiber. Romagna was conquered and even Florence sufficiently intimidated to pay Cesare a large bribe for sparing the city from attack.

Cesare, Duke of Romagna and supreme commander of the papal armies, then joined the French and marched against Naples. On the way, they captured Capua where 6000 people, including priests and children, were massacred in an act uncharacteristic of Italian warfare. Innumerable women were raped and 30 of the best looking were shipped back to Rome for Cesare's enjoyment. When Naples fell, Alexander seized the lands of his enemies south of Rome. He made a triumphal tour of his conquests, leaving Lucrezia to administer the Holy See, provoking universal scandal. Alexander's realm was secure on all fronts. All he lacked was an alliance with the strategic state of Ferrara. For that, he offered the widowed Lucrezia as wife to the son of the local prince. Although the prince hesitated to ally his house with such a notorious woman, the power of Rome and a generous dowry prevailed.

Cesare returned to Rome where, according to a contemporary, he 'surpassed the bestiality and savagery of Nero and Caligula'. Borgia spies were everywhere and any expression of discontent brought savage punishment. One critic had his tongue and hand cut off and nailed together, another was strangled and tossed into the Tiber. Poisoning and murder were rampant. In 1502 the Pope joined Cesare to inspect new fortifications that Leonardo da Vinci had designed, then Cesare set out for Urbino, whose Duke had been a loyal ally. Cesare asked him for 1000 men to attack a neighbouring city. When the Duke obliged, leaving Urbino defenceless, Cesare struck. The Duke escaped before his city fell.

Cesare's incessant treachery and growing power disquieted his equally treacherous mercenary captains. They feared, not unreasonably, that their lands would be the next to fall, and rose in a general revolt that cost Cesare some of his recent conquests. When they failed to gain help from the French King, and realized they could not trust each other, they made peace with Cesare who graciously renewed their contracts. He then summoned them to join him in attacking the small town of Senigallia. Once they were inside, expecting to celebrate, Cesare cornered them. Some he killed, but he arrested those belonging to the powerful Orsini family. The Pope had them killed, along with their relatives. Cesare's treachery in Senigallia was much admired in Italy.

With central Italy secured, Alexander and Cesare looked to replenish their war chest for further conquest. Cesare's gangs arrested Jews and converts and then allowed them to buy their freedom; a rich cardinal was poisoned and his property confiscated; a complaining secretary strangled. As usual, creation of new cardinals proved most profitable – there were always rich candidates. During this period, Cesare went about the city at night, usually wearing a mask to hide a face disfigured by syphilis. Father and son were at the height of their power and looking forward to the day when Cesare himself might succeed to the papacy, when disaster struck.

In August 1503, Alexander and Cesare fell mortally ill, some said from poison they had meant for others, but it is more likely they both contracted malaria. Cesare survived but the death of the Pope ended his hopes. A new Pope quickly took control, the network of alliances the Borgias had created collapsed, and conquered cities broke away. Cesare took refuge in Naples where his future looked promising until the King of Spain decided a Borgia meant trouble and had him imprisoned in Spain. He escaped after two years, but was by now a penniless adventurer. Fighting as a mercenary in Spain, he was killed in a skirmish in 1507 at the age of 31. Lucrezia, Duchess of Ferrara, famed for her piety and good works, survived him by 12 years. The family never rose again.

Selim the Grim

(1512–20)

'A carpet is large enough to accommodate
two Sufis, but the world is not large enough for
two kings.'

Grim is a translation of the Turkish *yavuz*, meaning tough, or inflexible, an apt description of a ruler who defeated the most powerful states of his day and slaughtered his enemies at home and abroad. He began with his own family, massacred thousands of heretics, and waged aggressive and successful wars that doubled the extent of the Ottoman Empire. He added the riches of Egypt and the holiness of Mecca and Medina to his realm. Building on Selim's work, his son Suleiman the Magnificent brought the Empire to its height of glory.

Selim was born in 1470, in the reign of his grandfather Mehmet the Conqueror who had taken Constantinople and built a powerful state based in the Balkans and Asia Minor. When he died, his son Beyazit had to fight a long civil war with his brother Jem, and as Beyazit himself aged, another struggle loomed between his three surviving sons. Beyazit favoured the eldest, Ahmet. Korkut had the support of the religious establishment, but the powerful Janissary army corps leaned toward the most militant, Selim, despite what they knew of his harsh nature. Since by tradition the Sultan's sons governed provinces, each of the three manoeuvred to obtain an appointment close to Istanbul, to be ready to move in the event of their father's incapacity or death. Selim, who was farthest away, directed successful campaigns on the eastern frontier that won him important military support, then moved to the Danube and started an active rebellion. He reached a compromise with his father that brought him a posting on the Danube, then had to face Ahmet who was about to march against him with the backing of the Grand Vizier (Prime Minister). At this point, the Janissaries rebelled and forced Beyazit to bring Selim to Istanbul. When he arrived, Selim deposed his reluctant father, who died on his way to retirement in 1512. Selim was now ruler, but still had to deal with his family.

At first, compromise looked possible. Korkut accepted a comfortable governorship and Ahmet was offered another. Ahmet, however, wanted much more and declared himself Sultan of Anatolia. He raised an army from among the Turcoman nomads and took over much of Asia Minor. Selim finally defeated Ahmet in 1513 and had him and his son strangled. By then, it was obvious that any surviving male relatives could pose a threat, so Selim took direct measures. He brought the five young sons of his two deceased brothers to Istanbul where they were promptly strangled, then surprised Korkut in his provincial palace and killed him. Selim's successors maintained the practice of murdering their brothers for the rest of the century. Safe at home, Selim was free to move against his enemies abroad.

Chief among those was the Safavid Ismail, who claimed descent from the Prophet and had gained control of Persia during Beyazit's reign. Ismail belonged to a Shiite sect that engaged in dynamic proselytism, especially among the Turcoman tribes of Anatolia. These tribes were susceptible to propaganda because their attachment to orthodox Islam was weak, while the tribes in eastern Turkey were disturbed by the constant expansion of the Ottomans, who threatened to engulf them. Ismail sent out hundreds of preachers to spread a message that the Sunni Ottomans saw as a political as well as a religious threat – because the tribes moved frequently and were spread throughout the Empire, the danger of subversion from Iran was very real. Shiism also challenged the orthodoxy that had supported most of Islam's ruling dynasties. Safavid missionary activity was at its height during the reign of Beyazit, who tried to convince Ismail to rein it in, only to see his adversary expand aggressively into Iraq, where he conquered Baghdad, massacring Sunnis and destroying their mosques and tombs. Selim, who became a fanatical champion of orthodoxy, had to act.

Before he could advance against Ismail, however, Selim faced a potential threat at home from the Red Heads, as the followers of Ismail were called from their distinctive red headgear. Selim had organized an extensive network of informers throughout his realm. They compiled lists of known Red Heads aged 7 to 70 in Europe and Asia. On the order of the Sultan, 40,000 of them were rounded up and executed. Many more were wiped out as the army advanced east in the spring of 1514. Real or accused enemies of the Sultan perished along with them. Meanwhile, Selim had begun economic warfare. He ordered an embargo on all shipments of silk from Persia via the Ottoman lands, to deprive Ismail of the revenue from his most profitable export.

Selim and Ismail met on the battlefield of Chaldiran in far eastern Turkey in August 1514. Thanks to his cannon and bulwarks of chariots chained together, Selim won a decisive victory. In the campaign that continued into the following year, he entered Ismail's capital Tabriz (in Persian Azerbaijan) where he captured 1000 valuable artisans and scholars. Although he did not hold the city, he did annex a large region of eastern Turkey and northern Iraq, inhabited mostly by Kurds. These lands became a buffer against renewed aggression from Ismail and controlled crucial trade routes between east and west.

During this campaign, the Safavid had tried to form an alliance with the other great power of the Moslem Near East, the Mamelukes of Egypt. These were a caste of slave soldiers, mostly recruited from the Caucasus, who had ruled Egypt since the 13th century. Selim's ambitions now reached their height, but before starting a war, he made sure he had the support of the merchants of the Syrian cities whose prosperity was closely tied to the Ottomans. Many Arab traders had lost faith in the Mamelukes, who seemed incapable of protecting them against a new and pressing danger. The Portuguese had found a route round southern Africa and begun to trade directly in luxury goods with India and the Gulf region. As they insisted that the goods should be carried in their own ships, they constituted a growing menace to the prosperity of local merchants and were even seen by some as having designs on the holy cities of Mecca and Medina. Selim did not need much persuading, although his religious authorities did, since, as the Mamelukes rightly claimed, he was proposing to attack an orthodox Sunni country. Selim responded that the Mamelukes were foreigners who were oppressing Islam and had allied themselves with the heretic Ismail.

The campaign went well. Selim smashed the Mamelukes in northern Syria in August 1516, using the same tactics that had brought victory at Chaldiran. Aleppo and Damascus simply opened their gates. In Syria and Palestine, Selim showed that he was building for permanence, not simply conquest. He organized an administration, conciliated local notables and granted autonomy to the Greek and Armenian churches. He then decided to march on Egypt, announcing his aim of bringing all Moslem lands under his protection. Gaza soon fell, but Selim faced the problem of getting his army across the desert of Sinai. Fifteen thousand camels loaded with water bags enabled him to cross in a week, and walk into Egypt. Once again, his superior firepower won the day. Selim entered Cairo in February 1517; by then, some 50,000 Mamelukes had been killed or executed.

After conquering Egypt, Selim received the submission of Mecca and Medina, which recognized him as Servant and Protector of the Holy Places, a title that gave him enormous prestige in the Islamic world. He appointed governors for Egypt, Arabia and Syria, and shipped several hundred potential troublemakers to Istanbul. Among them was the last Abbasid Caliph al-Mutawakkil, descendant of the family of the Prophet and successor to Caliphs who had ruled since the eighth century, but had transferred to Egypt when the Mongols destroyed Baghdad in 1258. Because of this, some called Selim himself Caliph, though as a foreigner he had no legitimate claim to the title, which he apparently never used. Much later, however, his successors revived the Caliphate as an effort to claim spiritual jurisdiction over the whole Moslem world. More tangibly, Selim received the sword and mantle of the Prophet, which were preserved in Istanbul.

Selim was a violent man whose advisers and high officials could never be sure what to expect from him. He went through seven Grand Viziers in his short reign, all of them beheaded. 'May you be Selim's Vizier' became a common Turkish curse, meaning 'drop dead'. Prudent officials made their wills before taking office. At the same time, Selim was highly cultivated, wrote good Persian poetry, and patronized poets and historians.

In 1519, a new rebellion of Red Head Turcomans disrupted Asia Minor and was only suppressed with difficulty by the Janissaries. It interrupted Selim's plans in the west, for he was building a fleet to attack the Christian islands of Chios and Rhodes. On his way east from Istanbul in September 1520 he was taken ill and died. He had conquered more territory than any of his predecessors and made the Ottoman Empire a world power.

Ivan the
Terrible

Josef Stalin was a great admirer of Ivan the Terrible. Both achieved absolute personal power, slaughtered their enemies, and developed a fearsome secret police force that terrorized the population. But both also reorganized the government, extended their rule over vast territories and laid the foundations for Russian power and expansion. Ivan was a determined modernizer, transforming Muscovy from a feudal state with a dominant landed aristocracy, to one where the Tsar's power was supreme. He owed his nickname to an unparalleled reign of terror that left a demoralized and virtually depopulated kingdom.

Ivan, son and heir to the Prince of Muscovy, was born in 1530. His grandfather, Ivan III, had established independent power by annexing the major city of Novgorod and defeating Russia's traditional enemies, the Tartars. He ruled with a landed aristocracy (boyars) who provided men for the army in exchange for grants of land. The leading boyar families constantly struggled with each other and with the ruler for domination.

At the age of three, Ivan IV took the throne under the regency of his mother and her lover, both from old boyar families. In 1538, they and many of Ivan's family were murdered. The young boy witnessed some of the killings, which brought the Shuisky and Belsky boyar families to power. Ivan never forgot the horrors of his childhood. He had his revenge in 1543 when he had the boyar leader Shuisky killed in his presence, but he allowed government to remain in the hands of his mother's family, the Glinskys.

In 1547, Ivan was crowned with the new imperial title of Tsar, derived from Caesar, reflecting the notion that Moscow was a third Rome, inheriting the dominion of both ancient Rome and Constantinople. In theory, he ruled by divine right, a doctrine fundamental to autocracy. In the same year, he married Anastasia Romanova, who exercised a calming influence on him. Not long after, a devastating fire in Moscow was blamed on the Glinskys, whom Ivan banished, concentrating their power in his own hands.

The next years, 1547–60, marked the positive period of Ivan's rule. He was a genuine reformer whose aim was to strengthen the kingdom by reducing the power of the boyars and bringing new classes into positions of authority. His advisers formed a 'chosen council' independent of the boyars, while an Assembly of the Land broadened his base of support. A new code of law, a land survey, tax reforms, laws against corruption and increased local autonomy followed. Ivan, well aware of the power of hostile neighbouring states, created a new cavalry, supplemented by infantry raised from the common people and armed with modern muskets.

This was also a period of successful conquest. In 1552, Ivan took the powerful Tartar base of Kazan, followed in 1556 by Astrakhan. Russia now controlled the whole Volga region, and began expanding into Siberia. Ivan wanted territory on the Baltic, to increase Russian trade and contact with the West. He failed, despite endless wars. He did establish relations with the West, however, when English ships reached

Russia from the north via the White Sea in 1553. Ivan exchanged ambassadors with Queen Elizabeth, who was amused to see the Russian envoy crawl across the floor to kiss the hem of her robe, as was customary in Russia. Ivan himself was so enamoured of his new ally that he even proposed marriage, and in his last years considered retiring to England.

Ivan's talents as a Renaissance man have been obscured by his darker reputation. He was familiar with classical antiquity and political philosophy, knew theology so well he could debate with leading Catholic and Protestant theologians, composed church music and wrote prayers. He sent students to learn from the West, introduced the printing press to Russia and advanced military technology. He patronized art and architecture, including the magnificent cathedral of St Basil in Moscow's Red Square, built to celebrate the capture of Kazan. However, he had the cathedral architects blinded so they could not repeat their creation elsewhere.

In 1553, Ivan became seriously ill and asked his boyars to swear allegiance to his infant son. He never forgot the betrayal of those who refused. After his wife died in 1560, he dismissed his reforming advisers, and his reign began to turn to violence and horror.

Ivan left Moscow suddenly in December 1564, withdrawing to his estate of Alexandrovna Sloboda, 60 miles (90 km) away. He left the capital ungoverned and wrote to the Archbishop denouncing the boyars and clergy and announcing his plan to abdicate. The people, fearful of civil war in a leaderless state, begged the Tsar to return. Ivan, who had stage-managed the whole performance, had no intention of giving up power. He agreed to return on condition that he should have a large territory to rule directly and that he could punish traitors and criminals as he wished. Russia then entered one of the grimmest periods of its history.

Ivan's personal lands, known as the Oprichnina, embraced about a third of Russia's territory. Here his word was law. He could bring anyone to trial, and determine the verdict and punishment himself. The rest of Russia, called Zemshchina, was ruled traditionally, but heavily taxed to support Ivan's projects. The Tsar organized his followers into a kind of hierarchic monastic brotherhood. The Oprichniki dressed in black robes (that often concealed finery) and lived a communal life, but ate and drank well. Their symbols were a broom and a dog's head. There were originally about 1000 of them recruited from the nobility, but numbers grew to 6000, mostly drawn from more humble origins. Ivan had absolute control over them and they would execute any order he gave. The Oprichniki were financed by confiscated estates, whose occupants were evicted. Their bases were the heavily fortified Alexandrovna Sloboda and a powerful new castle in Moscow. From there, they unleashed a degree of unprecedented savagery.

Ivan turned his new servants on anyone he disliked or suspected. Boyars, their relatives, friends, families and servants were the first victims. Nor was the clergy spared. The violence, which started in 1566 after the Tsar returned to Moscow, appeared to be indiscriminate. When a group of Zemshchina nobles petitioned to have the Oprichnina abolished, Ivan arrested 300 of them. Fifty were flogged in public and several had their tongues cut out. When the Metropolitan Archbishop objected he was arrested in his church and exiled. Oprichniki seized boyar estates, devastating whole communities and carrying out widespread torture and execution. The worst scenes were at Novgorod in 1570. Ivan, suspecting that the city was leaning towards his Polish enemies, slaughtered most of its population and brought several hundred of its leaders to his headquarters for a sham trial. After horrendous tortures, they revealed a (non-existent) conspiracy among the higher ranks of Ivan's advisers. More executions followed. The city of Pskov would have received the same treatment had not the deeply religious Ivan been stopped by a local monk renowned for his holiness.

As the Oprichniki grew in number, they became more violent. New recruits hated all aristocrats and never hesitated to indulge in public torture and execution. Their victims were soaked in boiling or freezing water, burnt alive, had limbs chopped off or were thrown to wild beasts. Things changed after 1571 when the Tartars suddenly attacked and burnt Moscow. Ivan hesitated to meet them in battle because his Oprichniki army was better at slaughtering civilians than fighting armed enemies. As he began to suspect treason among the Oprichniki, the torturers themselves became victims, but their executions were kept secret to maintain a high level of public fear. By now, disaffection was virtually universal as the Oprichniki struck with impunity and criminals, disguising themselves in the distinctive dress of the Oprichniki, added to the violence. In 1572, Ivan suddenly abolished the whole organization. It had done its job too well.

In Ivan's last years, Russia fell into economic crisis. The Baltic wars dragged on, consuming men and resources, taxes increased and whole areas became depopulated as people fled from the Oprichniki. With so many men away fighting, agriculture declined and the resulting fall in population made it harder to recruit soldiers. Ivan's solution to this problem had long-lasting effects. In 1581, he introduced the Forbidden Years, when peasants could not leave the land they worked. This produced a more stable rural population but eventually led to the system of serfdom that lasted into the 19th century.

Ivan's last years were almost as miserable as those of his subjects. In 1581, seeing his pregnant daughter-in-law wearing what he considered inappropriate clothing, he beat her so hard that she miscarried. When his son and heir protested, Ivan flew into a rage and beat him to death with the iron-tipped staff he always carried. The murder destabilized him altogether. He was suddenly filled with remorse, desperately seeking forgiveness for all his crimes. He sent lists of thousands of his victims to monasteries, requesting prayers for their souls. His forehead became bruised and calloused from being banged on the floor as he prostrated himself in prayer. He finally died in March 1584, probably poisoned by two trusted followers after he had tried to rape their wife and sister. His death ushered in a long period of chaos.

Bloody Mary

(1553–8)

'Her majesty cannot forsake that faith which the whole world knows her to have followed since her birth… and she desires greatly that her subjects may come to embrace the same faith quietly and with charity.'

Religious devotion led Queen Mary – the first woman to rule England in her own name – to commit the atrocities that have blackened her reputation and obliterated the memory of her many acts of clemency and generosity. Mary started life as a princess and heir to the throne, but fell into disgrace and saw her beloved Catholic church dismantled by her father and brother. As Queen, she was determined to restore Catholic worship, but her heavy-handed methods, combined with a bitterly unpopular marriage and her inability to produce an heir, doomed her to failure.

Mary Tudor, born in 1516, was the only surviving child of two Catholics, Henry VIII and Catherine of Aragon. She learnt to speak Latin, Spanish, French and Italian, studied Greek and science, and became an accomplished musician. She was in much demand as a bride: her father arranged her betrothal to Francis I of France, then to the Emperor Charles V, then to Francis's son – all before she was 12.

Trouble began in 1527 when Henry, realizing that Catherine would never bear him a son, and already enamoured of Anne Boleyn, asked the Pope to annul his marriage. However, Rome was occupied by Charles V, Catherine's nephew, whom the Pope could not afford to offend. The divorce struggle dragged on till 1533, when Anne Boleyn was pregnant and Henry was growing desperate for his heir to be born legitimately. Henry then broke with Rome and obtained his annulment from Thomas Cranmer, the Archbishop of Canterbury. Anne was crowned Queen and three months later produced a daughter, Elizabeth.

Mary and her mother were expelled from court and separated (Henry never allowed them to meet again). She lost her household and was sent to be lady-in-waiting to the infant princess. The Act of Succession of 1534 declared her illegitimate. Mary, who refused to recognize her own illegitimacy, or accept the title Lady instead of Princess, became Anne Boleyn's special victim. The new Queen would not allow her to appear in public, searched her rooms, read her letters and sent away her friends and attendants. Anne eventually suffered in her turn. Having failed to produce a son, she was divorced and beheaded in 1536. Henry then married Jane Seymour, who produced the desired boy, Edward. Mary finally submitted. She acknowledged her illegitimacy, accepted Henry as head of the church, and was granted her own household and palace. When Henry died in 1547, she was second in line to the throne.

The new king, Edward VI, was only nine years old and chronically ill. Thomas Seymour, head of the Regency Council, began to establish Protestantism in England. The Act of Unification of 1549 ordered the churches to use the new Protestant Book of Common Prayer. When Mary's request for private Catholic services was denied, she appealed to the Emperor, who threatened war. Mary was granted her priests, only to see the situation worsen when John Dudley, later Duke of Northumberland, took power in 1550. He enforced a more radical Protestantism and removed Mary's priests and retainers. Dudley's ambitions were unlimited. He persuaded Edward to disinherit Mary and Elizabeth and to name as his heir Lady Jane Grey, who was married to Dudley's son. When Edward died in 1553, Dudley proclaimed the reluctant Lady Jane queen and sent troops to arrest Mary. She escaped, then rode into London with her sister, to the acclamation of the public. Dudley's plan collapsed, he was executed, and the nine-day queen and her young husband were imprisoned in the Tower of London.

Mary was crowned on 1 October 1553 by the Catholic bishop of Winchester, Stephen Gardiner, because all the other high prelates were Protestants. Parliament then validated the marriage of Henry and Catherine (and therefore Mary's legitimacy) and abolished Edward's religious laws. Mary failed to understand how far Protestantism had advanced in England, but she made an important compromise. She allowed the gentry who had grown rich on lands confiscated from the church by Henry VIII to keep them, and swore not to persecute Protestants.

The Queen was now a 37-year-old virgin, anxious to marry if only to deny the succession to Elizabeth, whom she hated. Gardiner and Parliament advised her to marry a popular English nobleman, Edward Courtenay, Earl of Devon. Instead, she followed the advice of Emperor Charles V who proposed his own son, Philip, 11 years younger than Mary. England was appalled at the thought of a Spanish king. Lady Jane Grey was proclaimed again and Sir Thomas Wyatt rose in arms. Mary's powerful speech as the rebels approached London encouraged her supporters who quashed the revolt. Lady Jane Grey, however, lost her head, and Elizabeth was sent to the Tower, then put under house arrest.

In July 1554, Mary married Philip in Winchester Cathedral. The young prince found Mary unattractive and merely did his duty but Mary fell passionately in love with him. Philip became King of England but with extremely restricted powers. Mary wanted an heir and in September her doctors told her one was on the way. In November bells pealed in London in thanksgiving. Philip, who was anxious to leave to pursue war against France, stayed to await the birth. The Queen entered confinement at Easter 1555, but nothing happened. By June, all business was at a standstill. The clergy prayed for a safe delivery and Mary wrote birth announcements to the rulers of Europe, with the child's name and date of delivery to be filled in. Still nothing happened. Finally, in August, it became obvious that the Queen had had a false pregnancy. Philip departed, leaving Mary plunged in frantic grief.

Mary's pregnancy had made reconciliation with Rome more urgent. In November 1554, the Pope's legate Cardinal Pole arrived in London and a few days later Parliament formally requested Philip and Mary to restore the Catholic faith and repealed all anti-Catholic legislation. At the same time, virtually unnoticed, the medieval laws against heresy were revived. They ordained the church to identify heretics and to turn them over to the civil authorities for punishment.

Pole, now Archbishop of Canterbury, persuaded Mary to uproot Protestantism. Heresy trials began in January 1555. The first victim was John Hooper, Bishop of Worcester, who was burnt at the stake in February. The fire took 45 minutes to kill him, but despite his torments he prayed till the end. This began a campaign that consumed 283 lives, all recorded in gruesome detail by an exiled Protestant, John Foxe, whose *Book of Martyrs*, published in Elizabeth's reign, ensured that Mary and Catholicism would long be reviled in England. Heresy was generally regarded as the worst of sins, since it brought and could spread eternal damnation. Protestants also burnt Catholics, and the Spanish Inquisition, with which Philip was familiar, had long been at work. Mary's persecution, however, was unprecedented in England, and failed. The bravery of the persecuted Protestants only strengthened their cause.

Nevertheless, Mary and Pole persevered. Their most famous victim was Archbishop Cranmer who had granted Henry's divorce and supported Lady Jane Grey. He repented and accepted Catholicism, but too late. In February 1556 he was burnt, but at the last minute withdrew his recantation of his faith, dramatically thrusting his right hand, with which he had written it, into the fire. Cranmer's execution more than any other reflected badly on the government. Most of the victims, though, were poor and obscure people, who had been denounced by their neighbours or local justices, sent on to the bishops and turned over to the state. Many knew nothing of heresy and had grown up under Edward when Catholicism was publicly condemned. Execution of such obviously innocuous people stirred further resentment.

By 1556, public discontent was growing, as condemnation of the burnings was publicized in pamphlets the government could not suppress. Mary started to see treachery all round her. She still had Pole's support, but longed for Philip. He finally returned to England in March 1557, because he needed English money and allies to prosecute his war with France. He found Mary greatly aged and in poor health, although still alert enough to throw out the mistress Philip tactlessly brought in his entourage. In June England entered the war against France and the following month Philip left for the last time. Mary was convinced that she was pregnant again, but it was another false alarm. Disillusion, confusion and conflict ruled the court as Mary's health deteriorated while she realized that her efforts had failed. Churches stood in ruins and England was more Protestant than ever. Even worse, a new Pope who opposed the Emperor excommunicated Pole and summoned him to Rome. The Archbishop, who was growing senile, stayed in Canterbury.

The war with France was a disaster that cost England enormous sums of money and the loss of Calais, its last outpost on the continent, adding to the Queen's disillusionment. She agreed to name Elizabeth as her heir to avert a potential civil war. Eventually the ovarian cancer that had been responsible for her false pregnancies killed Mary as she was hearing Mass on 17 October 1558. Cardinal Pole died the same day. Elizabeth, whom Mary had enjoined to keep the Catholic faith, did the opposite: England remained Protestant.

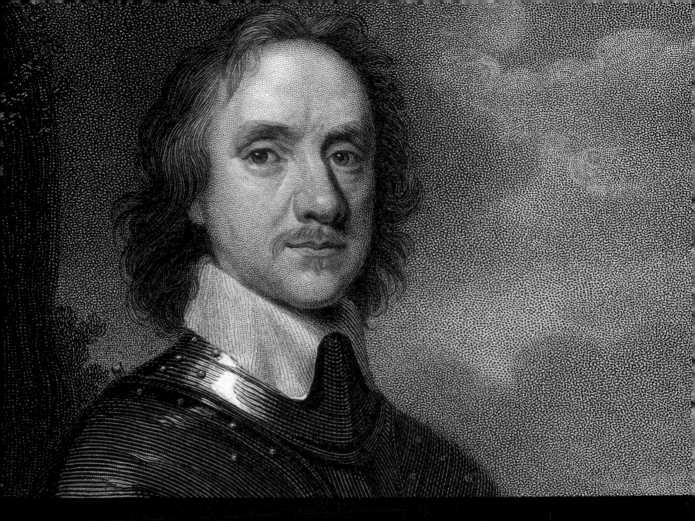

Oliver Cromwell

(1653–8)

'God has brought us where we are, to consider the work we may do in the world, as well as at home.'

Cromwell, England's only dictator, was driven by an intense religious faith. He might have remained only an obscure country gentleman had he not lived at a time of religious turmoil and conflict between King and Parliament. Cromwell wanted constitutional government. but when debate gave way to war, he raised a troop of cavalry and demonstrated the skills and commitment that marked him as a leader. As Lord Protector, he established a more arbitrary and despotic regime than England had ever known. He conquered Scotland and subdued Ireland in a bloody campaign that created long-lasting hatred. Although his rule was short, he paved the way for constitutional government in England.

Oliver Cromwell was born in 1599 in Huntingdon in eastern England, where Puritanism had taken root. This uncompromising doctrine stressed the insignificance of the believer before God, and the need for an intense personal faith to join the elect whom God had chosen. It was vigorously expounded at Sidney Sussex College at Cambridge, where Cromwell matriculated in 1616. He was more interested in sports than study, however, and withdrew after a year when his father died. He studied law briefly, married and settled down. Some time in his twenties, Cromwell had an intense religious experience that left him with an abiding sense of sin and convinced him that every decision involved a choice between good and evil. Faith dominated his life, with constant Bible readings and long family prayers.

As a member of the local gentry, Cromwell entered Parliament in 1628. He joined a faction that was working to reduce the privileges of the King, Charles I, and spoke in favour of democrats, Puritans and small landowners. The King dissolved Parliament the next year. Cromwell retired to the country, where as Justice of the Peace he defended small landowners against the rich. In 1636, when he was contemplating joining one of the new Protestant colonies in New England, he inherited a substantial estate and abandoned thoughts of emigrating.

In 1638, the Scots, antagonized by the increasingly high-church practices of the King, rebelled and occupied northern England. Charles was forced to recall Parliament in 1640 and Cromwell was returned as a member for Cambridge. This Long Parliament sat uninterruptedly for 13 years. Cromwell supported its successful efforts to oblige the King to rule with the consent of Parliament, to renounce the special taxes he had levied, and to allow the Parliament to meet until it willingly adjourned. Cromwell, who was never a great orator and was more interested in religion than politics, spoke so forcefully and impetuously that he had to be reprimanded. England seemed on a peaceful route to a constitutional monarchy, until the Irish revolted. Their massacre of Protestant settlers caused outrage in England but raised fears that the King, who needed an army to fight the Irish, might then use it against Parliament. Tension increased rapidly. When Parliament demanded control over the King's council and the army, Charles entered the House of Commons with armed guards to arrest Cromwell and other rebels. Cromwell escaped to the country where he raised money for fighting the King, who left London and mustered an army in defence of his divine right to rule. In August 1642, civil war began. Cromwell's first action was to seize the University silver that was about to be shipped to the King from Cambridge.

Cromwell had never served in the military but he had a gift for command. Taking the rank of Captain, he created a cavalry different from any other. He chose his officers by merit rather than birth, and his men joined not for adventure or reward but to do the Lord's work. Although subject to tough discipline that prohibited blasphemy, immorality or political dissent, they went into battle enthusiastically, singing hymns. Cromwell's troops drove the larger Royalist forces from eastern England, then played a decisive role in the great victory of Marston Moor in July 1644. Unlike the more conservative majority, the Presbyterians, Cromwell opposed compromise with the King. Thanks to the New Model Army, based on Cromwell's principles, but commanded by Sir Thomas Fairfax, Parliament won the victories that drove the King into Scotland in 1646.

In January 1647, the Scots turned Charles over to Parliament, who demanded control of the army, navy and ministries, confiscation of royal estates and the establishment of a Presbyterian church. Negotiations had hardly begun when the army revolted. With peace at hand, Parliament had proposed disbanding the army, but equivocated about the amount of back pay its forces were owed. In August, the army, claiming to represent the people, marched on London and entered discussions with the King. Charles tried to play the army off against Parliament, and finally escaped to launch a second civil war in March 1648. Cromwell rapidly crushed the King's Scottish supporters; then occupied London with his forces, demanding that the King be punished. Cromwell appointed the judges who tried the King and condemned him to death. Charles I was executed on 30 January 1649, an act Cromwell considered ordained by God.

England was now a Commonwealth governed by the Rump of the Long Parliament, which owed all its power to the army. Cromwell, serving as Lieutenant-General under Fairfax, first crushed the Levellers – democrats very popular with the lower ranks of the army – then set out for Catholic Ireland, which had taken the Royalist side. Cromwell defeated the Irish in a ten-month campaign that saw unparalleled atrocities. When the town of Drogheda resisted, he slaughtered 3500 of its inhabitants, including the garrison, priests and civilians, calling his actions 'the righteous judgement of God on these barbarous wretches'. In Wexford, 2000 were killed, including priests whom Cromwell believed represented the Antichrist. By May 1650, Ireland was wholly subdued. Thousands of Irish were sent as slaves to the West Indies, and Catholic landlords were expelled in favour of Protestants. Cromwell hoped the Irish would eventually convert to Protestantism but only succeeded in planting the seeds of enduring hatred. Scotland was next. Cromwell overwhelmed the last Royalist forces and placed the country under military occupation. The late King's son, Charles II, fled abroad uncrowned, the wars ended and Cromwell entered London in triumph in September 1651.

With the Royalist threat removed, Parliament became increasingly fractious. Its constant infighting so exasperated Cromwell that on 20 April 1653 he marched into the House of Commons with his troops and sent the members packing. England became a military dictatorship. The new regime took shape in December 1653 when Cromwell assumed the office of Protector, which gave him authority to be shared with a Council and a future Parliament. The reformist government built roads, promoted poor relief and education, and had a policy of religious tolerance, allowing Jews to reside in England for the first time since the 14th century. Parliament met in September 1654, only to be dissolved by Cromwell the following January when it proved as obstructive and unproductive as its predecessors. The Protector became more authoritarian than ever. He divided England into 12 districts, each ruled by a Major-General with a mounted militia to maintain order, enforce public morality, and exile Royalists and bad characters. By closing alehouses the Major-Generals stirred widespread resentment but followed Cromwell's Reform of Manners, which condemned gambling, idleness and frivolity and abolished horse races, cock-fighting and theatrical performances, all considered keys to damnation. Puritanism triumphed.

The next Parliament, called in September 1656, persuaded Cromwell to abolish the Major-Generals but recognized the need for firm central control. In April 1657 they suggested that Cromwell should be made King. He refused, after much hesitation, but did agree to be reinstalled as Lord Protector with a ceremony something like a coronation, and to accept virtually regal powers. He would command the army, name his successor, and appoint members of a new second House of Parliament. He had greater power than Charles I had ever enjoyed, running a regime that brooked no opposition, backed by armed forces, a bodyguard and efficient police and spies. When Parliament objected to the Protector's arbitrary taxes and arrests, he dismissed it.

Cromwell's foreign policy brought England tremendous respect. He aimed to support the Protestant cause, encourage trade and prevent a Stuart Restoration. His successful wars against the Dutch brought England control of the North Sea and laid the foundations for maritime dominance, and his fleets conquered Jamaica as they 'fought the Lord's battles' against 'Roman Babylon', and finally took Dunkirk from the Spaniards. That was his last victory. Cromwell died of malaria in September 1658. He had abolished the monarchy, disestablished the church and united the British Isles. When the monarchy was restored in 1660, Cromwell's body was exhumed and beheaded. His head was kept on public display until 1685. But British monarchs could no longer claim divine right and had to acknowledge the supremacy of Parliament.

Maximilien Robespierre

(1793–4)

'Terror is nothing but prompt, severe, inflexible justice. It is therefore an emanation of virtue.'

Most tyrants are associated with evil but Robespierre strove all his life for good. He was the unflagging champion of the 'virtue' that represented the will of the people and justified striking down anyone who disagreed or opposed him. A participant in every stage of the French Revolution, he oversaw the Reign of Terror when thousands of innocent lives were sacrificed on the guillotine in the first systematic political mass murder of modern times.

Maximilien Robespierre was born in 1758 in northern France. The local bishop helped Robespierre to attend a prestigious college in Paris, where he received an excellent classical education and was singled out, ironically, to give the welcoming speech to the new King Louis XVI in 1774. This was the age of the Enlightenment, which taught that government was a revocable contract between rulers and the people, and that the general will of the people, which was necessarily good, should determine a country's destiny. At the same time, political crises and wars brought Louis XVI's regime to bankruptcy. His only solution lay in calling the Estates General, representatives of the nobility, clergy and Third Estate (educated professionals) to Versailles in 1789.

By then, Robespierre was a lawyer who devoted time to literary societies and speaking, and worked to raise his public profile until he was elected to the Estates General, which became the Constituent Assembly. Reform soon yielded to revolution. The royal fortress of the Bastille in Paris fell to a mob on 14 July 1789, and on 6 October the King and royal family were dragged from Versailles to the capital where they were virtually prisoners. Robespierre gave over 150 speeches to the Assembly in two years, advocating freedom of speech, the press, and the individual citizen, and strongly opposing the death penalty. He also displayed arrogance, self-aggrandizement and priggish morality.

Robespierre's real influence grew behind the scenes, in the Jacobin Club, where radicals discussed measures that they presented to the Assembly. He was also popular with the people of Paris, whose rights he consistently defended. He rarely associated with the poor himself, however, and maintained a fastidious, old-fashioned appearance, with silk stockings, buckled shoes and carefully powdered and curled hair. By 1791, the revolution appeared to be over: a constitutional monarchy had been established, and the power of the nobility and the church had been destroyed. Robespierre accepted nomination to the powerful and lucrative office of Attorney-General.

The situation changed radically in June, when the King and his family attempted to flee Paris, hoping to rally support beyond the frontier. Instead, he was brought back in humiliation and republican support increased. In September 1791, the King signed the Constitution, and the Assembly, which had done its job, adjourned. Robespierre, crowned with oak leaves by the people, was carried home in a triumphal procession.

Robespierre did not sit in the Legislative Assembly, but made his opinions known through his newspaper, the *Defender of the Constitution*. He firmly opposed the moderate Girondin faction that controlled the new Assembly, denouncing their plans for war with Austria, which he feared would strengthen the King and the army. He was a prominent speaker in the left-wing Jacobin Club, and played an active role in the Paris Commune, the radical municipal government. In June 1792, the Girondins stirred a mob against the King who, unintimidated, fortified the Tuileries palace, raising fears that he was planning a coup. Detachments of patriotic fighters (one from the south introducing a stirring new anthem, the *Marseillaise*) were now arriving in Paris, where the Jacobins hosted them. Together, they planned a revolt in which Robespierre was deeply, although not openly, involved. On 10 August a mob stormed the Tuileries, forcing the King to take refuge with the Assembly, slaughtering his guards and looting the palace. Robespierre called it 'the most glorious revolution that has ever honoured humanity'. Three days later, the Commune imprisoned the royal family.

Robespierre's influence in the Commune brought him his first real power, which he used to control elections for a new assembly, the Convention. By now, the guillotine had been set up in the centre of Paris and thousands of royalists and other suspects had been arrested. Between 2 and 6 September, armed mobs invaded the prisons and slaughtered some 1300 people, ostensibly because Austrian forces were advancing on Paris, but really to intimidate the electorate. The strategy worked. Under Robespierre's manipulation, Paris returned a slate of radical Jacobins, who voted as a block and filled the public galleries of the assembly with their supporters.

Robespierre, the recognized leader of the left, became a dominant force in the Convention, which met on 21 September 1792 and abolished the Monarchy. He skilfully outmanoeuvred the Girondins and had the King put on trial and condemned to death. Louis's execution on 21 January 1793 was followed almost immediately by war with virtually every country in Europe and massive revolts in the provinces. The government responded with powerful emergency measures. On 12 March it established the Revolutionary Tribunal, which could try and execute suspects independently of the regular legal system, and on 5 April it set up the Committee of Public Safety, which met secretly to determine internal and foreign policy. For the time being, the ardent revolutionary Danton was the leader, and the Girondins still had a substantial presence in the Convention. Robespierre continued to denounce the moderates, claiming that the state needed a single will, that the only parties were the people and its enemies, and that all who conspired against the rights of man should be exterminated. His words and plotting provoked another coup, when a mob invaded the Convention on 2 June and arrested the Girondin leaders, leaving the Jacobins in complete control. On 27 July, Robespierre joined the Committee of Public Safety.

By the end of 1793, the Committee held supreme power in France. Since conscription for the huge revolutionary army had created considerable economic disruption, the Committee created a powerful centralized state that took control of every aspect of the citizens' lives. It abolished Christianity, introduced a new calendar, incorporated Jacobin Clubs into the government structure, requisitioned food for Paris, and ordered the arrest of anyone denounced by spies and informers.

Robespierre was only one of 12 members of the Committee, but if he was not actually dictator of France, his influence was overwhelming. His prestige among the Jacobins and the Commune made him the vital link between the Committee, the Convention and the people, while his unvarying, incorruptible moral stance ensured his domination. He was the real leader of the Reign of Terror that began on 31 October 1793 with the execution of the Girondin leaders and continued as long as Robespierre lived.

At the trial of the Girondins, Robespierre proposed that the tribunal not waste time with witnesses but ask the jury after three days whether it was satisfied with the evidence, and if so move to a decision. Swift justice became the rule, as did execution immediately after sentencing, for keeping condemned prisoners waiting for death was considered inhumane. The bloodiest work of the Terror was carried out by the Revolutionary Tribunal, staffed by Robespierre's men. They simplified procedures by trying people in batches: in some cases, the condemned did not even know one another. Aristocrats, priests, politicians or the rich had no hope of escape. Proof of guilt was as rare as real defence.

Robespierre now turned against his rivals. In March, the extreme leftists whose popularity had grown among the Parisians were rounded up and executed, then in April, Danton, who had spoken against the Terror, was sent to the guillotine along with his closest followers. The verdict against them, based on the feeblest evidence, was prepared and printed before their condemnation. Robespierre, who had no rivals and still enjoyed immense popularity, then went too far. Disturbed by the collapse of organized religion, which he feared would lead to immorality, he announced a new cult of the Supreme Being whose magnificent festival he led on 8 June. People started murmuring that he was becoming a god as well as a dictator.

Two days later, the Committee streamlined the Tribunal's procedure. If the jury had material or moral proof of the guilt of the accused, it could judge by its conscience. No witnesses or lawyers were allowed: the only verdicts were innocence or death. Robespierre's new law claimed 1376 victims within six weeks, a huge portion of the 2795 who had died since the Terror began.

For a month after the new law was passed, Robespierre stayed away from the Committee, plotting, his colleagues suspected, to send them to the guillotine. France was now winning its wars, and the emergency was diminishing, but thousands of people had been arrested as suspects, striking fear throughout society. Robespierre's colleagues planned carefully and moved before he could preempt them. On 9 July, he was unexpectedly shouted down in the Convention, arrested, and executed together with his closest followers the next day. The Reign of Terror came to a swift end.

Napoleon
(1799–1814)

'If I had succeeded, I would have been the greatest man known to history.'

A minor Corsican aristocrat who espoused the French Revolution and rose rapidly in the army, Napoleone Buonaparte became the Emperor Napoleon I and brought most of Europe under his control in a dizzying series of conquests. He ruthlessly exploited the areas he ruled and established a police state at home. He brought wealth and glory to France, but finally succumbed to his own grandiose ambitions and to the hostile powers of Europe. His Empire collapsed, but his laws and administration survived.

Napoleon claimed to have been born in August 1769, just after France acquired his native Corsica from Italy, but was probably born a year earlier, falsifying the date to make him a native French citizen. His father's connections enabled him to attend an excellent school and the Military Academy in Paris. His retentive memory, hard work and skill at mathematics enabled him to complete the two-year course in one. He read extensively (a habit he maintained all his life), including the Enlightenment writers and historians; his heroes were Alexander the Great and Julius Caesar. He studied at a time when France was modernizing its armed forces with the latest tactics and technology. After graduation, Napoleon witnessed enough of the Revolution in Paris to develop a contempt for mob rule and the weakness of the monarchy. He spent much of his time on leave in Corsica, however, hoping to lead a patriotic movement there. When that failed, he returned to France, where his loyalty to the Revolution and his excellent training led to rapid promotion. His first real breakthrough came with the Siege of Toulon, which had gone over to the English in 1793. His skilled use of artillery captured the city and earned him promotion to Brigadier at the age of 24.

The fall of his supporter Robespierre in 1794 brought a temporary eclipse to Napoleon's fortunes, but the influence of a new patron, Count Barras, the leader of the ruling Directory, brought him a command in Italy and also a wife, the Count's former mistress Josephine. The Italian Campaign of 1796 brought Napoleon real glory. With his speed and brilliant tactics, Napoleon drove out the Austrians, established republican regimes and seized treasures and works of art. He used the money he raised to reward his backers and to generate the publicity and propaganda that ensured his fame. France's main enemy, however, was England. Napoleon was offered command of invasion forces that he considered inadequate. He decided instead to take the war to Egypt, striking at England's imperial lifeline. His forces rapidly seized the country, completely reorganizing it and studying every aspect of its history and present culture. They were marooned, however, when the English naval commander Lord Nelson destroyed the French fleet.

In 1799, Napoleon deserted his men in Egypt and sailed back to France at a critical time. The Directory was in chaos, divided against itself and looking for a new leader, ideally a figurehead. Napoleon joined a plot that took over the regime in November. By the following month, he had outmanoeuvred his colleagues, to be named First Consul with a term of ten years. He had extensive executive authority in an extremely complicated administrative system, but no political experience. Rather than turn to the legislature for approval, he consulted the people in what became a trademark of his regime, a plebiscite that gave him three million votes. Only some 1500 opposed him.

Napoleon was in power, but with limits imposed by the constitution and legislature. He moved with great speed to remove them, bringing France under tighter control than ever. In February 1800, he established a system of Prefects to rule the Departments into which France was divided. Never local men, and always appointed from Paris, they replaced the last traces of local democracy. Later in the same year, an attempt on his life gave Napoleon a pretext to crush the radical Jacobin opposition, although he knew that royalists had organized the plot. By then he had repelled the Austrian forces in Italy yet again and soon made terms with France's remaining enemies. Peace finally arrived, for the first time in ten years, in 1802.

Peace gave Napoleon even greater prestige, which he used to call another plebiscite where the usual overwhelming margin made him Consul for Life, with the right to name his successor. He had achieved permanent, yet constitutional, power. Napoleon was determined to establish unity and harmony in France, but religion was a major problem. Although the Revolution had dispossessed the churches and tried to destroy Christianity, the French remained Catholic. To pacify his people and gain wider support, Napoleon entered into negotiations with the Pope. They culminated in the Concordat of April 1802 that restored the Catholic church but with conditions that effectively subjected it to the state. The church was to have one liturgy and one catechism (where loyalty to Napoleon featured prominently). It would also control primary education and every child would have the name of a saint. This proved a problem, as there was no St Napoleon. Scholars obligingly discovered a St Neopolis, forged a life for him (he became a martyr of early persecutions) and celebrated his feast on Napoleon's birthday, 15 August, replacing the great religious holiday of the Assumption of the Virgin.

Since Napoleon aimed to be a constitutional ruler, he appointed a committee of lawyers in 1800 to draw up a code of laws. He actively participated in their discussions, quoting whole passages of Roman Law from his prodigious memory. The new code was clear and simple, incorporating many of the rights proclaimed during the Revolution, with freedom and equality under a secular regime, but also adding Roman features that subordinated wives and children to the male head of the family. After being discussed by the Council of State – Napoleon's advisory body, composed of men of talent recruited regardless of birth or rank – the Code Napoleon was introduced in March 1804. It remains Napoleon's most lasting achievement.

Napoleon wanted to create a new model citizen who would perpetuate his ideals. The state therefore established a uniform system of education where the same lessons would be taught from the same books at the same time on the same day in every school in France. The children wore uniforms and received military training from the age of 12. Higher education became a state monopoly. No subversive ideas were to be taught, nor could they be spread in other ways. Most of the newspapers that had appeared during the Revolution were suppressed, leaving only one in each province and four in Paris, all of them taking the lead from the official *Moniteur*. Books, theatres and all forms of public expression were put under the supervision of the police.

A radical revolutionary, Joseph Fouché, ran the police and the network of spies that reached through the whole of French society. Mail was routinely opened and anyone might be secretly denounced. Fouché read foreign newspapers – not available to the public – so that he and Napoleon would have a wider view of events than was available from the censored French press. Napoleon had his own secret service that reported directly to him. He believed in creating overlapping or parallel organizations to ensure his personal control of his subordinates. Daily life in France became more dreary and there was a widespread sense of fear.

This system developed as Napoleon's power increased. In 1804, following discovery of a royalist plot, he kidnapped and executed a prominent member of the royal family, then crushed the royalist opposition. In its place, he created a royalty of his own. After the usual plebiscite approved, he became Emperor Napoleon I, placing the crown on his own head in the presence of the Pope, who had been brought from Rome for the occasion. He created a new aristocracy with pompous titles, but without the power and exemptions from the law that the old nobility had enjoyed.

The Emperor fought wars that lasted till the end of his reign. In 1805, he defeated Austria and Prussia, set up subsidiary kingdoms (usually ruled by members of his family) in Holland, Italy and Germany, moved into Spain and Portugal, and by 1810 dominated Europe as no one had done since the Romans. He never stopped working, supervising even the smallest details of running his vast Empire. He routinely allowed eight minutes for lunch and 12 for dinner, and even on campaign in Spain or Russia, was giving orders about the fountains in Paris or the programme for the state theatre. However, he never managed to defeat the British, whose control of the sea effectively frustrated the Continental System designed to block all British trade with Europe. These incessant wars required huge manpower, drafted from France and its dependencies, as well as money ruthlessly exacted from all occupied lands. Another unbeatable enemy was Russia, which Napoleon attacked in 1812 at the same time as a British force was making progress against him in Spain. The French took Moscow, but the campaign was a disaster. Of the 500,000 men who set out for Russia only 18,000 returned. After that, Napoleon's allies fell away, the occupied countries revolted and enemy forces advanced into France, forcing Napoleon to abdicate in April 1814. The generous allies allowed him to keep his imperial title and rule the small island of Elba from which he escaped in March 1815, returning to Paris, raising new armies and facing ultimate defeat at Waterloo in June. This time, he was sent to St Helena in the south Atlantic, where he died in 1821.

José Rodriguez de Francia

(1814–40)

'*You may have heard that my government is despotic and unnecessarily severe. I had only a choice between this severity and the anarchy of my country. I preferred the former.*'

José Gaspar Rodriguez de Francia, Dictator of Paraguay, was a great admirer of the French Revolution. He brought equality to his country by destroying the ruling elites, but liberty vanished as every aspect of life fell under his direct personal control. To avoid the corrupting influence of foreign ideas, he sealed his country off from the outside world. Yet he ran an honest and efficient regime that brought prosperity and stability and favoured the common people.

Francia was born in 1766 in a remote and undeveloped part of Spanish America. Paraguay had no important natural resources, little trade, and a native population trained in servility by Jesuits. A handful of Spaniards controlled commercial and political life, rigidly excluding Creoles like Francia. Educated by monks, Francia gained a doctorate in theology from the University of Córdoba (in present-day Argentina) in 1785, but after returning home, he turned to the law. Francia was attracted by the radical writers of the Enlightenment, especially Voltaire and Rousseau, and sympathized with ideals of the French Revolution. As a lawyer, he consistently took the side of the poor and weak. By 1809, he had been elected to the Municipal Council and become a judge, but could rise no further because Spaniards monopolized all higher posts.

Paraguay declared its independence from Spain in May 1811 without a fight. Many considered joining forces with the provinces of Buenos Aires, but Francia, who now became a prominent political figure, insisted that his country pursue its own independent course. The new government established a five-man junta, with Francia as Secretary. Because he was one of the most skilled and learned people in a country where higher education did not exist, he soon came to dominate his colleagues. On two occasions, he withdrew because the junta was extravagant or corrupt, and only returned when promised greater powers. In 1812, he took control of foreign policy and half the army.

Members of the junta and of the national Congresses, which were held annually, knew nothing about government, but some had read Roman history. The Congress of 1813, therefore, voted to make Paraguay a Republic, run by two Consuls. They chose Francia and Fulgencio Yegros, a prominent landowner. Francia arranged his term to coincide with the beginning of the next Congress and began to replace army officers with his own men. Together, the Consuls moved against the local Spaniards, forbidding them from marrying white women in an attempt to reduce their influence and with a view of extinguishing them altogether.

When the Congress of 1814 elected Francia as its President he proposed a one-man executive to deal with the general emergency caused by the wars of independence that were raging in South America. Francia took the new office of Dictator for three years. He removed high-ranking civil servants and army officers, replacing them with men of humble origins, loyal only to him, and started to bring the church under control by abolishing the Inquisition and forbidding night services, which might serve as a cover for plotting. The Congress of 1816 made him Dictator for life. He promised to hold Congresses in the future, but never did. Instead, he put a stop to political activity by banning any public gatherings except those for which he had given his specific permission. Paraguay had fallen under one-man rule.

Francia soon established a reign of terror whose worst manifestations followed the discovery of a conspiracy in 1820. A group of prominent citizens and army officers planned to assassinate Francia and install Yegros as ruler. Francia got wind of the plot, arrested 200 people, including Yegros, and sent them to the 'Chamber of Truth' where they were whipped until they gave the answers their torturers required, then taken out in batches to be shot. The executions, carried out by firing squad in public and watched by Francia from his palace window, continued for two years. The conspirators' property was confiscated and their families cut off from all contact with them. The next year, he arrested the 300 Spaniards living in the capital and held them for more than a year before releasing them on payment of a huge fine. That, together with the government seizing control of all commerce, reduced the surviving Spaniards to poverty. Francia had crushed the old ruling class.

He next turned his attention to the church and the remnants of local liberties. In 1824, Francia banned religious orders and closed the monasteries, confiscated the property of the church and took control of its finances. Priests were made to swear loyalty to the state, as Francia refused to recognize the authority of the Vatican. Instead, he made himself head of the church, which he had considered as a potential rival for power. He also closed down the municipal assemblies and appointed commandants to administer and judge each province. Francia himself made the laws, which were never published, not least because there was no printing press in the country. Laws were transmitted to the commandants and through them to the judges: the public never knew what they contained. Crimes against the state, however, as well as those committed by the military, were judged in person by Francia who actually gained a reputation for honesty and fairness. This was a regime capable of treating its followers well, as long as they never stepped out of line.

The Dictator himself was an isolated, mistrustful figure. An unsociable bachelor subject to fits of hypochondria, he lived austerely in a palace with few retainers and followed a regular schedule of work, walking, reading (especially French) and carrying out tours of inspection. He had no friends or confidants and never asked for advice. He lived in fear of assassination. Although he willingly gave audiences, he always kept weapons close at hand and forbade anyone to approach closer than three paces, and then they had to keep their hands down by their sides. When he rode out, doors and windows along his route had to be closed and his guards would strike anyone who approached too close with their swords. As a result, the streets of the capital were usually empty, but anyone who was caught in the open had to take off his hat and stand with bowed head. Those who did not own hats had to carry a simple circular brim, just to be prepared to raise it.

Francia did not like the narrow winding streets of Asunción and suspected that they, like the lush courtyards of private houses, could harbour assassins. In 1821, therefore, he drew up a new city plan, with broad streets set out in a rectangular pattern and ordered any house that stood in the way to be demolished. Many of them belonged to the elite. Francia was a great builder: roads, fortresses and public works adorned every part of the country. The provinces supplied the materials and only the master builders were paid. Prisoners did most of the work.

There was no shortage of prisoners, for the police constantly watched everyone, and the Dictator encouraged an army of informers. Every soldier and policeman was a spy for Francia and every citizen who did not report suspicious activities was himself considered guilty. Any comment that seemed to criticize the government or any delay in following orders meant arrest.

There was no freedom of movement and no privacy in Francia's Paraguay. No one was allowed to leave the country without a passport signed by the Dictator, and new arrivals were carefully watched. The postal service was suppressed because it offered easy communication. Letters that came by private post or from abroad were taken to Francia, opened and read. The government suppressed all commerce except for a necessary trickle of trade, exchanging Paraguay's raw materials for weapons. Ships that came into the country had to proceed directly to Asunción and could only unload their goods after careful inspection. In one case, when a ship arrived with a bill of lading in English, it had to wait until Francia, with the aid of a grammar book and dictionary, had learnt enough of the language to read it. The country became so isolated that virtually nothing is known of the latter part of Francia's reign. Rarely has a country been so effectively sealed off from the outside world.

The negative aspects of Francia's regime tend to conceal its merits. He crushed the ruling class and granted substantial benefits to the poor. Thanks to confiscation from the rich and the church, the state wound up owning half the land in the country. Some state land was rented to people for cultivation, while the rest became horse and cattle ranches. Profits from these activities enabled the state to reduce taxes dramatically, and so many animals were produced that they could be given away to the peasants. Internal sales of state products became the greatest source of revenue and led to virtual self-sufficiency. Isolation enabled Paraguay to avoid involvement in the wars of its neighbours, and to achieve complete independence. Francia ran an honest administration, very much in the interests of the poor, for whom he created a system of obligatory primary education.

The Dictator died in 1840, rejecting the last offices of the church. For months people refused to believe that he was dead, and were still afraid to mention his name long afterwards.

Shaka Zulu

(1816–28)

Shaka, an outcast from his tiny Zulu tribe, rose through military skill to command a powerful army that dominated southern Africa, striking fear far beyond the frontiers of the great nation that he created. He ruled his army through fierce discipline and his people by terror, forging a unity that had never existed before. The foundations he laid gave his people dominance for a half century after his death, until they succumbed to the modern technology of invading Europeans.

Shaka was born around 1785 in Kwa Zulu-Natal in what is now South Africa. His father was chief of the 1500-strong Zulu tribe. When he was six his parents quarrelled. Shaka and his mother were forced to take refuge with her tribe, the Langeni, where Shaka was a fatherless outcast, bullied and humiliated by the other children. In 1802, when food ran short, the Langeni expelled them. They were taken in by the Mthethwa, whose powerful chief Dingiswayo took a liking to Shaka and became his patron. Shaka grew up in a traditional pastoral society where cattle were the most important source of food and indicator of wealth. The tribes were patriarchal, with the father exercising complete control over the family. The individual was strictly subordinated to the group, which was collectively responsible for any individual member's misbehaviour. The tribes worshipped their ancestors. Diviners interpreted the will of the ancestors and had special powers to 'smell out' malefactors. Real or imagined offenders were killed by impalement through the rectum. The tribal chief had considerable powers, limited by consultation with leaders of the main families. In Shaka's time, traditional stability was being undermined by Europeans whose desire for trade and slaves, backed by their novel and powerful weapons, destabilized the region, while the growing indigenous population was putting an increasing burden on the land. Under these circumstances, warfare changed from ritual inter-tribal combat into a bitter struggle for survival.

Shaka spent his youth as a herdsman, developing a reputation for physical strength and bravery that made him desirable as a warrior. Rather than return to his father's or mother's clan, he joined one of the new regiments that Dingiswayo was creating. Instead of fighting with their blood relatives, the young men of the tribe were grouped into fighting units that drew on all the clans, and were posted away from home. Loyalty to their fellow warriors replaced the previously divisive attachment to their small kinship groups and allowed the creation of a larger, more stable army. Shaka rose rapidly to become a commander whose discipline and fighting spirit convinced Dingiswayo that he would make a valuable tribal chief and ally. When the leader of the Zulus died in 1816, Dingiswayo provided the manpower that enabled Shaka to take over his ancestral tribe.

Shaka forged the Zulus into a powerful fighting machine. He replaced the old ritualized fighting system, where warriors threw spears at one another, causing and suffering few casualties, into a tightly organized formation that aimed at absolute victory. Each fighter, armed with a short, deadly spear and a large shield, fought in coordinated, disciplined and rapidly-moving formations. Shaka drilled his men constantly and trained them through forced marches of 50 miles a day. They fought barefoot, as Shaka decided that shoes slowed operations. Soldiers who objected to discarding their sandals were executed on the spot, as were those who returned from battle without their spears or with wounds in their back. Shaka evolved a formidable new formation, the 'bull's horns', in which the main body, the 'chest', composed of the best fighters would charge the enemy while the younger men in the 'horns' would swoop round to encircle them, and the older men, 'the loins', would form a reserve to be sent wherever needed. The army moved fast: young boys carried the equipment, and the troops lived off the enemy's land. Tactics, discipline and mobility brought Shaka success, even though he started with a force of only about 400.

In 1817, Dingiswayo was captured and killed by his rival, Zwide, head of the powerful and aggressive Ndwandwe. Shaka saw his opportunity. He conquered a number of small neighbouring tribes, incorporating their men into his own army, then moved against the far more numerous Ndwandwe. The combination of guerilla warfare and his new tactics brought success. After one battle, Shaka's warriors surprised Zwide's kraal, where they impaled all the women and children. Zwide's mother, whose witchcraft was supposed to have caused Dingiswayo's death, suffered a special fate: she was shut in a hut with a hungry hyena who chewed off her limbs before the hut was burnt to the ground. This victory marked the beginning of Zulu expansion. Sending out raiding parties of 100 men or armies of several thousand, Shaka subdued 300 neighbouring tribes and incorporated them into his system. By 1820, his army of 25,000 controlled a population of 500,000 and he was the most powerful ruler in southern Africa.

Shaka ruled through fear and terror. Military discipline was imposed on his entire population, with violent and arbitrary punishments applied suddenly and mercilessly. In warfare, he took no prisoners, and even ordered his own badly wounded men to be executed. He is reputed to have slaughtered all married couples, together with children and even dogs of tribes that resisted, but retained single young men and women for his army and their services. His reputation was such that many tribes willingly submitted, paying a tribute of cattle and providing more men for the army. These, like the conquered tribes, were assimilated into the growing Zulu nation, which was organized for war. Every male from his teens to his forties served in the army. Young men could only gain the sign of manhood and permission to marry by 'washing the spear' – killing an enemy. As the army expanded, so did the need for conquest. Troops had to be kept busy, and the leaders rewarded, preferably with captured cattle. Incessant warfare created disturbances that affected all southern Africa in the so-called *mfecane* (crushing), a kind of chain reaction that forced tribes to flee out of Shaka's reach, attacking or displacing other tribes over a vast region.

Shaka ruled with absolute power through his efficient military system. His troops were organized in self-sufficient regiments that had their own villages and cattle provided by the state. They lived, fought and ate together, loudly praising Shaka during their meals. They were not allowed to marry until Shaka gave the order, when they could select from the units of young women who performed domestic duties for them. This usually happened on retirement, when the men had distinguished themselves in battle and reached their forties. By delaying marriage as long as possible, Shaka kept greater control of his men. Shaka's appointees ruled the regiments, carrying out the king's orders. They were chosen from outside the traditional aristocracy, and were dependent on his favour.

At home, terror ruled. Outside Shaka's headquarters was the 'Cowards Bush' where offenders were executed by wringing the neck, clubbing the head or in cases where witchcraft was suspected, by impalement. Executions were constant, even for the most trivial offences like sneezing in the King's presence. His own family was not spared. Since Shaka feared creating an heir who might threaten him, any of his wives who became pregnant were executed. The message was clear: total obedience alone would ensure survival. In addition to his executioners, Shaka employed an army of informers, a kind of secret service that could denounce anyone. Traditionally most denouncing had been done by the Diviners who claimed to have supernatural powers. Shaka saw them as a potential threat, since they could cite powers greater than his own, so he laid a trap for them early in his reign. Splashing ox blood over his dwelling, he called in the Diviners to ask who was responsible. The vast majority made accusations which, of course, were totally false. They were slowly tortured to death. Shaka also had no patience for the old or sick, whom he usually ordered to be killed on the grounds of their uselessness.

Shaka's violence became increasingly irrational, and reached a peak at the funeral of his mother in 1827. When huge crowds gathered to share the King's grief, those who did not lament adequately or went off to drink water were beaten to death as the frenzied crowd turned on itself. To ensure proper mourning, Shaka ordered that for a year no crops could be grown nor any milk drunk, and forbade sexual relations. Any woman found pregnant was executed with her husband, and thousands of cows were slaughtered so their calves would also know what it was to lose a mother. He was persuaded to relent after three months, by which time the Zulu were facing ruin.

Shaka's increasingly bizarre demands, which included slaughtering hundreds of women accused of witchcraft and sending his men off on lengthy campaigns without any support, eventually resulted in a conspiracy against him. In September 1828, Shaka was stabbed by his brother Dingane, who succeeded him in power. Shaka had forged a nation that survives to the present day, but at enormous cost.

Mutesa I of Buganda
(1856–84)

*'I warned you but you paid no heed. Now the
lion has devoured you.'*

Mukaabya, more usually known as Mutesa, the *kabaka* of Buganda – King of Southern Uganda – was the most powerful and sophisticated ruler in Central Africa at a time when traditional society was confronting the outside world. He ruled an organized hierarchical state that had functioned for centuries, but when the Arabs and English arrived in his territories, he realized the need for change. Mutesa veered between parties and religions in an effort to maintain his independence and increase his power. He succeeded, despite increasingly erratic behaviour, accompanied by what foreign visitors described as unspeakable cruelty.

When the English explorer John Hannington Speke arrived in Buganda in 1862, searching for the source of the Nile, he encountered a civilization that had grown in isolation from the outside world and was completely unknown in Europe. His detailed account reveals Mutesa and his kingdom on the eve of momentous change. Buganda was an ancient traditional society with a strong central government that had replaced local tribal chiefs some time in the remote, unrecorded past. Mutesa had complete power over the lives of his subjects, exercised through a complex hierarchy. He was advised by a council of chiefs led by a kind of prime minister. Chiefs, priests and courtiers attended the King, together with the dreaded Binders, ready with their cords to drag victims to execution. Wives, daughters and the powerful Queen Mother also advised the King. The state consisted of ten provinces whose governors, appointed and dismissed by the King, were like kings themselves in their own realms. The people lived in scattered homesteads and villages in a territory that stretched along Lake Victoria. There were about a million of them, supporting an army of 30,000. The only city was the capital, with 30–40,000 inhabitants. The state was large and organized, but had no system for writing or telling the time and had not discovered the wheel or the plough.

Speke was amazed by Mutesa's capital, with its broad roads and a complex of large and graceful thatched huts around a central compound where the King lived and held court. Bells on the gates warned of intruders. Musicians greeted Speke, who brought wonders from the outside world: a watch, a telescope and guns. Mutesa was so intrigued with the guns that he gave one to a page with orders to shoot someone in the outer court. The page returned, mission accomplished, and Mutesa became devoted to this new technology. The King ruled by traditional means, in which fear was a major element. No one could sit or speak in his presence. When he spoke, all threw themselves flat on the ground shouting out their gratitude and devotion. When he walked in his peculiar fast tiptoeing gait, which was supposed to imitate a lion, all followed behind. He had an elite bodyguard and was constantly on the watch for sedition. His informers made sure he knew everything that happened in the capital, and messengers constantly went back and forth to the provinces.

Speke, like those who followed him, was struck by the violence and cruelty he saw or heard. Girls who spoke too loudly, pages who forgot to shut a door, and others guilty of seemingly trivial offences were seized by the Binders at a sign from Mutesa, and carried off screaming to the execution ground. Women of the royal palace suffered the same fate, sometimes as many as two or three in a day. No one was allowed, on penalty of death, to talk about the King's ancestors or neighbouring countries, to cast an eye on his women, or to possess any foreign object other than beads or brass wire. On one occasion, when one of his favourite wives presented him with a fruit she had just picked, Mutesa flew into a rage and sent her off to die. He blew out the brains of a female attendant to show how good his aim was, and shot another woman whom he saw tied up for punishment. Torture was also routine. When an official complained that Mutesa had given him only one slave, Mutesa ordered him cut to pieces on the spot. Such arbitrary killings were not unknown before Mutesa, who used his power of life and death to create an atmosphere of awe and dread. Late in life, when he seemed to be growing mild, some of the chiefs complained about the decline in executions. The cruelties, however, seemed centred on the court. Most of the population lived in prosperity and often peace.

Speke's visit, the first ever by a European, stimulated Mutesa's interest in the outside world. Arab traders, already known in Buganda, became more frequent in the 1860s. They brought valuable goods, but also introduced trade in human beings, which had previously been unknown, even though slavery was well established. In 1869, the Sultan of Zanzibar, chief figure in the slave trade, exchanged embassies and gifts with Buganda. The wealth and power of the Arabs evidently impressed Mutesa, for he spontaneously adopted their religion. He had already reduced the power of the traditional priests and abandoned some ancient customs, but now took on Islam with enthusiasm. He learnt Arabic, wore Arab dress, introduced the Islamic calendar, built a large mosque at the court (others followed in the villages) and held Koran readings. The new practices were enforced: dozens were executed for failing to address him with the proper Arabic formulas. The Ramadan fast was also obligatory. Mutesa sent inspectors round the country to make sure it was being observed, and during Ramadan in 1875 executed 200 for not adopting his religion.

The famous English explorer Henry Morton Stanley found a changed society when he reached Buganda in 1875. Mutesa was no longer unsophisticated and ignorant of the outside world. He had a new capital whose elegant thatch buildings covered several miles of hills, with splendid accommodation for visiting caravans, and ruled a realm that could raise an army of 150,000, many of them armed with guns. Manufactured goods were now common, and bloody executions at court no longer in evidence. Mutesa liked Stanley, who tried to persuade him to abandon Islam and adopt Christianity. Mutesa agreed to receive missionaries. When they arrived in 1877, they found the King in Arab dress reclining on a Persian carpet, with a bodyguard in trousers and tunics. The missionaries set to work, but the Arabs warned Mutesa that under Christianity he would have to give up all his wives but one, could no longer keep slaves, and could not raid other communities for women and cattle.

The Arabs were right, but Mutesa hardly listened, for he had lost his enthusiasm for Islam. By now, envoys from General Charles Gordon, who was helping the Khedive of Egypt to extend his domains southwards, started to put pressure on Mutesa. They were greeted by the public execution of 30 men. Strict Egyptian Moslems also arrived and quickly pointed out the deficiencies in Mutesa's version of Islam. His mosques faced the wrong direction and his prayer leaders were not circumcised. When some of the King's pages followed the new strict teaching and refused to eat meat killed by non-Moslems, Mutesa began a persecution that took 1000 lives. He was now ready to listen to the missionaries, but their work was complicated by the rivalry between Protestants and Catholics, who seemed to Mutesa to represent two different religions. Mutesa needed the weapons and technology associated with the missionaries (some of whom were extremely skilled mechanics), so he started to play the Christians off against the Moslems. He allowed missionaries to hold services and print tracts, held Bible readings in the palace, and ordered Sunday to be observed. Christianity's stock rose when missionaries successfully treated the King's chronic gonorrhea, but there was real opposition from his mother and the Prime Minister, and serious dogmatic obstacles, for neither Protestants nor Catholics would tolerate the polygamy and slavery that were ingrained in Bugandan society. Mutesa did make one concession, however. After exchanging embassies with Queen Victoria, he announced that he would abandon all his wives if the Queen would give him one of her daughters in marriage. Finally, in 1879, he turned back to his ancestral gods, closed down the mission services, and began to kill Christians. On one infamous day, 2000 were burnt alive as a sacrifice to the sprit of Mutesa's father. The following year, as the result of a dream, he turned back to Islam, but let his people follow whatever religion they pleased.

Mutesa's last years were miserable as he strove to deal with foreign powers and domestic problems, exacerbated by the plague and epidemics that decimated the population. Debilitated by advancing venereal disease, he faced discontent and conspiracy from his people. He responded by sending out many more raiding forces than customary, hoping that chiefs would be killed in the process. That did not work, nor did the cures offered by his priests, and in 1884 Mutesa died. He had kept his country united and independent, at incalculable cost to his own people.

Francisco Solano López
(1862–70)

'Only by war could the attention and respect of the world be secured to Paraguay.'

Francisco Solano López would probably be forgotten today if he had not succeeded in virtually destroying his own country. He ruled Paraguay, a small nation dwarfed by its enormous and rich neighbours, Brazil and Argentina. López involved Paraguay in a war with both of them simultaneously and, in the process, caused the death of a greater proportion of his country's population than any other tyrant in history. But although he ruled them with spectacular brutality and cruelty, his people stuck by him to the end.

López, who grew up under the dictatorships of Francia and then of his own father, Carlos Antonio López (1844–62), knew nothing of democracy. Born in 1827, he was a spoilt child, educated by priests, and became a notorious womanizer. He was made a general and Minister of War when he was very young, and in 1854 was put in charge of operations against Argentina. The army saw no action and López developed a well-deserved reputation for cowardice. He was fortunate that his father had supreme power and was determined to keep it in the family. Carlos Antonio had taken over a state whose treasury was overflowing thanks to the efficient austerities of Francia. He used the money to turn Paraguay into a military powerhouse, with a well-trained army of 30,000, modern gunboats and a string of fortifications along its lifeline, the Paraguay River.

Carlos Antonio wanted to impress the world with the importance of his remote and obscure country and to acquire modern weapons and machinery. To that end, in 1854 he sent Francisco, who was being groomed for the succession, to Europe to represent his father and to acquire knowledge of the world and a taste for civilization. The younger López visited England, observed the Crimean War (from a distance), and was dazzled by the glittering sophistication of Paris. Because he was important and rich, he attracted numerous women, including a 19-year-old Irish girl, Elisa Lynch, who had come to Paris after an unsuccessful marriage and saw López as the romantic heir to a powerful state. She returned with him to Paraguay and never left his side. They eventually had four children, but could not marry because of complications with her divorce. Europe changed López: he adopted very fashionable, almost flashy, dress and became extremely ambitious, constantly encouraged by Mme Lynch. No clothes, however, could conceal the fact that he was short and fat, but he spoke well and fluently unless he had drunk too much, when he would fly into uncontrollable rages.

When the elder López died in 1862, Francisco went though the motions of democracy, convening the Congress that would choose the new President, but before it could meet, he showed his true colours. The Chief Justice was arrested, officials throughout the country were replaced, and guards were stationed around the capital. López then announced the discovery of a conspiracy headed by his own brother and the late President's confessor. Both were arrested. The Congress unsurprisingly chose Francisco López as President. Only one mildly dissenting voice was raised when a Senator questioned the propriety of hereditary succession. He was arrested and never seen again.

Initially, López followed his father's policies of public works and military strength. He paved the capital's dusty streets, built roads in the country, installed South America's first telegraph system and began construction of an opera house and a grandiose palace. Most of his work, however, was directed towards the army, which he concentrated in a new camp near the capital, while fortifications were built or improved, most notably at Humaitá, Paraguay's main port of entry.

Foreign relations brought López to disaster. In 1863, a revolt supported by Brazil broke out in Uruguay, which appealed to López for assistance. Francia and the elder López had resisted previous attempts to involve Paraguay in the affairs of its neighbours, believing that isolation was the surest guarantee of independence. López, however, took a fateful step by announcing (quite wrongly) that Uruguay's independence was essential for the security of Paraguay, and ordered a general conscription that increased his army to 60,000, the largest in South America. Neither Brazil nor Argentina had anything comparable. When Brazil invaded Uruguay in September 1864, therefore, López seized a Brazilian ship, arrested its crew and passengers, and then attacked the Brazilian province of Mato Grosso, accessible only via the Paraguay River. In a fortnight he had occupied it, capturing huge military stores that kept him supplied throughout the war. He looted the towns he captured, tortured the rich for their money and killed his prisoners.

López now requested Argentine permission to cross their territory in order to invade southern Brazil. When that was refused, he moved anyway, capturing two Argentine gunboats. War inevitably followed. In May 1865, Argentina, Brazil and Uruguay (occupied by Brazil) signed the Triple Alliance against Paraguay. At first, López appeared to be in a strong position. He had a large well-trained army, adequate munitions, and would be fighting along internal lines, while the resources of his enemies were widely dispersed and would take time to mobilize. Had he struck immediately, he might have been able to take Montevideo or Buenos Aires and impose terms on his adversaries. Instead, he sent two armies against Brazil; both were ultimately defeated, with the loss of 20,000 men. His enemies had huge reserves and the industrial base to replace any losses. They also had 20 times the population of Paraguay. López's army looked good, but was desperately short of qualified officers since appointments had been made for political rather than military reasons, and it lacked reserves. Ambitious aggression was to turn into a grim struggle for survival.

After the failure of the attack on Brazil, López called a Congress in the capital, Asunción. The delegates gave him the title of Field Marshal and agreed to place their lives and property at his disposal. Mme Lynch organized the women to contribute their jewellery to the war effort, while the regime forbade them to mourn their relatives, but join in processions and festivities. Most of the jewellery found its way to Mme Lynch, who held court on a magnificent scale. López now moved his headquarters to an orange grove outside Humaitá. He rarely left, and never visited the front lines. Mme Lynch lived with her children in a neighbouring house. Not far away was the military court where prisoners were tortured and executed.

In April 1866, the Allied forces crossed the Paraná River into Paraguayan territory. López's losses were staggering, as he had no idea of tactics, strategy or engineering, but sent his men on suicidal attacks, ordering them to fight to the death. Those who failed to obey were considered traitors and the families of deserters were punished. The troops received no encouragement or reward, only execution if they failed, but they fought on. By this time, all males from between the ages of ten and 60 were being drafted, while female 'volunteers' aged between 16 and 40 were put to forced labour. These policies led to further problems, because there were no men left to farm, and the country was blockaded. Shortages of food and supplies became desperate.

The following year, when the army had been reduced to about 20,000 men, López announced that he would fight to the bitter end, rejecting generous terms for ending the war because they would oblige him to go into exile. He was ready to sacrifice his country rather than sacrifice his office. In 1868 Humaitá and other strategic points fell. López, who was sinking into madness, ordered the survivors of their garrisons tortured and executed, even though they had fought with incredible bravery. He left his camp, after killing all prisoners of war, and proceeded to Asunción. He had the capital evacuated and drove its population into the countryside. This had been the city of his dreams, where even then a new palace was being built with the labour of 9- to 13-year-old boys.

López moved off into the wilds of the interior, after discovering imaginary conspiracies that led to the torture and execution of what civil or military leadership remained. During the retreat, López and Mme Lynch rode in carriages ahead of the pathetic remnants of their army (mostly young boys and old men), rising late, eating well and drinking plenty of champagne. They hoarded money, food and salt, of which their troops had no share. Constant losses forced López further into the interior during 1869. He still found time to put most of his family, including his mother and sisters on trial, but kept them alive under constant torture. In February 1870, he had reached the far northeast of Paraguay, where on the last day of the month, he ordered the execution of his mother. The next day, Brazilian forces captured him. For the first time in his life, he fought back but was rapidly overcome and killed. Mme Lynch dug him a shallow grave. The war came to an end. Only 220,000 Paraguayans out of a pre-war population of 525,000 were left alive and of them only 29,000 were adult males.

Leopold II

(1865–1909)

'The Congo Free State is unique in its kind. It has nothing to hide and no secrets and is not beholden to anyone except its founder'

As a constitutional monarch, Leopold II had no possibility of becoming a tyrant in Belgium. He could dismiss Parliament, but had to sign the bills it submitted to him, and to rule in consultation with his ministers. He did not even have a coronation, but an inauguration where he swore before Parliament to obey the Constitution. Yet Leopold had tremendous ambitions. He dreamed of a Belgium that could stand among the European powers, and for that he deemed colonies a necessity. By clever and stealthy means, he managed to gain control of a vast realm in Africa, the Congo, much of which became his personal property. Here, he indulged his desire for profit by exploiting the native population more ferociously than anyone before him. His excesses finally became so notorious that Belgium took control of the colony, giving the country the empire Leopold desired, but blackening his memory.

When Leopold was born in 1835, Belgium was deeply divided. The Flemish speakers were at odds with the French Walloons, and the Liberals opposed the conservative Catholics. This was a time of rapid progress: industry flourished, and Belgium came to have the densest railway network in Europe. Militarily, though, it was weak, and its leaders focused on local problems rather than the international scene.

As Prince, Leopold travelled worldwide at a time when vast colonial empires were being constructed. He became convinced that Belgium, too, needed colonies, not just for wealth, but to rise above party strife. He investigated places where Belgium might gain a foothold, but neither people nor Parliament was interested. When he became King, he determined to push Belgium along the lines he advocated.

Leopold was a man of tremendous energy and firm ideas. He rose at 5 a.m., consumed an enormous breakfast of half a dozen eggs and a whole pot of marmalade, and worked incessantly. He lived simply in a vast unheated palace and worked to overcome what he considered the small-mindedness of his people. Duplicity and ruthlessness drove him on. After the premature death of his only son in 1869, family mattered little to him. He lost interest in his Queen, and grew to despise his daughters.

As King, Leopold searched actively for colonies. He looked to the Philippines, East Africa and southeast Asia but found nothing suitable. The interior of Africa seemed to offer real possibilities, but it was almost totally unknown. Leopold eagerly followed news from explorers and forwarded (and covered) his ambitions by calling a Geographical Congress in Brussels in 1876 where he proposed establishing a network of scientific and medical outposts in Central Africa that would serve as bases for abolishing slavery. He became a leader of philanthropic efforts to bring European civilization to Africa.

The next year, Henry Morton Stanley's emergence at the mouth of the Congo after traversing the continent caused a sensation. Leopold, sensing a spectacular opportunity, raised the possibility with Stanley of extending exploration and establishing humanitarian stations in the Congo basin. They would not become a colony, for Leopold's ostensible aim was to bring justice and order and abolish slavery. Stanley received a large subsidy to buy land, establish settlements and bring local chiefs under control of the philanthropic Committee for Study of the Upper Congo, the front for the King's ambitions. By 1884, the groundwork was laid, but Leopold needed international recognition for his acquisitions. The Berlin Conference of 1884, which convened representatives from all the major European countries, did the job: the powers recognized Leopold's control of the Congo basin, where he promised free trade to all, neutrality, the end of slavery and improved conditions for the indigenous population. Belgium's Parliament, however, wanted nothing to do with it. Instead, in 1885, they allowed Leopold to rule the million square miles of the Congo Free State in his own name. It was an enormous personal triumph.

Leopold considered Belgium a small country with small-minded people. Growing hostility between Catholics and Liberals, focused on religious or secular control over education, together with the rise of socialism and the workers' increasingly violent struggle against low pay and squalid conditions, kept them from paying much attention to the Congo, where Leopold began to establish himself in force.

From the beginning, the Congo Free State was under firm central control, with all policies made in Brussels and no shadow of representative institutions. It needed money for development. Leopold poured in his own fortune and managed to obtain loans from Parliament, but could not collect tax in the Congo because it did not have a money economy. He wanted to develop private enterprise and trade, but that would take time. Instead, he turned to direct and ruthless exploitation. He divided the Congo into three zones: concessions to companies that would organize trade and business; his personal property (an area ten times the size of Belgium); and an area provisionally reserved for the state. Since many of the companies operating in the country were fronts for the King's interests, he controlled most of the economy and profited hugely from it.

Already, in 1885, all 'vacant' land was assigned to the Free State – that included the hunting grounds where ivory-bearing elephants roved, and the forests where wild rubber vines grew. In 1891, the Free State received a monopoly of these products. Native Congolese were forbidden to hunt outside their villages, and it was a criminal offence to buy ivory or rubber from them. That resulted in a state monopoly of the most valuable products, based on fierce exploitation of the local populations. Since there was no money in circulation, tax took the form of forced labour, nominally 40 hours a month. The worst atrocities, committed more by the companies than by Leopold's agents, were associated with rubber production. High fixed quotas were established, remuneration was a tiny fraction of the product's worth and villagers were flogged, mutilated or killed if they failed to meet the quotas. Women (who were often raped) and children were held as hostages. Raids on recalcitrant communities were common. Agents brought back baskets of severed hands to show how many had been killed (they had to account for every cartridge fired). The Congolese were helpless. The Free State broke down the existing tribal systems, chiefs lost all power and Belgian agents (usually backed by African troops) had a free hand. All this brought incredible profits, which went straight to Leopold.

In the decade 1893–1903 he made a huge fortune. Meanwhile, Parliament cancelled Leopold's debts and continued to avoid dealings with the Congo, for fear of expensive and complicated involvement. It also recognized that Leopold spent lavishly at home. His great building plans enhanced Brussels, Ostend and many other places, while he continued to live in relative simplicity, although he did maintain a large yacht and several properties on the French Riviera.

Leopold abolished slavery by bringing the eastern Congo, where Arab slavers had flourished, under Free State control, and did all he could to expand his territory to the north and south, but opposition from the European powers made him back down. He had no better luck in Morocco, but did manage to bring Belgian enterprise to China, where he built its first long-distance railway. He was constantly looking for ways and places to expand his empire.

Word of the atrocities in the Congo, however, could not be suppressed, and opposition started to arise, especially in England. The Free State became a watchword for horror in 1903, when Britain's first Consul to the country, Roger Casement, published his famous Congo Report, which detailed the atrocities he had witnessed. He found whole areas depopulated, natives who fled at the sight of white men, Congolese driven deeper and deeper into the jungle to look for rubber, and forced to work not 40 hours but 20 days a month without pay. He saw a regime devoted entirely to profit, all directed from Brussels. Leopold, a master of public relations, responded with plausible explanations, but an International Commission confirmed Casement's findings and discovered that Leopold had done nothing for the Congolese, spent nothing on infrastructure, and not even planted new rubber vines. The Commission's report stirred demands in the Belgian Parliament to take control of the Congo from Leopold. In 1906, Leopold withdrew to his yacht in southern France where he drew up plans to hide as much of his fortune as possible, and to disinherit his legitimate but rejected daughters. By now, his popularity was at a low ebb as he was living openly with a girl he had met when she was a 16-year-old prostitute in Paris (a city he frequented for such pleasures, as well as business). Vulgar, but loyal, she bore him two children, and only added to the scandals associated with his name.

Finally, in 1908, Belgium took control of the Congo. Leopold kept much of his fortune, but died the following year, days after marrying his young mistress and signing a bill authorizing conscription for the Belgian army. He never visited his African kingdom.

Abdul Hamid II

(1876–1909)

'*I will soon settle those Armenians. I will give them a box on the ears that will make them smart and relinquish their revolutionary ambitions.*'

Abdul Hamid ruled the Ottoman Empire, which had once terrorized the western world, but in his time declined to become the so-called 'sick man of Europe'. Faced with enemies abroad and demands for reform at home, Abdul Hamid used every possible means, including intrigue, dissimulation, treachery and a vast army of spies, to maintain his Empire. When he turned to mass murder, the blood of slaughtered Armenians earned him notoriety as the Red Sultan. Although hated in Europe, and detested by his Christian subjects, his clever use of Islam kept the loyalty of his Moslem population for over 30 years. He preserved the Empire by playing his enemies off against one another but ultimately succumbed to rebellious army officers who benefited from the progressive education he had himself established. Although he held absolute power over millions, he lived in a state of constant fear.

Abdul Hamid was born in 1842 in the harem of his father Abdul Mejid (1839–61). He grew up in an atmosphere of jealousy and intrigue, for the women of the harem were in desperate competition, and one who gave birth to a son could gain enormous influence. His mother, however, had no such luck. Seven-year old Abdul Hamid watched her die of tuberculosis. Another of his father's wives taught him the exquisite manners he always maintained, but the quiet, gloomy child was shown no favour by the Sultan who preferred his older, more outgoing son, Murad.

This was a time of tremendous change for the Empire. Faced with constant military defeats, the Turks had been trying to modernize since the beginning of the century. This involved improved secular education and increased contact with Europe, whose progressive ideas inevitably accompanied the desired technology. Demands for a more liberal government joined outside pressure for reform, especially as the Empire fell increasingly into debt to pay for its often extravagant programmes.

By 1875, the situation was desperate. Ottoman credit collapsed, the Balkans rose in revolt, and Sultan Abdul Aziz (1861–76) became hopelessly senile. The troops restored order with the savage Bulgarian Massacres that resounded through Europe. When the European powers demanded extensive reforms, however, they received an unexpected shock: on 23 December 1876 the Ottomans proclaimed a Constitution. This was the work of the reforming Prime Minister, Midhat Pasha, who saw the crisis as a road to real change. Midhat had deposed the recalcitrant Sultan Aziz, and passed the throne to Murad, for whom the reformers had great hopes until his nervous disorders developed into real insanity. They then turned to Abdul Hamid, who guaranteed his support and was proclaimed Sultan on 1 September 1876. With the acceptance of the Constitution three months later, he became the first constitutional monarch in Ottoman history. The new ruler basked in his popularity as a reformer, but was actually biding his time until he could regain absolute power. For that he needed to eliminate Midhat whom he hated for reducing his authority, abolish the Constitution, and somehow neutralize the great European powers.

He first had to deal with Russia, which was crushing his forces in a bitterly fought war. Abdul Hamid summoned the new Parliament and called on other European countries to mediate. The British, together with Germany and Austria, restrained the Russians, in the process helping themselves to Cyprus (the Austrians got Bosnia) and inserting a clause into the 1878 Treaty of Berlin providing for reforms in the Armenian provinces, to be supervised by British Consuls. By then, the Sultan had prorogued the Parliament, abolished the Constitution, and exiled Midhat. In 1881, however, he lured Midhat back to Turkey, put him on trial on fabricated charges, and sent him to Arabia, where he was murdered soon after.

Absolute power did not bring security. The Sultan lived in a state of fear, especially after May 1878 when rebels tried to restore the demented Murad to power. From then, Abdul Hamid shut himself up in the heavily guarded Yildiz palace overlooking Istanbul, a vast fortified compound with secret underground passages, steel doors, parrots in every room to screech at strangers, and a complex floor plan that only he knew. He rarely emerged, except for Friday prayers in the nearby mosque. Within the walls lived his harem, the court, and hundreds of servants, all in mortal fear of their ruler, who always carried a pistol (and used it with deadly effect). Yildiz was the nerve centre of the Empire, the place where all decisions had to be made. The Sultan, who had a prodigious memory, was obsessed with the most trivial details and worked extremely hard. He employed an army of spies through his vast realm and spent a great deal of time reading their reports, which he carefully recorded. He had a map of the Empire at its glorious height in his study, reminding him of the encroachments of the hated Europeans. He ate little and simply, smoked incessantly, and for relaxation played Offenbach or Meyerbeer on the piano.

Technology helped tyranny. Abdul Hamid was terrified of electricity, but took great advantage of the telegraph whose network rapidly spread, allowing his orders to reach the most remote provinces with unprecedented speed, and enabling him to exercise ever-tighter control over his subordinates. He succeeded in creating a police state where the whole population lived in fear of informers.

Neither spies nor peace could prevent further disaster: in 1882, the British occupied Egypt, the richest province of the Empire. To keep hold of the rest, Abdul Hamid increasingly turned to religion, not because he was an ardent believer (astrology and the occult had greater attractions), but as a means of ensuring the loyalty of his Moslem subjects and potentially stirring up trouble for European empires with Moslem populations. He made sure there were government agents in every Islamic establishment in the Empire.

This policy generally worked, as did his friendship with the new German Kaiser, whom he entertained royally in 1889. When he chose to be, Abdul Hamid was a man of great charm, capable of putting on a magnificent banquet and dispensing splendid gifts. The Kaiser's wife believed she had walked into the Arabian Nights. The depth of her understanding showed, however, when she asked the Sultan's chief eunuch whether his father had been a eunuch also.

The Treaty of Berlin had given the Christian Armenians hope of reform. When nothing materialized, they began to organize revolutionary parties for their own protection. Abdul Hamid, convinced that foreigners were subverting his subjects, created a special Kurdish cavalry to quell any disturbances. He finally decided that he could only solve the Armenian problem by eliminating the Armenians, so in 1894 he ordered his governors to suppress the 'rebellion'. At the sound of a bugle (this was no spontaneous action), mobs and troops attacked Armenian quarters, looted shops, destroyed property, raped women and killed men. Everything happened on a large, coordinated scale and some 200,000 perished in the bloodbath. The reaction of the European powers was furious, especially after Armenian terrorists took over the Ottoman Bank in Istanbul, holding staff members hostage and provoking a retaliatory massacre of tens of thousands of Armenians in the streets of the capital. The British Prime Minister William Gladstone denounced Abdul Hamid and President Clemenceau of France referred to him as 'the Red Sultan'.

Germany, however, stood aside, and the rest of Europe was soon distracted by troubles elsewhere. In 1898, the Kaiser and his Empress returned, met on the dock by Abdul Hamid who was now so afraid of assassination that he wore a shirt of mail under his clothes. The imperial couple enjoyed a splendid reception while most of the public lived in fear, especially those civilians who were rash enough to have any unauthorized contact with Europeans. By now, however, Germans were training the Ottoman army and numerous secular schools had been opened to educate the officers and civil servants. Dangerous liberal European ideas began to spread.

Trouble started in the ever-turbulent Balkans, where rebellious subjects formed secret revolutionary societies and army officers were plotting to overturn a regime that seemed to be losing control. Their central organization, the Committee of Union and Progress, rose in revolt in 1908 demanding that Abdul Hamid restore the Constitution. To save his throne, he obliged, to the immense joy of the entire population. Christians, Jews and Moslems danced together in the streets. This time, however, real power passed to Parliament and the army, and the Sultan was obliged to sign decrees he had not issued. Reaction was not slow in coming, stirred by the more extreme Moslem elements. In 1909, the Sultan briefly regained power, but he could not hold back the forces marching against him. His retainers and troops slipped away, leaving him with a few servants and female companions who calmed his nerves by reading him the latest adventures of Sherlock Holmes.

The final blow came on 27 April, when Abdul Hamid calmly accepted his deposition, saying only, 'It is fate.' He was shipped off by train (his first such journey) to Salonica, lodged in a palace and treated well until he was tricked into signing away the fortunes he held in European banks. Soon after, the Balkan wars broke out and the ex-Sultan had to be evacuated back to Istanbul where he spent his remaining years in a palace on the Bosporus, attended by ever fewer women, and finally dying peacefully in January 1918 in the arms of one of them, just in time to avoid seeing the defeat of Turkey in World War I.

Vladimir Lenin

(1917–24)

*'Liberty is so precious that it must
be rationed.'*

Lenin was probably the most influential leader of the 20th century. He devised and spread a doctrine that dominated half the world and influenced or menaced the rest. A politician and theorist, he knew how to seize and maintain power and how to convince people that slavery was freedom. The totalitarian state he created lasted for more than 70 years.

Vladimir Ilyich Ulyanov was born in Simbirsk on the Volga, where his father was Director of Education. In 1887 his older brother was executed for participating in a plot to assassinate the Tsar. This trauma turned Ulyanov to Marxism. After he joined student demonstrations he was expelled from Kazan University where he was studying law. He continued to study privately and qualified as a lawyer in 1891.

In 1895, Ulyanov visited leading Russian Marxist exiles in Geneva, and founded a Marxist group on his return. The authorities discovered it and sent him to Siberia, where he began his prodigious output of books and articles. After his release in 1900, he joined exiles in Geneva and founded a newspaper, *Iskra* (*The Spark*), the organ of the new Social Democratic Labour Party, which aimed to destroy Russia's autocracy. In 1902 he published a pamphlet entitled *What Is To Be Done?* that laid the foundations for a new interpretation of Marxism. Lenin (the name he nowed assumed) argued that the proletariat was too primitive to lead a revolution by itself, but needed the guidance of a professional elite. Its corollary, Democratic Centralism, obliged everyone to follow the party line once the leadership defined it. His notions were much discussed at the Party Congress of 1903, where the Marxists split. Although he only won by one vote, Lenin cleverly began to call his faction the Bolsheviks ('majority') while his rivals became Mensheviks ('Minority').

When the first Russian Revolution broke out in 1905, Lenin returned to St Petersburg, but his group was too small to make much impression. He ordered his followers to participate in the newly-established Parliament where they formed a small noisy faction. Party finances improved thanks to rich supporters and 'expropriation' – armed robberies carried out by gangs, especially in the Caucasus where they were led by a young enthusiast named Stalin. Lenin used the money to print revolutionary literature and to influence the growing industrial trade unions.

Lenin left Russia in 1907, moving between Switzerland, France and the Austrian Empire until 1914, when he settled in Zurich. He longed for violent revolution, but believed it would only come with war, which was unlikely in the near future. When World War I did break out, Lenin was shocked that socialists of all countries joined the fighting instead of forming a solid class front for peace. He hoped Russia would collapse in civil war. In fact, the war brought such enormous losses of men and material, shortages of food and crippling inflation that the workers of Petrograd began a strike. It turned to revolution in March 1917. The Tsar abdicated and a Provisional Government took over pending elections for a constituent assembly.

Early in 1917, Lenin had said that he would probably not live to see the Revolution; it occurred a month later. Because he spent his time with intellectuals and theorists, rarely dealing with the common people, Lenin was often wrong in predicting events. He led a single-minded, austere existence. Politics determined his activities, his friends and where he lived. He was absolutely convinced that he was right. When he was proved wrong, he had the singular ability to shift quickly to the opposite point of view and expect everyone to follow. He wrote incessantly about theory, but always advocated action, the more violent the better.

The liberal Provisional Government proclaimed liberty but faced the immediate problem of German advance. Their determination to continue the war stirred widespread opposition, especially from the socialists whose Councils of Workers' and Soldiers' Deputies (the Soviets) rapidly turned into a rival government. The Soviets, who were influential in the trade unions and armed forces, wanted to end the war. Profiting from the confusion, the Bolsheviks began to infiltrate them.

The Germans saw Lenin, who consistently opposed the war, as a key figure. In April 1917, they sent him back to Russia and subsidized his party. When he arrived in Petrograd, Lenin announced his position: no cooperation with the government; immediate peace; seizure of land by the peasants and factories by the workers, all encapsulated in the slogan 'All Power to the Soviets'. In May, Russia launched an offensive against the Germans that failed miserably. The Bolsheviks then attempted an uprising in July, but it was easily suppressed and Lenin barely managed to escape to Finland. But in September, when the government faced a right-wing military uprising, it had to call on the Soviets for help. Lenin returned to Russia and insisted that the Bolsheviks aim to take power immediately. The party agreed and on 7 November seized the government headquarters in the Winter Palace in a swift military coup. The next day, Lenin became chairman of the ruling Bolshevik Council of Peoples' Commissars. This was the Great October Revolution, so called because Russia used a different calendar from the rest of Europe.

The Bolsheviks moved fast. By the end of 1917, land was nationalized, opposition parties suppressed, and factories turned over to the workers. The courts and the legal profession were abolished, banks nationalized and private accounts confiscated. The state seized church property and forbade religious education. On paper at least, Russia was a Communist, atheist, one-party state. Some of this was show, for the Bolsheviks were only a small minority whom many opposed, but they gradually got the upper hand. They showed their true colours in January 1918 when the newly-elected Constituent Assembly tried to meet. Bolshevik representation was small since they had only won a quarter of the vote. As the Assembly convened, Red Guards marched in and disbanded it. Democracy came to a sudden end.

Meanwhile the Germans were advancing into Russia. Lenin, who thought the war would end when the new socialist state won round the workers, was disappointed. He finally overruled the objections of his colleagues and accepted the treaty of Brest-Litovsk in March 1918, conceding huge territories to the Germans or their newly independent satellites. In a sense, he was paying the Germans back for installing him in power. By then, however, opposition was turning into civil war. The Red state was attacked on all sides by White armies favourable to monarchy or any alternative to Communism, and backed by western allies. Soviet territory was reduced to the heartland of Russia. Thanks to the skill of the Red Army commander, Trotsky, and irreconcilable divisions among the Whites, Lenin was able to reunite the country by the end of 1920. By then, industrial and agricultural production had fallen to half their pre-war levels.

Lenin thought he could establish Communism fast. He sent troops out to the countryside to seize crops for the cities in what he termed Communist Distribution. Hostility to this policy helped stir the civil war. More effective was War Communism, which gave the state control of trade and production. Workers had to work and slackers went to concentration camps along with uncooperative 'former people' – priests, nobles and the bourgeoisie. The key to Lenin's power was the Cheka, the secret police he created in December 1917, whose agents were given the power of execution without trial. After an attempt on Lenin's life in August, he unleashed the Cheka against intellectuals and the educated middle-classes. Terror became universal as the government gained complete control.

In 1918, Russia adopted a new apparently democratic Constitution where local Soviets elected regional councils that selected delegates to the All-Union Congress of Soviets. The Congress in turn elected the supreme Council of Peoples' Commissars. However, only workers and peasants could vote, ballots were open rather than secret and there was only one Communist candidate for each office. Other parties were forbidden, and all media were under government control. In practice the Politburo of the Council, headed by Lenin, ran the state, the superior bodies chose the candidates for lesser offices and the Communist Party monopolized power.

The civil war left Russia in ruins. The sailors in its main naval base, Kronstadt, previously the most loyal backers of the Revolution, had had enough. In March 1921, they revolted, joined by many workers. Lenin sent in troops who crushed this final attempt to establish democracy. Ever adaptable, he recognized that Communism had failed and essentially abandoned it. His New Economic Policy restored private ownership of land and small businesses, allowed free trade, and brought forced requisitions and much of the terror to an end. After the great famine of 1921–2 (which American aid helped to end), the new policies brought recovery. By 1927 production had returned to pre-war levels – but Lenin never saw that. The strokes he suffered in 1922 and 1923 ended his active role and he died in June 1924. Against his will his body was embalmed and enshrined in the heart of Moscow.

Benito
Mussolini

Mussolini rose from humble origins, made a career in journalism and became a persuasive politician. He created the Fascist Party whose violence intimidated the Italian government into making him Prime Minister. He transformed Italy into a one-party dictatorship. He was a master of propaganda, with grandiose ideas derived from the Roman Empire. Mussolini was fatally convinced that he was always right and that Italy was a great military power. He squandered the country's resources on a useless Empire, then blindly followed Adolf Hitler into the war that led him to disaster. After being dismissed from office, he ran a German puppet regime in northern Italy.

Benito Mussolini, the son of a blacksmith, was born in a small town in the Apennines in 1883. He was expelled from school for stabbing a fellow student but eventually qualified as a teacher, drifting until he found his true vocation in politics. He studied revolutionary literature and began to give talks and write articles. In 1909, he took a job as a journalist, where he learnt that it was possible to fabricate news without anyone noticing. As a result, he began to despise the uncritical masses. In 1911, when Italy invaded Libya, Mussolini's outspoken opposition to the war made him famous and led to his arrest. While in jail, he wrote his autobiography. After a speech he gave to the Socialist Congress in 1912 he was made editor of the party newspaper, *Avanti* (*Forward*). Its circulation doubled under his aggressive and outspoken leadership. Mussolini followed the party line in opposing entry into World War I, then, when he saw that public opinion favoured war, he switched sides, and immediately lost his job. From that point he hated socialism.

Mussolini started his own newspaper, *Il Popolo d'Italia* (*The People of Italy*), funded by Italian agrarian interests and backed by the War Ministry. During the war, he fought on the northern front until he was wounded in 1917. Italy in the post-war period was in chaos. Three million demobilized soldiers were searching for work, and the socialists, enthused by the Russian Revolution, aimed for drastic change. They terrified the ruling classes by occupying factories and land. In March 1919, Mussolini founded a new party, the *Fascio di Combattimento* (Combat Group, later called the National Fascist Party) and recruited veterans eager for a fight. His men burnt down the offices of *Avanti*, but the Fascists did poorly in the November elections. As economic and political crises worsened, Mussolini directed his forces to the country, where they helped landowners drive out the socialists. The party's gangs beat their opponents or tortured and humiliated them by forcing castor oil down their throats. These efforts were so successful that the Fascists were brought into government in 1921 by a Prime Minister who saw them as potential allies against socialism. Mussolini only had a few seats but gained a valuable political platform. The politicians who thought they could tame him were totally mistaken. Political violence continued the next year as the Fascists threw the socialists out of city governments, proclaiming that only they could restore order. In 1922, Mussolini formed a Fascist militia and announced that they were going to march on Rome. The government declared a state of emergency, King Victor Emmanuel III equivocated, and the politicians negotiated. As a result, Mussolini became Italy's youngest Prime Minister in October 1922. He arrived in Rome wearing the party's black shirt and told the King, 'Your majesty will forgive my dress – I come from the battlefields.' The Fascist march was staged anyway.

Only 4 of 14 ministers were Fascists, but Mussolini personally took the Interior Ministry, which gave him control of the police and enabled him to establish a secret service. His government ended the post-war chaos and generated huge enthusiasm. Youthful and dynamic, Fascism seemed the wave of the future and stirred great interest abroad. In November, Mussolini entered parliament in full military dress and gave a violent speech that liberals supposed was directed only against the far left. They soon found out that Mussolini totally lacked principles and subordinated everything to his enormous ambition. He was a showman and he knew how to tell his audience what they wanted to hear. He had few clear ideas (everything he wrote was contradicted somewhere in his own works) but was obsessed with the glory of ancient Rome. Mussolini ruled extra-constitutionally through the Grand Council of Fascism, made up of party bosses (he rarely solicited their advice) and the Voluntary Militia for National Security, a private Fascist army paid by the state. The regular army remained subordinate to the King, who wrote about numismatics, disliked politicians and was happy to leave Mussolini in charge. Mussolini aimed for total control. He forced through a measure to give two-thirds of the seats in parliament to any party that obtained one quarter of the vote in the 1924 elections. During the debate on his bill, armed Fascists guarded the doors and militia brandished their machine guns in the gallery. The bill was passed, but it was hardly necessary: Mussolini won 65 per cent of the votes in the last free election to be held for 20 years.

Within a few months the regime faced its first crisis when Fascist thugs murdered an outspoken socialist member of parliament, Giacomo Matteotti. He had objected to Mussolini's policy of pushing through hundreds of laws without discussion. There was a great public outcry. Mussolini accepted ultimate responsibility, then took steps to ensure that his government would never be vulnerable again. He had leading opponents arrested, dissolved parliament, censored the press, and replaced elected local officials with appointed Fascists. After an attempt on his life in 1926, opposition parties were banned, revolutionary tribunals were established for political offences, and capital punishment was reinstated (it was rarely used, however: this was not a bloodthirsty regime). The Fascist Party was supreme, but Mussolini could raise or destroy its members at will. He envisioned an all-powerful party that would create a new kind of disciplined fighting Italian.

Mussolini conciliated the power centres he did not control. The King rarely interfered but the Catholic church was potentially a much more dangerous rival. In 1929, Mussolini's agreement with the Pope established the independent Vatican state and brought the regime new popularity. In the following elections, the Fascists presented 400 candidates, to be approved or rejected as a block. They obtained 98 per cent of the vote. Mussolini wanted to control the economy by establishing the

Corporate State where employers and workers would function together by industry, guided by the State. He also aimed for self-sufficiency, especially in the Battle for Grain which raised wheat production, at the expense of other crops. The regime did have one great success: it accomplished what Caesar had begun by draining the malarial marshes near Rome to create new agricultural land.

Mussolini surrounded himself with sycophants and encouraged adulation. His image was everywhere, his title *DUCE* (leader) had to be printed in capital letters, and his favourite slogan was '*Mussolini ha sempre ragione*' ('Mussolini is always right'). He modelled himself on Caesar and Augustus and embarked on a grandiose rebuilding plan for Rome. Flattery and the concentration of power in his hands made Mussolini ever more isolated from reality. Officials told him what he wanted to hear, and the government was often paralyzed, waiting for the dictator to give an order which was often so vague that anyone but he could be blamed if things went wrong.

Mussolini wanted to create a new Roman Empire. Italy had Libya but controlled very little of the country. Mussolini sent in a ferocious governor who broke local resistance through massacre and the establishment of concentration camps. Mussolini's lust for conquest led to Ethiopia where the Italian army had been defeated in 1896 and which even Augustus had not conquered. In 1935, he sent a huge army that used poison gas and extreme brutality to subdue the country. In May 1936, on Rome's sacred Capitoline Hill, Mussolini solemnly proclaimed the restoration of the Roman Empire. His regime was at the height of its popularity. But the war consumed a year's national income, diverted the army, and seriously weakened the country as a greater conflict loomed.

The hostile reaction of Britain and France to the Ethiopian war pushed Mussolini into the arms of Hitler, with whom he concluded the Pact of Steel in May 1939. He had already helped Germany by mediating at the Munich conference that dismembered Czechoslovakia, although he was not pleased when Italy welcomed him back not as a conqueror but a peacemaker. He followed Hitler's lead by introducing extremely unpopular racial laws against Italy's Jewish population. When World War II started, Mussolini held back until France collapsed and then jumped in hoping for a share of the spoils. His insistence on running the war effort himself led to disaster: the British sank most of his naval fleet, his forces were beaten in North Africa, and his sudden attack on Greece led to a humiliating defeat from which he had to be rescued by Hitler. By 1943, Italy was on the verge of collapse. When the Allies landed in Sicily that year, the Fascist Grand Council met on 24 July and gave Mussolini a resounding vote of no confidence. The next day, when he went to meet the King, he was dismissed from office and arrested.

Mussolini had one last inglorious period of power; the Germans rescued him from prison and installed him to rule the Italian Social Republic in northern Italy. He turned from Fascism to socialism but was under the thumb of the German commander. When the Allies drew near, he tried to escape to Switzerland but was caught and assassinated by Italian partisans in April 1945.

Josef Stalin

(1929–53)

'*There are no fortresses that Bolsheviks cannot storm.*'

Josef Stalin was probably the most successful dictator in history. He brought a vast country under such direct personal control that he was able to kill millions of his own citizens with impunity. He made the Soviet Union one of the world's greatest powers. He won wars, imposed his regime on Eastern Europe and saw the triumph of Communism in China. He died in his bed after a long time in power.

Iosif Visarionovich Djugashvili grew up in poverty in Georgia, where he was born in 1879. After his father, a drunken cobbler, died he was raised by his devout mother and a priest who sent him to a church school. He graduated to the Orthodox Seminary, intended to prepare him for a career in the church, but his interest in Marxism and his activity in radical student groups led to his expulsion in 1899. He turned to political agitation, spreading revolutionary Marxist messages to workers in Georgia and the neighbouring regions. Djugashvili was constantly on the run from the police, living the dangerous life of a conspirator and learning never to trust anyone. Nor could anyone trust him – he was also an informer for the Russian secret police. He joined the Bolsheviks in 1904 and attracted the attention of Lenin, who needed a tough man of the people to balance the party's intellectuals. Stalin (Man of Steel), as he came to be called, led bank robberies that provided funds for the Party. Lenin brought him on to the Central Committee in 1912 and asked him what Bolshevism should propose for the innumerable ethnic groups who lived in Russia. Stalin's solution was that national proletariats, not the bourgeoisie, should gain autonomy. In 1913 he was exiled to Siberia where he stayed until 1917.

When Stalin returned to St Petersburg, he was made editor of the Communist Party newspaper, *Pravda* (*Truth*). He played no significant role in the October Revolution, but did become Commissar for Nationalities in the new Bolshevik regime. Totally loyal to Lenin, Stalin was one of the few party leaders who backed the humiliating treaty of Brest-Litovsk, which entailed the loss of Russia's western territories. He fought in the civil war and in the subsequent war against Poland, but his role was far less important than that of Trotsky, who led the Red victory. Instead, Stalin was busy with the party apparatus where he worked hard, mastered the intricacies of the bureaucracy and was generally seen as a harmless plodder, good at boring routine matters. Stalin joined the powerful Politburo, the state's central executive body, then assumed a crucial new position as General Secretary of the Party in 1922.

After Lenin's unexpected stroke in 1922, Stalin was made his guardian, controlling access to the ailing leader. He was so rude and overbearing that Lenin recommended removing him from all leadership positions, but died in 1924 before he could take action. The chief contenders to succeed Lenin were Trotsky and two of Lenin's old comrades, Kamenev and Zinoviev. Trotsky lost face when, thanks to Stalin's manoeuvring, he missed Lenin's funeral. He was so popular that the others willingly ganged up on him. Stalin exploited their differences and took advantage of his position as General Secretary to install his own men in strategic party posts. He was a skilled politician with a superb sense of timing and an effective speaker. Trotsky resigned as War Minister in 1925. The next year he and Zinoviev were removed from the Politburo but remained on the Central Committee. Stalin turned to the secret police who falsified a report that Trotsky and Zinoviev were planning a revolt. Both were expelled from the Party. Stalin's victory culminated in the 1927 Congress that condemned any deviation from the line he laid down. The executive offices were filled with Stalin's men, and his close ally, Kirov, ran Leningrad. Since the Party was young and inexperienced, Stalin had powerful human resources to mould and direct.

During these years, the Soviet Union followed Lenin's New Economic Policy, which had restored many aspects of capitalism. Stalin opted for Communism. In 1928, he announced the Five Year Plan to industrialize Russia at breakneck speed. This would involve complete reorganization of the economy and require stupendous expenditure. Only agriculture could generate the necessary revenue, but for that the state needed to buy the agricultural surplus at a low price and sell it abroad. Stalin took his cue from what he read about the United States: large-scale mechanized farming would require less manpower, releasing people to work in industry. The farmers' land would be consolidated into collectives, where all worked together and divided the profits. Private ownership would be abolished. Before he could impose a solution that would change the face of Russia, Stalin had to crush the last opposition from 'rightists' who advocated a more gradual approach. With that, in October 1929, he had undisputed control.

Collectivization first smashed the prosperous farmers, then herded millions into collectives. Those who resisted faced starvation as the government confiscated all the wheat it could find. Some five million people perished in the man-made famine of 1932–3. The peasantry was crushed and the state acquired their grain for virtually nothing. Millions of people flocked to the cities where they worked for low pay in horrendous conditions. A system of internal passports kept the peasants in place and forced the rest to work if they wanted to eat. Much of the Five Year Plan was accomplished by the slave labour of peasants and dissidents who were sent to concentration camps, then organized by the secret police for unpaid work on canals, in the mines and forests, and building transport. The death rate was high, but there was no shortage of 'criminals' to be 'redeemed' through labour. Stalin directed the Plan, which generated enormous enthusiasm at home and favourable attention from other countries plunged in the Depression.

With the industry and peasantry under control, Stalin started a new wave of repression. First came experts whose projects had failed or fallen behind schedule. They were put on trial as 'wreckers' and shot. Stalin's real opportunity came when his ally Kirov was assassinated in 1934 (quite likely by his own orders). The regime responded with a law on terrorism, allowing swift trials with no right to appeal and imposing capital punishment. For the first time, terror struck the Party. Old leaders like Kamenev and Zinoviev were arrested and put on public trial. To the horror of the world, they confessed to conspiracies against Stalin and the Soviet Union. Few knew that they had been tortured and forced to memorize scripts often written by Stalin himself. The secret police had quotas of people to be shot. Footsteps in the hall and loud knocks on the door in the middle of the night struck fear into the whole population as millions of innocent people were sent to prison camps in Siberia. The slightest sign of dissidence could mean death. The army, the last conceivable threat to the regime, was next. Starting in 1936, Stalin had 30,000 officers, including 80 per cent of higher-ranking generals and colonels, executed.

He could not have done this at a worse time. Having become an unlikely ally of his nemesis Hitler in 1939, Stalin reeled when the Germans attacked Russia two years later. The Red Army fell back to Leningrad and Moscow, but Stalin held firm in the Moscow underground, directing the victorious resistance at Stalingrad, then crushing the German army. The end of the war saw Stalin in control of all eastern Europe and half of Germany. He had restored the empire of the Tsars, but at tremendous cost. He was universally regarded as a great hero.

Russia needed to be rebuilt after the war. People were put back to work under an increasingly personal dictatorship where Stalin ruled through his own secretariat and a core group whose members were remarkably long-lasting, a tribute to the loyalty the ruler inspired and his skill at choosing competent and effective administrators. He kept them divided and interned their wives or relatives, to ensure maximum control. Stalin never gave direct orders, but left his subordinates to draw their own conclusions about his intentions (which ensured they could be blamed if they were wrong). He related directly to each minister (the normal government offices were powerless) and intervened arbitrarily, though often effectively, thanks to his incredible knowledge of the state. In these years, he ruled from the dinner table, where he drank very little but forced his cronies to consume so much that some became alcoholics. On such occasions, Stalin could be a man of great charm – convivial, entertaining and humorous, with an excellent singing voice. He was enthusiastic about the cinema and also found time to read 500 pages a day.

During these years, Stalin boosted Russia's morale by building the atom bomb and encouraging his people to believe that they had invented everything from the radio to the automobile, long before the hated West acquired them. He was glorified as never before as an infallible leader and great teacher. His works had to be cited by all and his image was inescapable. He had great plans: dams, canals, new cities and even a belt of 300 million trees that would change Russia's climate.

As he aged, Stalin became suspicious of everyone. His food was tasted and the air in his official residence filtered. Terror began again in 1949, with a move against Jews in the Party. In November 1952 he had the Kremlin doctors arrested, supposedly the first step in eliminating the Soviet Union's Jews altogether. But before he could act, he suffered a fatal stroke, possibly provoked by poison, in March 1953. He had built the Soviet Union on such firm foundations that his system outlived him by 35 years.

Rafael Trujillo

(1930–61)

Rafael Leónidas Trujillo Molina ruled the Dominican Republic, an insignificant country that he built into a regional power under a tightly controlled personal dictatorship. Installed by the United States, he governed for 30 years until his American patrons helped to have him assassinated. He reinforced his political power by taking ownership of most of the country, rising from poverty to be one of the richest men in the world.

Trujillo, a mulatto of middle-class origins, was born in a provincial town in 1891. He was a serious student noted for his meticulous appearance. After leaving school, he became a telegraph operator then, it seems, cattle rustler. In 1916, he took a job as guard in a sugar plantation, became head of its security and two years later joined the National Police, the only armed force in a country then under American military occupation. Trujillo had good relations with the Americans, who turned the national police into the national army and named Major Trujillo its commander when they withdrew in 1924. The departing Americans established a democratic government that soon succumbed to factional fighting. Finally, in 1930, a military coup was followed by an election where Trujillo intimidated the opposition candidates into withdrawing. When the politicians complained to the Supreme Court that Trujillo had received more votes than the number of registered voters, armed thugs occupied the chamber and the case collapsed.

A fortnight after Trujillo assumed office, Santo Domingo was devastated by the worst hurricane in its history. Trujillo's efficient response won him great popularity, but he hardly needed it, as he moved fast to ensure total personal control. He installed his own men, usually obscure people without a following of their own, in high office, while established politicians were killed, exiled or forced into retirement. He had a loyal and well-trained army to enforce his will. He won the 1934 election with 100 per cent of the vote.

Trujillo's first crisis came from Haiti, a traditional enemy. Thousands of Haitians had crossed the border and settled in Dominican territory. Trujillo had 15,000 Haitian immigrants massacred in 1937, ostensibly because he had discovered a Haitian plot against his regime. Faced with international outrage, he paid blood money to the Haitian government, which promptly stole most of it. He made a nominal commitment to democracy by not running for office in 1938, but showed the reality of power by installing the new President in a tiny room next to his own grand suite. Trujillo felt so secure that he travelled to the United States in 1939, where he made a treaty that returned control of the nation's finances to the Dominicans. Trujillo maintained warm relations with the US during World War II when vastly increased demands for Dominican products produced such wealth that he could pay off the country's entire national debt in 1947.

Trujillo nominally turned the Republic over to his brother Hector in 1952 but in fact continued to run it. He made several trips to the United States, which regarded him as a valuable bulwark against Communism, and visited Rome where he signed an agreement with the Pope. This granted considerable freedom to the Dominican church, and ensured him Catholic support.

During the post-war years, Trujillo ran the country as he liked. He embarked on a huge programme of public works. The capital, now called Trujillo City, was cleaned up and modernized, hospitals, schools and roads were built, and every locality had clean drinking water. Trujillo celebrated 25 years of power with a great international fair that cost a fortune but failed to attract the anticipated foreign participation.

Trujillo came to power through the army, which by the 1950s consumed 25 per cent of the national budget, not because it faced external threats, but as a means of control. Army and police personnel were kept happy with high salaries and ample opportunities for graft: gambling and prostitution paid for protection while employers willingly contributed the fees that guaranteed a peaceful workforce. State security kept the people in line by coordinating secret service agencies and running a huge network of informers. Taxi drivers, maids and waiters were favoured recruits. Anyone might be a spy, subjecting people to the law of 1933 that forbade spreading subversive information or defaming the government.

Trujillo's Dominican Party's motto – Rectitude, Liberty, Work, Morality – reflected the initials of the dictator's name. All government employees had to join the party and donate ten per cent of their salaries to it. Its innumerable branches helped administer justice, organize charity and encourage literacy and culture. But its most important job was to spread propaganda, transmit Trujillo's orders, and keep files on the population. The party was part of a political façade in which a Congress functioned, according to the constitution. The President, however, could serve as many terms as he liked, could initiate or veto legislation, and could dissolve Congress. Trujillo made the laws and Congress passed them.

Trujillo constantly shuffled his subordinates so that none could build a power base. All government employees, from janitors to university presidents, had to sign undated letters of resignation, and were constantly watched. Officials who stepped out of line found themselves denounced in anonymous letters to the government newspaper. Since they knew Trujillo wrote them, they could only hope that grovelling protests of loyalty would keep them out of the dictator's dreaded prisons. Trujillo used public humiliation as a way of controlling his subordinates, even his seemingly closest allies. People never knew what lay behind Trujillo's smile, or how long they would remain in office. A favourite tactic of Trujillo's, following the arrest or murder of one of his opponents, was to visit the man's wife in tears, offer his condolences, and promise to investigate. Likewise, when a woman's reputation was ruined by an anonymous letter (that he himself had written), he would be full of indignation and insist on trying to find its author.

Trujillo liked plump mulatto women and respectable virgins. Every week, his officers would bring dozens of women from whom Trujillo would choose his bedmates, dismissing them with gifts after a night or two. Providing women for

Trujillo was a sure way to obtain his favour. Trujillo brought his enormous energy to every activity he undertook, rising at 4 a.m. and working all day. He did not drink, hated gambling, but was a fastidious dresser who had at one point 2000 suits and 50 pairs of shoes. He could be charming when needed and had many associates but no friends. He trusted no one and had no scruples.

Trujillo increased his power through control of the economy. Starting with monopolies on salt and tobacco, he built his holdings to include ranches, slaughterhouses, sugar mills, shipyards, airlines and automobile sales. He ran the national lottery and the state insurance company (all employers had to insure their workers). If his businesses failed, he sold them to the government. He awarded himself a commission of ten per cent on everything the state bought or sold. Working through his family and anonymous front companies, he eventually owned half the farmland and more than 60 per cent of the country's sugar industry, as well as 80 per cent of business in the capital. His fortune amounted to $800 million – and he was exempt from taxation. This meant that 75 per cent of the population worked for Trujillo. No dissent was possible because of the risk of losing a job.

From the beginning of his rule, Trujillo controlled the media. Their job was to praise the regime and transmit its orders. Trujillo's 'Thoughts' appeared every day, part of a personality cult that began in the first year of elementary school in textbooks that Trujillo himself wrote. Teachers were under constant supervision and there were student spies in every classroom. But this was not an ideological regime. The only common belief was in Trujillo. The motto 'Trujillo is Head of this Household' adorned every living room, hospitals claimed 'Only Trujillo Cures Us', village pumps were adorned with 'Only Trujillo Gives us Drink', and the sign 'God and Trujillo' marked the entrance to the harbour at Santo Domingo. Cynics were surprised that God's name came first. On a more sophisticated level, Trujillo influenced foreigners by employing professional New York public relations agencies and inviting Congressmen for lavish junkets. He soon needed their support.

After 1955, Trujillo faced one crisis after another. Jesús de Galíndez, a Spaniard settled in the Dominican Republic, went to Columbia University in New York to write a thesis exposing the Trujillo regime. He disappeared shortly before publication. Trujillo was suspected, and when a US citizen, a young pilot who obviously knew too much about the case, died mysteriously, he was denounced in the US Senate. This happened at a time when America was ending support for Latin American dictators. More trouble loomed when the liberal Romulo Betancourt became President of Venezuela and started denouncing Trujillo, who responded by trying to have him assassinated. Betancourt persuaded the Organization of American States to vote sanctions on the Dominican Republic, a fatal blow to a country whose military expenses were rapidly growing. As dissatisfaction spread, Trujillo responded with increased repression, to no avail. A conspiracy of businessmen, professionals and army commanders plotted to remove him and the CIA supplied the weapons that killed Trujillo as he was heading for the house of his current girlfriend in May 1961.

Adolf Hitler

(1933–45)

'*The party must not become the servant of
the masses, but their master.*'

Hitler is probably the world's most notorious tyrant. His name is virtually synonymous with evil. Rising from obscurity and failure, he found inspiration in the German army and entered politics after World War I. His Nazi Party became the largest in Germany, leading to his appointment as Chancellor in 1933. Within a year, he had turned Germany into a dictatorship. He built up the economy while establishing a police state based on terror. He pushed his country into World War II where his aggressive leadership produced spectacular victories until opposed by the Soviet Union and the United States. During the war, he ordered the murder of six million Jews and other minorities. With his country collapsing around him, he committed suicide.

Adolf Hitler was an Austrian, born 20 April 1889 in a border town where his father was a customs official. Rejecting the discipline of school and the bourgeois ideals of his father, Hitler left for Vienna, the imperial capital. He lived there from 1907 to 1913. His mediocre talent frustrated his artistic ambitions, while lack of formal qualifications kept him from studying architecture. He drifted in and out of jobs, living a marginal existence selling paintings of popular views and staying in hostels. He developed a passion for the opera and for politics, although he despised parliamentary government. During this period, he seems to have been celibate and on friendly terms with the Jews he knew.

Hitler moved to Germany to escape Austrian conscription, but enthusiastically joined the German army when World War I broke out. He served as a messenger, earning two Iron Crosses, but he was considered to lack leadership ability and never rose above the rank of Corporal. After the war, the army sent him to investigate political movements in Munich. In the insignificant German Workers' Party he discovered the opportunity and latent talents that brought him success. He left the army, joined the party, and rapidly became its most skilled speaker and propagandist. Under the name National Socialist German Workers' Party, (NSDAP or Nazis), it held its first large public meeting in 1920, when Hitler denounced democracy, capitalism and the Jews. The next year, facing a split within the party, he resigned and only returned when he was given complete control. He established the 'Führer Principle' of unquestioning obedience that marked the rest of his career. As his following grew, he attempted to seize power in Bavaria in 1923. He failed and went to prison. There he wrote the autobiographical *Mein Kampf* (*My Struggle*) that blamed all the ills of society on the Jews and laid out plans for a future totalitarian state. After his release, he re-established his control of the NSDAP but made little progress until he redirected it away from the generally socialist workers to small towns and the lower middle class. His stress on traditional German values and denunciation of Jews and Communists brought him increasing support, especially as the Depression struck Germany. The Nazis seemed the only party willing to take drastic action to revive the economy. Hitler worked incessantly, giving vague but powerful speeches that played on the emotions of his audience. He also built practical support in the form of the Storm Troopers, thugs in brown shirts who spread party propaganda and disrupted meetings of its opponents. By 1933 the Nazis were the largest party in Germany.

After a series of crises, Germany's political leadership turned reluctantly to Hitler, who became Chancellor on 30 January 1933. The politicians foolishly thought they could control him. Instead, he moved rapidly to turn the republic into a dictatorship through a series of legal manoeuvres. When the parliament building burnt down in February, Hitler suspended civil rights while his storm troopers moved to crush opposition. Elections in March gave the Nazis 44 per cent of the vote. With nationalist support, they had enough votes to pass the Enabling Act that allowed the government to rule by decree. State governments were put under central control, trade unions were suppressed and in July the NSDAP was declared the only legal party. Hitler still had potential rivals. He co-opted big business with a programme of public works and pleased the army with a massive military expansion. Only the Storm Troopers, who were more left-wing than Hitler, remained a threat. He had their leaders murdered in June 1934. Two months later, when President Hindenburg died, Hitler took over as Chancellor and *Führer* (leader). All soldiers and government employees swore an oath to him personally. Ninety per cent of the voters approved him in a national referendum.

Hitler had no superior, and there was no appeal against him. The only alternative to obedience was imprisonment or death. He ruled Germany through the regular government and the increasingly powerful Nazi Party whose organizations reached every level of the population. The regime looked simple and streamlined, but Hitler, who believed in the survival of the fittest, encouraged competition among his subordinates, often appointing two people to very similar jobs, so that they would have to come to him for resolution. He rarely consulted his cabinet but relied on a loyal coterie headed by Heinrich Himmler, chief of the elite SS troops and the *Gestapo* (secret police), Hermann Göring, commander of the air force and Joseph Goebbels, Minister of Propaganda. Hitler was the ultimate amateur, a skilled politician with no education but a photographic memory that enabled him to intimidate his officers. He distrusted educated specialists and believed he was right about everything. He met with his cronies over tea where he would indulge in endless monologues – tea, because he was a vegetarian and teetotaller who also firmly discouraged smoking.

The regime regulated every aspect of life. Workers had to join the Nazi union, but received free holidays, recreation and, most importantly, jobs. Hitler built motorways and industries useful for the military. He had grandiose architectural ambitions that would have transformed Berlin into Germania, a colossal imperial capital, filled with pompous buildings in the Roman style. Hitler encouraged education but made sure it had a propagandist agenda. The Nazi Party organized activities for the young, who had to join the Hitler Youth. Every society or organization was taken over by the party. Hitler hoped to create a new society where the men would be devoted to the Nazi ideal, and the women would stay at home and produce more Germans.

Hitler ruled with the threat or reality of terror. From the beginning, the regime built concentration camps for its political enemies. Anyone who spoke out was certain to find themselves in the hands of the police, the *Gestapo* or the dreaded SS. People acquitted by the courts (where all judges were Nazis) could still be sent by the *Gestapo* to a camp from which they were unlikely to emerge. Spies were everywhere, and even private conversations were dangerous, but there was relatively little dissidence: fear worked, as did the rising economy and the censoring of information, as the party controlled all the media.

Hitler directed his venom against Communists, homosexuals, the handicapped and especially the Jews. In 1933, Jews were expelled from the professions. The Nuremberg Laws of 1935 dealt with the difficult question of defining a Jew, because the German Jewish community was largely assimilated and many had married Gentiles. Real persecution began in 1938 when Jewish business activity was restricted, and all Jews were forced to take the names Israel or Sarah. It reached a climax in *Kristallnacht*, a night in November when Jewish businesses were ransacked (the expression referred to the thousands of broken shop windows). A huge fine was imposed on the Jews for the damage. By then, emigration had left the Jewish community poorer, older and more vulnerable.

Nazi ideology demanded expansion. It began peacefully in 1938 with the annexation of Austria and the occupation of strategic parts of Czechoslovakia following the Munich Conference, when Britain and France adopted a policy of appeasement. Hitler soon took over the rest of Czechoslovakia and cast his eyes on Poland. Before moving in that direction, however, he accomplished his most astonishing diplomatic triumph by striking a deal with his ideological enemy, the Soviet leader Josef Stalin. On 1 September 1939, Nazi troops invaded Poland, triggering World War II. By now, Hitler had taken supreme control of the army and believed that he knew better than his generals. His boldness worked for two years. He conquered much of Europe, and then made a fatal decision to attack his ostensible ally, the Soviet Union. German troops reached the outskirts of Moscow, the Volga and the Caucasus but their defeat at Stalingrad in 1942 marked the turn of the tide.

During the war, persecution of the Jews turned into extermination throughout all the occupied territories. The Nazis established death camps in which six million Jews perished, along with political opponents, homosexuals, the handicapped and Gypsies. The killing continued uninterruptedly, despite the war effort. By 1944, however, with German forces in retreat everywhere, the Nazis made unsuccessful efforts to hide what they had been doing.

As Germany's cities were pulverized by British and American air attack, and the Red Army advanced, Hitler took refuge in a bunker deep below Berlin. He had lost any sense of reality, blaming everyone but himself for the catastrophe and trusting in imaginary armies to save him. Recognizing defeat, he finally committed suicide on 30 April 1945. He had destroyed Germany and much of Europe. His regime perished with him, never to be revived.

Francisco Franco
(1936–75)

'*The defence of internal peace and order constitutes the sacred mission of a nation's armed forces and that is what we have carried out.*'

Francisco Franco was born in 1892 to a conservative Catholic family, and grew up in a time of disillusionment with the political system following the disaster of the Spanish-American War (1898). After graduating from the Army Academy, in 1912, he was posted to Spanish Morocco, saw active fighting, and demonstrated real leadership skills as head of the tough Foreign Legion. Franco won rapid promotion during a time of political crisis that led to the departure of King Alfonso XIII in 1930 and the establishment of a republic the following year. The conservative Catholic army officers viewed the Republic with such misgivings that Franco even contemplated marching on Madrid. His rise had been rapid: he was made Brigadier in 1926 at the age of 33 – the youngest in Europe – and the next year became Director of the new Military Academy in Saragossa.

Franco supported the Republic, although it reduced the army, and sent him off to the Balearic Islands. Elections in 1934 left Spain even more deeply polarized. Rebellion broke out in Barcelona and among the radical miners of Asturias. Franco directed a long and bloody suppression, striking a blow, in his view, against the forces of chaos and subversion. As a reward, he was named Chief of the General Staff, where he became aware of a widespread conspiracy to defend the army against civilian reformers. In February 1936, the Left, united in a Popular Front, won the national elections. The chaos Franco feared began: anarchists and Communists occupied factories and estates and started burning churches and killing clergy. Before he left, Franco met other officers to organize a resistance movement under General Emilio Mola. Franco himself followed orders until 13 July, when the assassination of a leading conservative figure precipitated a crisis. He then joined the conspiracy, flew to Morocco, took over the army in Africa, and rose in rebellion on 18 July. He appealed to the Generals in Spain to save the state from anarchy.

The rebels planned to seize Madrid, but the capital remained loyal to the Republic. Franco commanded Spain's most powerful army, but was isolated in Morocco because the navy and most of the air force joined the Republic. Help from Mussolini and Hitler enabled him to bring his army across to the mainland. Franco's prestige increased when he returned to Spain and rescued the besieged nationalist garrison of Toledo, seat of the Military Academy and the Spanish church.

A Committee of National Defence composed of seven generals commanded the revolt. They put the areas they occupied under martial law, and cleansed them of leftists: some 50,000 people were eventually killed; the Republicans liquidated a comparable number. The generals soon realized the need for central authority. On 28 September, they made Franco *Generalísimo* (Supreme Commander) and Head of Government of the Spanish State. He was acceptable to all the nationalist factions – conservatives, monarchists, Fascists and the church – but was no ideologue. Franco's potential rivals disappeared one by one. The republicans executed José Antonio Primo de Rivera, head of the fascist Falange, while General Sanjurjo, who had organized the conspiracy, and General Mola both died in plane crashes.

In April 1937, he merged the Falange and the other right-wing factions into the movement that he commanded.

The Republic received extensive help from the Soviet Union, whose tanks held off assaults on Madrid, and from 35,000 foreign volunteers. For Franco, Italian troops were less crucial than the airborne German Condor Legion that committed the most notorious atrocity of the war by firebombing the historic Basque town of Guernica in April 1937. International outrage deflected attention from Barcelona where Communists and socialists were fighting their own civil war. Stalin's secret police soon dominated the Republic.

Franco won the war on 1 April 1939 when Madrid surrendered. Some 200,000 had been killed in action, while a comparable number of civilians died. Every part of the country was devastated. For the next four years, Communists, anarchists, union leaders and supporters of the Republic were sent before military tribunals or hounded by secret police. Only those who could prove loyalty to the regime were given ration cards or the possibility of a job. The 230,000 political prisoners had little hope and tens of thousands were executed. The economy was a shambles, and essential goods in short supply. Franco withheld reconstruction funds from the areas that most opposed him, and suppressed the use of languages other than Spanish. His aim was unity at all costs.

As World War II loomed, Hitler and Mussolini expected Franco to join them, while the Allies hoped to keep him neutral. Franco successfully played off both sides. He made a commercial agreement with Britain to secure supplies of oil and wheat, and told Hitler that he would enter the war if he were given Morocco and huge quantities of military supplies. He repeated his demands when he met the *Führer* in October 1941. Hitler came away claiming he would rather visit the dentist than repeat the experience. Franco remained neutral but did send 27,000 men to fight on the Russian front and continued to export crucial war materials to Germany until 1944.

At the end of the war, the United Nations excluded Spain, and called on its members to break ties with a country considered fascist. Most of them did, with the notable exception of Argentina, whose leader Juan Perón sent his wife Evita on a lavish visit to Spain in 1947. Franco, however, had two great advantages: he ruled an extremely strategic country, and he was unshakably anti-Communist. The Cold War saved him. In 1950, the United States began to explore military cooperation, and the UN revoked its condemnation.

Franco ruled Spain, but not as a Republic. The Succession Law of 1947 defined the country as a monarchy, although it recognized Franco's power for his lifetime. He intended to name Juan Carlos, grandson of the late King Alfonso XIII as his successor, although he waited another 22 years before naming him. Franco called a plebiscite that approved his succession plans by a huge margin. He termed this (and similar votes) his 'democratic mandate': no other forms of democracy were needed.

Franco was always cautious and considered all options before making up his mind. Reserved and suspicious, but courteous and proud, he rarely revealed his feelings. But a peculiar book he published in 1952 exposed his thinking. *Freemasonry* blamed the problems of the world on Spain's enemies, Freemasons and Communists. For him, Roosevelt, Truman and Churchill were all Masons, part of a destructive tide only temporarily held back by Hitler and Mussolini. When the western leaders met Stalin at Yalta and Potsdam, they had confirmed Franco's worst fears. These erratic views were not widely publicized abroad.

Spain gradually emerged from isolation. In 1953, Franco signed agreements with the Vatican and the Americans who were given military bases in Spain in exchange for substantial aid. All this culminated in President Eisenhower's triumphal visit in 1959. By now, Franco had relaxed and liberalized the economy, turning increasingly to technocrats who brought real prosperity to the country in the 1960s.

Franco celebrated 25 years of peace in 1964, basking in a cult of personality that called him 'the man sent by God and made leader' or 'hero of the hosts of heaven and earth'. Although he was less active in the government, he was still very much in charge. His beliefs never changed: freedom would lead to corruption and Communism, and the state should be based on the family, the towns and the party. For the first time, Franco defined his view of the state in the Organic Law (1966): a monarchy whose only political activity was Franco's movement, whose head had extensive powers that could be challenged but not threatened by an assembly. Strikes, student unrest and regional problems, however, made it clear that his ideas were not compatible with a modern state that needed representative institutions to deal with ever more complex problems.

In 1969, when he began to suffer from Parkinson's Disease, Franco finally named Juan Carlos his successor. Four years later, Carrero Blanco, Franco's long-term right-hand man, was assassinated by Basque terrorists. Franco's new administration allowed a free press, political association and strikes, which produced more anti-government activity, and in turn led to tougher repression. When international outcry followed the execution of a group of leftists, Franco presided over a huge demonstration of popular support. That was his last public appearance. He died in November 1975. Juan Carlos inherited a consumer society demanding political liberalization, with long-suppressed internal conflict becoming evident. Franco's stubbornness had kept his regime going, but Juan Carlos soon dismantled it.

Kim Il Sung

(1945–94)

'North Korea has vigorously advanced along the road of national independence and progress while South Korea has fallen into the road of colonial slavery and reaction.'

No modern tyrant ruled as long as Kim Il Sung. For almost half a century he was the only ruler his country knew. His invasion of South Korea in 1950 brought him to the brink of disaster, but he was rescued by his allies and removed internal opposition through bloody purges. He turned his country into one of the most industrialized and regimented on the planet. The personality cult surrounding him reached unparalleled heights. North Korea's economy collapsed with the end of the Soviet Union, but Kim did not live to see the mass starvation that followed.

Kim Il Sung was born to poor parents near Pyongyang in 1912. He grew up in Manchuria where his father ran a herbal pharmacy. Expelled from secondary school for subversive activities, he became a Communist and in 1932 joined partisans fighting the Japanese occupation of Manchuria. When the Japanese crushed the guerrillas in 1940, Kim and the 300 men he commanded fled to the Soviet Union. He was seconded to a reconnaissance unit of the Red Army, and spent the war in Khabarovsk, where he married and where his son Kim Jong Il was born.

When the Russians occupied the northern half of Korea in August 1945, they were determined to create a Communist state. For that they needed a leader; Kim was a reasonable choice. The Russians knew him and he commanded an organized body of tough guerrilla fighters. Kim arrived in September, and infiltrated his partisans into the security services. Yet as a guerrilla who had spent most of his life in Manchuria, he was a stranger in his native land. On 14 October, Pyongyang welcomed its Soviet liberators. They presented Kim to the Korean public, who had trouble believing that the unknown 33-year-old was a great hero of the resistance. The Russians built up his image and created the Korean Workers' Party in 1946. Kim was Prime Minister, Stalin its honorary Chairman.

Kim followed Soviet orders to redistribute land, improve working conditions, ensure sexual equality and establish heavy industry. These popular measures strengthened his position but, most importantly, Kim controlled the security forces. His partisans dominated the army, which gained valuable battlefield experience in the Chinese Civil War. Kim's power was secure by 1948, when the Soviets withdrew. They had set up a ruler, an army, a party and the Democratic People's Republic of Korea.

Kim was determined to reunite his divided country. In April 1950, he travelled to Moscow and received Stalin's blessing for an attack on South Korea. North Korean forces struck hard on 25 June. They were in Seoul within three days, and by the end of July had pushed the South Koreans and Americans into the southeast corner of the country. Kim made no plans for prolonged fighting, because he had not anticipated US intervention. He had no experience of major battles, and no knowledge of strategy apart from surprise guerrilla attacks. His forces were rapidly cleared out of the south, where they had divided their efforts between land reforms and the massacre of political opponents. By the end of October, UN troops reached the Yalu river. Kim panicked, and North Korea would have collapsed completely without Chinese intervention. The war degenerated into a bitter stalemate until an armistice was finally concluded in July 1953. The Chinese had pushed Kim aside and taken control. Their forces remained in Korea until 1958.

Kim blamed the failures on everyone – officers, potential leaders or rival Communist factions – except himself. Within five years of the war, 90 per cent of the generals who had fought in it were executed or exiled. Any possible opposition was ruthlessly crushed. Purges extended throughout society in the campaign of 'Thought Examination'. Agents sent from the capital rooted out suspects, 'spontaneous' denunciations were made in public meetings, 'confessions' written by the authorities were extorted and recited. The victims were then taken out to be shot or sent to forced labour in the mines or digging tunnels under the Demilitarized Zone. This campaign, which claimed thousands or even hundreds of thousands of victims, reached its height in 1956–8.

The regime achieved total control over the population, who were bombarded with propaganda. The slightest sign of dissent meant arrest, confiscation of property, exile to a remote village or worse. The universal presence of informers subdued the people. The Party told them that they were living in a paradise, presided over by a beneficent ruler of stupendous genius. Politically loyal and technically competent bureaucrats ran the country alongside the Workers' Party, which was totally subservient to Kim. None of this changed as long as the Great Leader lived.

Kim added his own touch, 'on-the-spot guidance', to the Stalinist policy of industrialization. He supposedly made 1300 visits to share his superhuman knowledge of industry and agriculture between 1954 and 1961. Whatever the benefits of this guidance, North Korea recovered swiftly after the war, and grew rapidly throughout the 1960s. After the death of his patron Stalin, however, the Soviets seemed to be deviating from the true path, while their split with the Chinese forced Kim to manoeuvre carefully to obtain the aid he needed from both sides. He had the impossible goal of building industry, agriculture and the military while trying to achieve self-sufficiency.

Kim turned to the outside world. He travelled extensively, and invited foreign potentates to sample the glories of his socialist regime. By 1974, he was doing more business with the West than with the Communist world. But when North Korea failed to repay its $1.2 billion debt, credits and trade dried up. Although Kim had played an international role, his country was simply too small and remote to be a world leader.

North Korea was given a new Constitution in 1972. The Great Leader, President Kim Il Sung, ran the state and the army, and issued the laws; the Supreme People's Assembly could only approve. *Juche* – political independence, economic self-sustenance and military self-defence – was the official ideology. Self-sufficiency was to be achieved by the working people, guided by ideology and a supreme leader. Although this claimed to be a Marxist doctrine, it was really nationalism. It contradicted a basic tenet of Marxism, that the course of history was determined by material conditions, not by the actions of individuals. By postulating a powerful leader, it even deviated from the theory (if not the practice) of Maoism. But *juche* gave Kim justification for anything he chose to do.

Kim wanted his system to last, and his place in history to be assured. Since the fate of Stalin (and later of Mao) showed that he could not entrust those goals to the Party, he turned to his own family. His son, born in the Soviet Union in 1942, returned to Korea to complete his schooling and graduate from Kim Il Sung University. He rose rapidly in the Party hierarchy and was put in charge of propaganda in 1972. The Sixth Party Congress of 1980 ratified the choice of Kim's son as his successor. Kim Jong Il entered the Party Secretariat, the Central Committee, the Politburo and the Military Commission. For the first time, a Communist state was being turned into an hereditary monarchy.

The Great Leader's 70th birthday in 1982 featured universal celebrations and unveiling of glorious new monuments. The centre of Pyongyang was transformed by a triumphal arch, bigger than the Arc de Triomphe in Paris, to celebrate Kim's liberation of Korea in 1945, and a tower taller than the Washington Monument to advertise *juche*. Every city was adorned with gigantic statues of the Leader, whose image was inescapable. History was rewritten to give him and his family a central role. No expense was spared to glorify Kim.

Officially, North Korea was an extremely prosperous industrial state. It generated 95 per cent of its energy, and agricultural production was at an all-time high. The country supported an enormous military establishment. If the figures could be believed, *juche* was working, but crisis was at hand. The collapse of the Soviet Union devastated North Korea, which, despite *juche*, depended heavily on Soviet food, fuel and weapons. To make matters worse, China established relations with South Korea in 1992, although it maintained a flow of aid to North Korea. The new economic situation brought a drastic fuel shortage. Factories were closed and the economy contracted at a dangerous rate. Kim turned to large-scale production of missiles and development of nuclear technology, to raise funds and, implicitly, to pose a threat that the international community would have to ward off by a large payment. This produced a crisis with the US, finally defused by the visit of ex-President Jimmy Carter in June 1994. The Great Leader surprisingly agreed to stop development of the nuclear programme, and seemed about to embark on a new opening to the West, when he suddenly died on 8 July. After 49 years in power and 30 or more as undisputed dictator, Kim expired peacefully, his control of the country unshaken. His funeral was enormous and the mourning genuine, as North Korea faced a future without the only ruler it had ever known.

Juan Perón

(1946–55)

'*Democracy in the European form is not applicable in Argentina.*'

Juan Perón was a tyrant who did not slaughter his opponents. He rose to power through the military, then was freely elected President of Argentina. He transformed the Republic into a personal dictatorship that he and his wife Evita dominated by force, persuasion and genuine social benefits. They helped the poor but stirred the hatred of the traditional ruling class. Perón, a master of propaganda, allowed no contrary opinions. After his wife died, his behaviour became so erratic that he was deposed in a coup. Unlike most ex-dictators, Perón managed to return to power, for one last inglorious spell in office.

Juan Domingo Perón was born in a small rural town in 1895. He lived in different parts of Argentina, shared the life of farmhands and ranchers and wanted to be an engineer. Instead he entered the military academy, finished the course in record time and was commissioned as Lieutenant in 1913. His only careers were the army, which he loved, and politics, which he mastered. Perón became an army fencing and boxing champion and developed a real rapport with the common soldiers, unlike most of his more aristocratic fellow officers. He was intelligent and hard working, with an extraordinary memory and powers of organization. He liked to lecture and write papers. He was genial and persuasive, calm, polite and even-tempered, but he never made close friends or shared his private life.

In 1929, Captain Perón was posted to the General Staff in Buenos Aires where he came into contact with officers who were plotting to institute a Fascist-style military regime (Italy's leader Benito Mussolini had a considerable following among Argentina's large Italian population). The revolution of 1930, which installed the Argentine military in power, gave Perón his first lessons in practical politics. He saw that careful secret organization was essential for a coup, but that mass support alone could guarantee success. During the next decade, he taught military history and wrote textbooks. In 1939, he went to Italy to work with its mountain troops. His visits to Rome and Berlin, where he admired the military efficiency of the Axis powers (those nations opposed to the Allies during World War II) and Mussolini's ability to sway huge crowds, left a lasting impression (although he did not have an interview with Mussolini as he claimed: Perón and the truth were not always close allies). On his return, he was posted to the Andes under General Edelmiro Farrell.

During World War II, Argentina came under pressure from both sides. The army favoured the Axis, but when it appeared that the government was going to support the Allies, they seized power in a coup in June 1943. The officers' success rested on a secret organization that Perón and Farrell had formed. Starting with small cells, it gradually incorporated the most powerful officers and had no trouble subverting the army, then the state. The military moved fast. They banned political parties, censored the media and took over the trade unions. At the same time, they coopted the church by restoring religious education in the schools. Thanks to Perón, they gained unprecedented public support. He exploited the minor post of Secretary of Labour and Social Welfare to pass the country's first significant social legislation, forging an alliance with the unions. By 1944, he had achieved great personal popularity. That year, he became Minister of War under Farrell, who was now President, and met a woman who was destined to leave her mark on Argentina.

Eva Duarte, born in 1919, was an illegitimate child who grew up in poverty. She became a dreamy teenager, obsessed with movies and their glamorous stars and determined to follow in their footsteps. In 1935, she made her way to Buenos Aires and struggled until she found her true talent in radio. Eva became a star and acquired a series of important gentlemen as patrons, including high-ranking military officers. In January 1944, she contrived to sit next to Colonel Perón at a benefit gala. She went home with him that night and never left his side. Meanwhile, as the fortunes of the Axis powers declined, opposition to the dictatorship rose, culminating in the biggest protest march in Argentine history in September 1945. Farrell decreed a state of emergency during which Perón's enemies in the army had him arrested. He had antagonized too many by flaunting his mistress and allowing her to influence his choice of appointments.

Perón's supporters went to work. On 17 October 1945, hundreds of thousands of workers poured into the elegant centre of the capital demanding Perón's restoration. The government capitulated and called elections. The day was a landmark, for never before had the common people played such a role; 17 October became the regime's great public holiday. Perón now married Evita, the affectionate pet name she was given by the people, threw himself into the campaign for President, and in February 1946 won a relatively free election.

Perón consolidated his support into the Peronist party, which he provided with a complex ideology intended as a middle ground between capitalism and Communism. Perón personally controlled the party, branches of which transmitted his orders to the population. Its members formed a solid block in parliament where Perón allowed a façade of democracy, but the other parties fell under increasing repression and never had any influence. Politicians who spoke out could be sure of exile, at best. In 1946, Perón took over the universities, but abolished fees, as he genuinely believed in helping the poor. In 1947, members of the Supreme Court were impeached. After Perón's men were installed, he had no problems with the law. In 1949, a new constitution expanded the President's powers and allowed him to be re-elected. It proclaimed civil rights but ominously stated that the state did not recognize the freedom to threaten freedom. It guaranteed rights for workers, families and the old, and promised a free education.

Perón defined freedom. He used the federal police to enforce the new laws on 'disrespect' (controlling virtually any expression of opposition), treason and sabotage. His political police supervised government employees, and had spies and informers everywhere. Voicing opposition could be dangerous, even at home, as domestic servants were likely to be in the pay of the regime. Everyone needed a 'good conduct' document issued by the police in order to get a job, study or marry. Political prisoners were tortured or exiled, but Perón closed concentration camps in

1946: his best weapon was fear. It took longer to silence the press. Although opposition papers were suppressed or sold to government supporters, and the state pumped out an astonishing quantity of printed propaganda, Buenos Aires' oldest and most respected paper, *La Prensa*, held out. Perón finally closed it in 1951, silencing the last opposition but stirring an outcry that badly damaged his reputation abroad.

Perón wanted to create a powerful country based on social justice. He used the huge surplus the country had accumulated during the war to build industry and nationalize foreign companies, most notably the railways. Military spending increased dramatically, but so did token government jobs for good Peronists. Perón entrusted the welfare of the people to Evita, who won women the vote in 1947 and founded the useful Women's Peronist Party. Her greatest achievement was the Eva Perón Foundation, a vast organization with thousands of employees. Eva personally interviewed long queues of the needy, to whom she handed out gifts ranging from a sewing machine to a new house. Every gift proclaimed the regime's concern for the poor. The foundation also built and operated hospitals, old age homes, hostels and a whole children's city. It eventually had assets of $200 million, some provided by the government, much the product of more or less willing contributions. Businesses that failed to contribute could face government inspection of their premises or huge tax bills. Eva's favourite technique involved the unions. When their leaders requested a pay rise, she would see that they received more than they asked for, provided that a percentage went to the Foundation, which never kept accounts. Eva was the humane, popular face of the regime. Perón's fortunes sank rapidly after she died of cancer in 1952.

To secure the future, Perón wanted control of secondary school students. He formed a union for them, and began to take great interest in their leisure activities, particularly the girls' sports. His residence was soon filled with teenage girls in shorts taking lessons in fencing, swimming or driving from the President himself. This stirred vicious rumours, not helped when the dictator took on a 14-year-old as his mistress. Since the church had its own youth activities, Perón moved to bring the church under control too. In 1954, he legalized divorce and prostitution and ended the church's role in education. These measures inflamed the Catholic population. In June 1955, the navy revolted and bombed the capital. Peronist mobs retaliated by burning down the cathedral and many other churches. As Perón gave ever more inflammatory speeches, the army decided things had gone too far. They revolted and Perón went into exile in September.

Normally, exile would mean the end for a dictator, but Perón never ceased agitating from abroad. He had made Argentina ungovernable by spoiling the workers, who longed for his return. Perón had avoided organized violence, but the military regimes that followed his departure were very different. Finally, after numerous coups and elections, Perón was brought back to Argentina in 1973 for a triumphant re-election. He tried to steer between left and right, but was in such poor health that he died the following year after only eight months in office.

Mao Zedong
(1949–76)

'*A revolution is not a dinner party, or writing an essay, or painting a picture, or doing embroidery. A revolution is an insurrection, an act of violence by which one class overthrows another*'

Mao Zedong had more power over more people for a longer time than anyone in history. He was also a mass murderer, responsible for more deaths than any leader in history. Mao developed a new form of Communism, founding his revolution on the rural poor. He established a Soviet state in a remote corner of China, then finally united the country after a devastating civil war. From the beginning, he massacred millions of opponents, but the greatest destruction followed his plan to build China by making steel in its backyards: tens of millions starved in the aftermath. His Cultural Revolution followed, destroying much of China's heritage. The subject of supreme adulation, Mao died peacefully of old age.

Mao, the son of a prosperous peasant, was born in Hunan Province in 1893. His father wanted him to work in the fields but he wanted to study. His arguments with his father taught him that determined resistance paid off. From 1913–18 he attended a teacher's training school and started to envision a reform that would scrap useless aspects of the past but preserve Chinese identity. He was tall and strong, swam and took long hikes through the countryside. He became a student leader and started to write. In 1918, he moved to Beijing where he learnt about Marxism. Mao joined the fledgling Chinese Communist Party in 1921 as an activist who led study groups and organized workers.

Mao became ill in 1925, and returned home to recover. While there, he investigated conditions in the countryside. He became convinced that China was ripe for a revolution based on the peasantry, a radical deviation from Communist doctrine that focused on the urban proletariat. His detailed studies of rural life led to his appointment as head of the Party's Peasant Training Institute. When the Soviet Communist leader Josef Stalin ordered uprisings in Chinese cities, Mao participated in his native Hunan, but all were easily crushed. Mao escaped into the Jinggang Mountains, where he displaced landlords, redistributed land and destroyed temples. He employed Stalinist terror, with torture, confessions and executions, believing that any action taken against counter-revolutionaries was justified.

Mao's guerrilla tactics held off attacks from nationalists led by Chiang Kai Shek until 1934, when the Communists were forced to evacuate. They marched 3000 miles to Yenan in the far northwest, where they built a new state. On the way, the Reds acknowledged Mao as their leader. They occupied a desperately poor region, blockaded by the nationalists and under Japanese threat. They survived by producing opium, whose use they publicly condemned. Mao cemented his power in Yenan through an effective secret police and the Rectification Campaign of 1942, which allowed no deviation from Mao's version of Party orthodoxy. Dissension invited a long and painful process of 'brainwashing'. The 1945 Party Congress solidified his triumph by making 'Mao Zedong Thought' the official doctrine.

When Japan surrendered at the end of World War II, the Russians moved into Manchuria, China's industrial heartland, and supported Mao in the ensuing civil war. The US supplied aid to the nationalists, but it was squandered through their incompetence and corruption. Mao's forces, who pursued a strategy of taking the cities by controlling the surrounding countryside, entering Beijing in January 1949. There, on 1 October, Mao proclaimed the People's Republic of China. He put the country under military rule and went to Moscow to celebrate Stalin's 70th birthday, his first trip abroad. Negotiations with Stalin were difficult but produced a treaty of aid and friendship.

Mao had always advocated land reform. During the regime's first year land was turned over to peasants and a million or more landlords were wiped out. Collectivization in 1953–6 completed the take-over of agriculture. Since Mao's forces were largely rural he lacked the skilled manpower to run a complex economy. Businessmen, government employees and teachers from the old regime kept their jobs. Mao intimidated them in campaigns against counter-revolutionaries and corruption that liquidated more than a million potential dissidents by 1953. These were mass campaigns, involving workers, youths, women and others, mustered in national organizations that could mobilize their members swiftly. China was now pacified.

In 1954, a new constitution gave Mao the novel office of State Chairman. He ruled China from the imperial compound in Beijing, surrounded by guards. He demanded total loyalty from his subordinates, none of whom ever became his friends. He played them off against each other and arbitrarily promoted or demoted officials for no apparent reason. Everyone was anxious to please, but Mao's careful questioning and checking usually enabled him to keep track of situations and overcome flattery. He kept on the move in his private train, staying in touch with provincial authorities and ensuring their loyalty. Until 1966, he rarely appeared in public. Mao wrote theoretical works and poetry. He had enormous energy and intelligence, slept little, kept irregular hours and never bathed or brushed his teeth. He spent most of his time in bed or by his swimming pool, wearing only a bathrobe. In private, he enjoyed the attention of numerous girls supplied by the Cultural Work Troops. He liked simple peasants who were honoured to be invited to the Chairman's bed and would bring their sisters with them. These activities were kept top secret.

Two events in 1956 shocked Mao – the new Soviet Premier Khrushchev's secret speech denouncing Stalin and the Hungarian revolution. Mao believed that Communism might collapse if it made concessions. He never forgave Khrushchev and became even more suspicious of the kind of intellectuals who had destabilized Hungary. Early the following year, in a seemingly liberal move, Mao invited open criticism of the Party: 'Let a hundred flowers bloom. Let a hundred schools of thought contend.' When they did bloom, and complaints spread, Mao cracked down with a vicious anti-rightist campaign that heralded 20 years of disaster. He guessed that there were one to ten per cent of 'rightists' in the party. His minions, charged with the investigation, compromised by identifying five per cent in their work units. Totally innocent people were beaten, tortured or driven from their jobs, as even party members came to realize that speaking out could be fatal.

Mao liked turmoil that kept people on their toes, but knew nothing of economics or production. In 1958, he announced that China was going to pass Britain in steel production, and initiated the Great Leap Forward. The whole country mobilized behind Mao's orders to make steel in huge earthen furnaces in cities and the country. By October that year, a hundred million people, most of them taken from agricultural work, stoked a million furnaces. Trees were cut down and metal objects were smelted. Pots and pans were no longer needed, as the population was organized into vast communes where they ate in common halls and had virtually no family life. Since all officials wanted to be seen as fulfilling their quotas, figures for agricultural and industrial production were grossly inflated while crops rotted for lack of people to tend them and the 'steel' produced turned out to be worthless slag. The regime, believing the false figures, confiscated whatever crops were available and exported them. The result was a man-made famine that killed at least 40 million people. By 1960, Mao's prestige was at an all-time low. He turned the government over to the pragmatic Liu Shaoqi and Deng Xiaoping and withdrew, nursing his resentment. However, Mao never gave up control of the army and still retained real power.

Mao finally struck in 1966 when he unleashed the Great Proletarian Cultural Revolution against the 'Four Olds': culture, ideas, customs and habits. He mobilized millions of school and university students and sent them out against the Olds. Education collapsed as teachers and administrators were humiliated and beaten. Young Red Guards ransacked homes and destroyed ancient monuments. Mao soon set them on the Party. Together with workers they stormed Party headquarters in Shanghai and elsewhere, setting up Revolutionary Committees in their place. The army chief Lin Biao, together with Mao's wife Jiang Qing, egged them on. They finally broke into the central government compound and attacked Liu, who eventually died in captivity. Finally in 1986, Mao called off the students and sent them to the country to learn from the peasants. For most, that meant years of hard labour. The Cultural Revolution had disrupted the country and destroyed all faith in the old Communist morality. The army was supreme and its head, Lin, was revered as Mao's heir. By now, Mao was growing old and more erratic. He rarely emerged from his quarters and his female minders controlled access to him. In 1971, Lin decided it was time for a change. He planned a coup, then tried to escape when it failed. His plane crashed and with it went much of China's faith in Chairman Mao.

Mao restored the pragmatists, though he never stopped finding ways to attack them through new, but much smaller campaigns. He enjoyed one last triumph when US President Richard Nixon visited China in 1972. After that, Mao's health rapidly deteriorated and he died in 1976. His successors turned away from Mao's unpredictable but unproductive doctrines and set China on its successful road to capitalism.

Sukarno

(1949–66)

Sukarno created the independent nation of Indonesia and held it together through political and international crises. A skilled speaker, writer and organizer, he transformed the presidency to which he was elected into a dictatorship. His most ambitious policies failed, but he brought greater coherence and prosperity to the country than it had ever known. Sukarno's regime collapsed following the violent suppression of a Communist coup. Although not himself a murderer, Sukarno was at least indirectly responsible for the greatest massacre in Indonesia's history.

Sukarno (he only used one name) was born in Java in the Dutch East Indies in 1901, the son of a schoolteacher who was descended from the minor aristocracy. He received an elite education. During secondary school, he lived with a family friend who was a political activist. Sukarno met the leaders of the popular Islamic People's Party and associated with leading Marxists. He studied engineering and architecture in the College of Technology and began writing articles for newspapers. He soon became a political activist himself, known for his left-wing views and his attempt to reconcile Communism and Islam. Sukarno opposed capitalism and imperialism and advocated nationalism, independence and non-cooperation with the colonial authorities. He edited a political periodical while working as an architect and teaching mathematics.

In 1926, after an attempted revolt, the Indonesian Communist Party was outlawed. This left a gap in the political spectrum that Sukarno filled by forming and leading the Indonesian Nationalist Party. He worked hard to unite the various nationalist factions in an extremely disparate country, envisioning one independent Indonesia stretching from Sumatra to New Guinea. His vision and his skill as a public speaker who could address the concerns of the common people built the party into the biggest in the country. His anti-colonial speeches, however, prompted the Dutch to arrest him in 1929, but the speech he gave at his trial made him a popular hero. He was eventually released, then arrested again and sent into internal exile, where he remained for eight years. Sukarno used the time to study, but his political movement fell apart under pressure from the Dutch who ignored his pleas to release him in exchange for abandoning political activity.

In 1942, during World War II, the Japanese conquered Indonesia. They needed local support to ensure order and the smooth flow of petrol to Japan. As Sukarno was a noted opponent of colonialism, they brought him back to Jakarta, where he became an enthusiastic collaborator, hoping the Japanese would eventually grant Indonesia independence. Later, he refused to talk about his wartime activities, which included travel to Tokyo to receive a decoration from the Emperor, and well-publicized participation in the Japanese effort to recruit 'voluntary' workers for slave labour in the homeland. He spoke on Japanese radio and helped to build a puppet Indonesian army. In 1945, the Japanese created a Committee for Indonesian Independence, to weaken the colonial powers. They made Sukarno its Chairman, and two days after Japan surrendered in August, he proclaimed the Indonesian Republic. He became

President and announced the *Pantjasila*, the Five Pillars of the regime: nationalism, internationalism, democracy, social justice and belief in God.

The Dutch, however, had no intention of giving up their rich colony. Negotiations and fighting dragged on until 1948 when the Dutch captured Sukarno and his government. They had effectively won the war, but international pressure, particularly from the United States, forced them to acknowledge the independence of Indonesia in December 1949. This was succeeded a year later by the Unitary Republic of Indonesia. Sukarno was President of both. Meanwhile, Communists had tried to set up a Soviet regime in Java. The fiercely anti-Communist army crushed it.

Sukarno headed a parliamentary regime often mired in conflict between nationalists, Islamists and Communists. He had no patience with democracy, which he saw as a western import, but favoured a traditional Indonesian method of lengthy discussion leading to a consensus. Although he resisted the proposal of army chief Nasution to take dictatorial powers, he relied heavily on the army for support. At the same time, the Communists provided him with a popular base. He admitted them to the government and moved closer to China and the Soviet Union. He wanted to organize what he called the New Emerging Forces against *Nekolim* (neocolonialism, colonialism and imperialism).

Sukarno made his debut on the international stage when he hosted the Bandung Conference in April 1955. This was the first meeting of the so-called Non-Aligned Nations, attended by the leaders of 29 independent countries, including Nehru of India, Zhou Enlai of China and Tito of Yugoslavia. Its ostensible aim was to strengthen solidarity against the competing superpowers, but in fact Sukarno, like the other leaders, leaned towards the Communist bloc. The attention Sukarno received from his new friends, and his constant travel, led him to fancy himself a kind of international political messiah, who could straddle the gulf between the West and the Communist regimes.

Sukarno returned from a visit to China and the Soviet Union in 1956 with a vision of 'guided democracy' that he believed could more effectively serve the people than the turbulent Indonesian parliament, where the Communists had become the largest party. In June 1957, after Islamic and military uprisings, he used a state of emergency to suppress opposition and to nationalize remaining Dutch businesses. Together with a decree that forbad resident Chinese to trade in Indonesia, and obliged them to move out of the rural areas, his policies seriously disrupted the economy.

In July 1959, Sukarno assumed a revolutionary power to rule by decree. His opponents were sent into exile, and the following year the elected assembly was replaced by one he appointed. Sukarno banned political parties that did not follow the regime's 'left progressive ideology'. In 1963, he was named President for Life. Indonesia had become a dictatorship, which Sukarno controlled through the uneasy collaboration of the army and the Communists. He advocated a policy of *Nasakom* (nationalism, religion and Communism), thinking that his powers of persuasion could overcome its intrinsic contradictions. He used celebrations, symbols, endless rhetoric and a grandiose building programme to advertise his dedication to what he called an ongoing revolution and to distract the public from a rapidly deteriorating economy.

Foreign policy was a prime distraction. In 1961, Sukarno started agitating for control of Dutch New Guinea, whose population was unrelated to the Indonesians. The Dutch proposed autonomy after a referendum, but the US and UN forced them to turn the territory over to Indonesia. Sukarno advertised this as a great triumph. Two years later, when Malaysia gained independence, Sukarno protested that the British were trying to encircle Indonesia and were threatening its revolution. Troop mobilization and guerrilla attacks lasted two years until Sukarno finally had to back down, withdrawing in anger from the UN in 1965. Relations with the US deteriorated seriously. His only ally was China, which he courted enthusiastically with the support of his enormous domestic Communist Party.

By 1965, the generals had lost their sympathy for Sukarno after learning that he planned to import millions of small arms from China to supply a new people's militia of workers and peasants. Indonesia seemed about to become a People's Republic, when Sukarno fell extremely ill. The Communists then began to worry because their success depended entirely on the President. They made plans for a coup that began on 1 October. Communist forces seized key points in Jakarta and captured six generals, who were tortured by Communist youths, then tossed down a well. Whether Sukarno was privy to the plot is not known but plainly he did not disapprove. General Suharto, Commander of the Strategic Reserve, crushed the revolt. Reluctantly, Sukarno gave Suharto permission to restore law and order when both the army and the public rioted at the funerals of the murdered generals. The army demanded revenge, but when Sukarno refused to ban the Communist Party, the generals took matters into their own hands.

The result was one of the largest massacres in history. The army, backed by Islamist mobs, destroyed Communist headquarters and Chinese offices in the capital, but the main activity took place in the country where the Communists had deep and widespread support. In Sumatra, troops massacred Communists. In Central Java, where Communist forces made a stand, they were crushed. By the end of October, the military was in full control. It then began its clean-up operation, recruiting youth groups, especially nationalist Moslems, to find and kill Communists with their families and sympathizers. The locals identified Communists and the army was helped by lists supplied by the Americans. Local resentments added to the death toll, as atheists and Chinese were also attacked. The government admitted to 78,000 deaths but the real figure was probably over 200,000.

Sukarno fell out with the Communists. In March 1966 he was forced to transfer his powers to Suharto, who put him under house arrest. He died without being released, in 1970.

'Papa Doc' Duvalier

(1957–71)

'God and the people are the source of my power. I have twice been given the power. I have taken it, and damn it, I will keep it.'

François Duvalier was the most monstrous ruler of a country that had a long history of tyranny. He stayed in power far beyond his elected term by terrorizing the population with an infamous secret police and by exploiting the more sinister aspects of the local Voodoo religion. He ruled through fear and corruption but provided an anti-Communist stability that ensured him the essential support of the United States. Under his administration, the country deteriorated to become the poorest in the western hemisphere. He built his power so well that he died in office and was succeeded peacefully by his son.

When Haiti, the first black republic, gained its independence from France in 1804, it inherited a legacy of harsh rule backed by military force and of bitter hostility between the majority of ex-slaves and the dominant mulatto (mixed-race) minority (whites had been massacred during the war). The first century of republican government was marked by an endless cycle of presidents trying but failing to gain dictatorial powers. Haiti had 22 presidents between 1843 and 1915. Only one completed a full term of office. In 1915, when a new president murdered his political rivals, and German economic interests in the country became threatening, the Americans occupied the country. They brought stability, public works and public health, and finally withdrew in 1934. Their mulatto collaborators stirred increasing resentment from the black population.

Election in 1946 of a black President, Dumarsais Estimé, brought real change. He taxed the rich, helped the rural poor, and gave Voodoo the same standing as Catholicism. His Minister of Labour and Public Health was a well-respected doctor, François Duvalier.

Duvalier, born in Port-au-Prince in 1907, developed an early interest in politics. In high school, where Estimé was one of his teachers, he was already writing newspaper articles denouncing the US occupation. He attended medical school, practised in rural areas where he became very popular, and served from 1943–6 with an American medical mission. By then, he was regularly expressing his political ideas in a journal he had founded, and in books that he wrote. He stressed Haiti's African heritage and identified the country's central concern as the racial struggle of blacks versus mulattos.

Estimé went the way of his predecessors, thrown out in a coup led by the pro-American Colonel Paul Magloire. Duvalier soon went into hiding, only to emerge when he helped organize the coup that toppled Magloire in 1956. In the election that followed, he presented himself as the heir of Estimé and, with the help of the army, won a large majority on 22 September 1957. On 22 October (Duvalier considered 22 his lucky number) he gave his first presidential address, a conciliatory speech. No one expected anything extreme from the shy and modest family doctor.

They were wrong. Soon after his inauguration, when the mulatto shopkeepers of Port-au-Prince closed their shops in a show of opposition, Duvalier called in hooded gangs from the slums to smash them all. At the same time, he shut down opposition newspapers and destroyed their premises. He arrested a hundred leading politicians. Some were taken to the grim Fort Dimanche and tortured to death, while the lucky ones fled into exile. When the workers' leaders spoke up, Duvalier seized control of the unions, threatening to crush any popular movement but his own. Only the army remained a potential threat. He neutralized that by constantly changing its commanders, and creating an independent Presidential Guard. Most effectively, he removed the army's weapons and ammunition to the presidential palace.

Duvalier's most effective means of controlling the population – one that became a watchword for terror – was the dreaded Voluntary Militia for National Security. Its ironic title, *Tonton Macoutes* (Uncle Knapsack – *tonton* is an affectionate French nickname for an uncle) told all: at Christmas good Haitian children receive presents from Uncle Christmas, but bad children are stuffed into a bag and carried off by the cruel giant Macoute. Under Duvalier, those bags were filled with adults. The *Tonton Macoutes* were easily recognized by their fashionable clothes, reflective sunglasses and barely concealed pistols. They had arbitrary power over the public, from whom they extorted their pay. The all-black *Macoutes* included better-off peasants, small businessmen, ex-soldiers, criminals and Voodoo priests. There were about 25,000 of them. They often left the bodies of their victims exposed in public as a warning. They cultivated ties with Voodoo, encouraging people to see the *Macoutes* as demons. Likewise, 'Papa Doc' (a reference to his early medical training) in his unvarying dark suits reminded people of Baron Samedi, the Voodoo guardian of graveyards, who dressed in a frock coat and top hat.

The regime faced its first crisis in 1958, when a tiny opposition force in a hijacked minibus took over the barracks next to Duvalier's palace before being wiped out. More seriously, in May 1959, Duvalier had a serious heart attack that incapacitated him for four months. Clément Barbot, his closest associate and head of the *Tonton Macoutes*, ran the country and willingly stepped down when the President recovered. Duvalier, however, suspected his ambitions and had him arrested the following year. Dissidents and exiles, though, were far less important than relations with the US. Duvalier handled the Americans with great skill, constantly demanding financial aid and military support. He played a racial card by claiming that the black Haitian republic was being neglected, and exploited his role as a bastion against Communism during the Cold War. He maintained at least the tacit support of the Americans, including President Kennedy, who had wanted to replace Duvalier with a more representative government but finally gave 'Papa Doc' his support.

Duvalier was 're-elected' on 22 October 1961: his party was the only one to stand in the election, and his name was printed at the head of every ballot paper, allowing him to claim that he had been elected unanimously. He succeeded where his predecessors had failed, as the opposition was fragmented and demoralized and the army was under firm control. Enemies who dared to voice opposition were soon crushed. In 1963, someone took a shot at a limousine that was carrying Duvalier's children. 'Papa Doc' responded with a wave of terror, but suspicion fell on the army's champion marksman, who fled into the Dominican Embassy. Duvalier was about to attack it when the Dominicans threatened war. He backed down and then discovered that the culprit was his old friend Barbot, whom he caught and executed. The next year, a mulatto force called Young Haiti launched a guerrilla resistance that was quickly defeated. In reprisal, Duvalier sent the *Macoutes* against the largely mulatto town of Jérémie, where hundreds, including whole families with small children and grandparents, were massacred. Altogether, his regime killed some 30,000 people in 14 years.

In 1964, responding to orchestrated popular demand, Duvalier produced a new constitution that appointed him President for Life and allowed him to name his successor. A referendum approved it by 2.8 million votes to 3000. A wave of adulation followed, with Duvalier the subject of a new prayer: 'Our Doc, who art in the national palace for life, hallowed be thy name by future generations; thy will be done in Port-au-Prince as in the provinces…' The regime's most widespread poster showed Jesus Christ standing with his hand on the seated Doc's shoulder, proclaiming, 'I have chosen him'. At this time, however, he was under threat of excommunication for denouncing foreign priests who had opposed Voodoo. He retaliated by expelling the Jesuits, but settled matters with the Vatican in 1966 when the Pope agreed that Haiti should have a native clergy. Duvalier now controlled the church.

'Papa Doc' found ingenious ways of looting his country. He established a Movement of National Renewal to transform the town where he had practised medicine into grandiose Duvalierville. Businessmen who were slow to contribute at least $5000 had their establishments wrecked and the really recalcitrant were arrested and tortured. Contributions were deducted from the salaries of government employees while informal roadblocks made sure that motorists paid their share. Few buildings were ever erected. Duvalier controlled the tobacco monopoly, which was extended to alcohol, flour, sugar and cars. All profits went to the President. In 1966, he generously introduced old age pensions: workers would contribute three per cent of their salaries to receive a guaranteed pension at 65. At the time, the average life expectancy in Haiti was 40. The 20,000 workers sent to cut sugar cane in the Dominican Republic were also a source of revenue as Duvalier charged the Dominicans $10 a head to employ them and took a cut of their salaries. Not surprisingly some 80 per cent of foreign aid also wound up in Duvalier's pockets.

On 22 February 1971, a referendum approved Duvalier's choice of his son Jean-Claude to succeed him as Life President. Somehow one negative vote was cast out of 2.3 million. Two months later, 'Papa Doc' died. His body was guarded by 22 soldiers and 22 *Macoutes* and his son succeeded without a problem. However, when 'Baby Doc', as he was known, fell in 1986, 'Papa Doc' Duvalier's body was dug up and beaten 'to death'.

Nicolae Ceausescu

(1965–89)

'*I have done everything to create a decent and rich life for the people in the country, like in no other country in the world.*'

The anti-Russian stance of one of Communism's most unpleasant dictators meant that Ceausescu was well regarded in the West, while he terrorized and impoverished the Romanian people. He rose through the ranks of the Party, then used an effective secret police to stay in power for decades until Communism collapsed around him and the Romanians revolted. He was executed after a summary trial, despite his claims of bringing great benefits to the country.

Nicolae Ceausescu, born to a poor peasant family in 1918, moved to the Romanian capital Bucharest to work as a shoemaker's apprentice when he was 11. In 1932, he joined the illegal Romanian Communist Party, and was arrested the next year for calling for a strike and distributing subversive literature. He was sent back to his village after two more arrests in 1934, officially branded as a 'dangerous Communist agitator', but soon returned to underground work in Bucharest, where he absorbed important lessons in conspiracy and distrust. In 1936, he was sent to the prison for Communists, where he read extensively and made good Party connections, though by all accounts he had an unattractive and vindictive personality. During a short period of freedom in 1939, he became secretary of the Communist Youth Organization. Late in 1940, he was back in jail where he met the Communist leader Gheorghe Gheorghiu-Dej, who became his patron. He finally escaped in 1944, just before Soviet troops invaded Romania. Ceausescu was by then a hardened and experienced worker for a Party whose small membership was pressed into service to run the country. Ceausescu became a member of the Central Committee in 1945, then Party Commissar of his home province, then member of the Grand National Assembly, Romania's parliament. In 1946 he married Elena Petrescu, a fellow Party member. Considered vulgar and stupid by those who knew her, Elena worked as a secretary in the Ministry for Foreign Affairs.

In 1948, the Communists seized power and proclaimed a People's Republic with a Stalinist constitution. Ceausescu was named Deputy Minister of Agriculture, then Chief Political Officer of the army in 1950, with the rank of General (although he had never served in the armed forces). Gheorghiu-Dej, now head of state, appointed Ceausescu Secretary of the Central Committee, a post that allowed Ceausescu to fill the Party with members loyal to himself. He joined the supreme decision-making body, the Politburo, in 1955.

When Gheorghiu-Dej died in 1965, the senior Party leaders chose Ceausescu as leader, largely because he was an outspoken critic of the Russians. At the age of 47, he became the youngest head of state in the Communist world. He remained consistently anti-Russian, refusing to participate in Warsaw Pact activities, denouncing the 1968 invasion of Czechoslovakia, recognizing West Germany and maintaining friendship with Israel after the Six Days War. These moves made him popular at home and abroad. Ceausescu became a pivotal figure in the Cold War, with the western powers praising and supporting his independent stand. His reputation reached a peak when US President Richard Nixon arrived for a state visit in 1969.

But though foreigners might view Ceausescu as a modernizing liberal, Romanians knew better. From the beginning, he imposed tight personal control. He had listening devices planted everywhere, monitoring them from a room next to his office. He soon disposed of a dangerous potential rival, Alexandru Draghici, the all-knowing head of the secret police. Ceausescu cleverly removed him by rehabilitating victims of the vicious purges that Draghici had managed for Gheorghiu-Dej. By appearing to be liberal, Ceausescu was consolidating his power. Its main bulwark, Ceausescu's creation, was the dreaded Securitate that opened mail, tapped telephones, broke into homes and arrested and interrogated suspects, all with total impunity. It became the largest secret service, in proportion to the population, of any Communist state.

Ceausescu had little consistent ideology, but many erratic ideas, notably that Romania needed a much greater population. In 1966 he forbad abortion and divorce, with no regard for the consequences – a drastic increase in infant mortality and countless unwanted children. Many wound up starving in orphanages. Ceausescu's policy during these years has been described as 'rule by frenzy': he was constantly shuffling the government and rushing around the country in unproductive tours where he would receive the staged acclamations of thousands.

Ceausescu became much more oppressive after he visited China and North Korea in 1971. Mao's Cultural Revolution and Kim Il Sung's subservient population provided inspiring models. The first manifestation was a mini Cultural Revolution directed against intellectuals, hippies and western music. The population of prisons and psychiatric hospitals grew rapidly and inmates routinely were beaten and tortured. At the same time, Elena Ceausescu began to assert herself, rising through the Central Committee and Politburo to reach its all-powerful Executive Committee in 1977. Her qualifications, like those of the Ceausescu children and relatives who rose with her, were non-existent.

Ceausescu himself was 'elected' to the new office of President in 1974. Ever intolerant and distrustful, he surrounded himself with sycophants and basked in a cult of personality. As the 'Genius of the Carpathians' or 'visionary architect of the nation's future' he formed a political triad with Elena and the Communist Party. Huge staged rallies greeted him wherever he went. Security forces in the front row dressed as workers would lead the cheering. The meetings, which featured a speech by Ceausescu, could last all day; he would leave believing that the people loved him.

China inspired Ceausescu's 'systematization' project, which aimed to move 11 million farmers from their traditional villages to concrete blocks in 500 'agro-industrial centres'. This project, designed to release capacity for industry and increase agricultural land, was bitterly unpopular. It never came near completion. A similar project demolished elegant and historic districts in Bucharest to produce the titanic House of the People, with rooms as big as soccer pitches and corridors as wide as streets. Ceausescu promoted a Stalinist drive for industrialization but many of its results were useless: the Danube-Black Sea Canal was barely used, and the inefficient steel mills consumed so much electricity that the population was forbidden to use bulbs brighter than 40 watts. The country plunged into debt while agricultural production fell. Ceausescu blamed western imperialism, as foreigners began to criticize his human rights record. His love affair with the West had culminated in a state visit to Queen Elizabeth II in 1978. Ceausescu was received at Buckingham Palace, Parliament and 10 Downing Street but the Queen was not amused when her guest insisted on having his food tested by his habitual tasters and washed his hands with alcohol after any physical contact. Nor did he make a good impression when he withdrew with his entourage to the palace gardens, supposing that their rooms were bugged.

Internal conditions deteriorated drastically in the 1980s when Ceausescu insisted on paying off Romania's foreign debt, which meant exporting food, fuel and other essentials. Romanians lived in the cold and dark while Ceausescu lived in luxury. He had 40 villas, his favourite at Snagov near Bucharest where Count Dracula was buried. The staff underwent daily medical examinations and anyone with even the mildest ailment was excluded. Ceausescu, the ultimate hypochondriac, suffered from diabetes that he would not allow his doctors to control. His deteriorating health may account for his increasingly bizarre behaviour.

The Romanian people lived under increasing supervision and control, manifested in 1983 when anyone who had a typewriter had to register it with the police, explain where it came from, how and why it was used, and leave a sample of its typeface. Popular dissatisfaction, usually disguised behind slavish even enthusiastic obedience, finally came to the surface in 1989. By then Ceausescu held all the top political posts, surrounded by his numerous relatives and dominated (rumour claimed) by his wife who had to be addressed as Comrade Academician Doctor Engineer, ironic distinctions for a woman who had failed elementary school. Although the Ceausescus seemed oblivious to the collapse of Communism around them, the people learnt what was happening in their country from foreign media, which published scathing criticism of Ceausescu. Despite this, however, in November 1989 Ceausescu was re-elected head of the Party.

Meanwhile, a Hungarian priest in the western city of Timisoara had been speaking out. When the regime responded with intimidation and beating, the locals gathered to defend him. Five thousand marched to the city centre on 17 December, sacked Party headquarters and burnt stacks of Ceausescu's works. The Securitate fired on the crowd, but the regime lost control of the city. As trouble spread to the capital, Ceausescu responded by calling a huge rally, believing that he could stir the people's love for him. Instead the crowd heckled, whistled, and shouted him down. When the population lost its fear of Ceausescu, the regime was finished. The army joined the revolt, Ceausescu fled but was captured and put on trial. His objections that the trial was illegal were to no avail. He was found guilty and shot with Elena immediately after sentencing, on Christmas Day 1989

Joseph-Désiré Mobutu

(1965–97)

'Go and steal as long as you don't take too much.'

Mobutu rose from poverty and obscurity to rule a vast country. Profiting from the Cold War, he remained in power for more than 30 years, draining the wealth of the Congo to maintain himself and his cronies. He gave a new meaning to kleptocracy but declined rapidly after he was no longer useful to his foreign backers. His activities converted an enormously rich country into a failed poverty-stricken state.

Joseph-Désiré Mobutu was born in 1930 to a small tribe, the Ngbandi, in the Belgian Congo. Local missionaries helped him to receive a good education. He was an outstanding student, but a troublemaker whose behaviour led to his expulsion in 1949. He joined the army, where he rose to sergeant-major, the highest rank open to a native Congolese. Mobutu then studied journalism, which he adopted as a career in 1956, rapidly becoming editor of a newspaper, and a public figure. The colonial administration sent him to Brussels, where he met the rising politician Patrice Lumumba and attended meetings preparing Congo's independence. He apparently funnelled information he learnt there to Belgian intelligence.

Mobutu grew up in a profitable colony that Belgium planned to keep, but in 1959 a wave of destructive riots in the capital Leopoldville prompted Belgium to grant the Congo independence. The country was totally unprepared. There were no Congolese in high posts in the administration and only 30 university graduates in the whole country. But there were two major political leaders. The charismatic Lumumba favoured a strong centralized regime, while Joseph Kasavubu advocated federalism for a country that had some 200 ethnic groups. When independence arrived in June 1960, Kasavubu became President, Lumumba Prime Minister and Mobutu Minister of Defence.

Chaos followed. In July, the army mutinied against its Belgian officers. Mobutu quelled the revolt through his skills of persuasion and immense personal courage. The same month, the mineral-rich province of Katanga seceded under Moise Tshombe. Lumumba asked the UN to intervene, threatening to call in the Soviet Union, and the Congo became a battleground in the Cold War. When Lumumba, marked as an enemy of the West, fell out with Kasavubu, the government was paralyzed. In September, Mobutu intervened. Lumumba was placed under house arrest and the Soviets given 48 hours to leave the country. The CIA paid Mobutu's troops and provided him with a jet plane. He turned Lumumba over to Tshombe, who had him killed in February 1961.

Mobutu now returned power to Kasavubu who appointed him Commander in Chief of the Congolese forces. Meanwhile, Tshombe had ended his secession and joined the government, but when rivalry between him and Kasavubu exacerbated the chaos, Mobutu moved again. In November 1965, he seized power, proclaiming himself President and promising elections in five years. A long dictatorship now began, backed consistently by the United States.

At first, Mobutu seemed to be a reformer, but in March 1966 he took all powers away from parliament, abolished the office of Prime Minister and ruled by decree. Two months later, he arrested and executed several former Cabinet Ministers, demonstrating the fate that awaited anyone who opposed him. A façade of democracy returned in April 1967 when Mobutu created a political party, the Popular Movement of the Revolution. Other parties, however, were banned and membership of the PMR was made obligatory for all. In the first elections in 1971, a green ballot symbolizing Progress could be cast for Mobutu, or a red one, signifying Chaos, for the non-existent opposition. Only 157 votes in the whole country went against Mobutu. The new constitution cast him as the 'embodiment of the nation' and placed his decrees outside its control. Provincial legislatures were abolished, and all Governors were members of the Party, appointed personally by Mobutu. These changes had one positive aspect. Since Mobutu was from a minor tribe, he could not create an ethnically based regime. The single party actually united the population as citizens of one supra-ethnic nation.

Mobutu's original contribution was the programme of 'authenticity' designed to remove the accretions of foreign influence. In 1971 the country, its major river and its currency were all renamed Zaire. Belgian city names disappeared along with colonial statues, and even a new type of clothing, resembling a Mao jacket, became universal. Mobutu adopted it, along with his characteristic leopard-skin hat and carved walking stick. He also took a new name, Mobutu Sese Seko Kuku Ngbendu wa za Banga, 'The all-powerful warrior who, because of his endurance and inflexible will to win, will go from conquest to conquest leaving fire in his wake'. The citizens began to see themselves as part of one great nation.

In 1973, Mobutu nationalized industry, farms and businesses. The properties were handed out to the Party faithful, or used to co-opt potential opponents. The President himself owned plantations that produced a quarter of the country's cocoa and rubber, but Mobutu was careful to parcel the goods out to all ethnic groups. These valuable favours won him greater support, but wrecked the economy. The new proprietors were not competent to run businesses that more often than not they simply looted.

Handing out favours was Mobutu's prime method of retaining power. Government service also spread wealth. During Mobutu's 35 years in power, Zaire had 52 governments, each one with new ministers and officials who received high salaries, official cars and loans that were never repaid. The regime eventually employed 600,000 civil servants for jobs that required about 50,000. The greatest source of wealth was the copper of Katanga, which generated $700–900 million a year in the early 1970s. Mobutu's share often reached $200 million. So much was stolen, while the infrastructure was neglected, that profits dropped to nothing by the early 1990s. Mobutu turned to the diamond mines of Kasai province, where the government monopoly skimmed off more than $1 million every month. When that ran dry, Mobutu resorted to the primitive tactic of printing money, rushing the new notes to the market for exchange before their value collapsed. This produced an inflation rate of 4130 per cent by 1991. He used the country's wealth to reward his cronies, defuse the opposition, and guarantee his control. He let his associates steal as much as they wanted, but his prodigious memory and active secret service stored information that he could use when needed against 'corrupt' officials. Mobutu was a man of great intelligence, with a sense of humour that strengthened his rapport with the common people, a shamelessness that enabled him to tell outrageous lies, and a view of human nature that recognized greed as a powerful motive. He survived by exploiting the country and virtually everyone in it.

Economic chaos eroded Mobutu's position in the 1970s, and revolts in Katanga posed a serious threat. Mobutu's Western backers helped him suppress them, because he was playing a valuable role in Angola's civil war (and embezzling millions from foreign aid destined for Angola). In 1977, under Western pressure, he allowed relatively free elections for the legislature but made sure it had no real power. He was re-elected unopposed in 1977 and 1984. By the end of the 1980s, however, people were starving and the infant mortality rate reached 50 per cent in some areas. Vast quantities of foreign aid disappeared, leaving the country with a stupendous debt that Mobutu kept finding excuses for not repaying.

By 1990, Mobutu's world was collapsing around him. With the demise of the Soviet Union his foreign backers, impatient with his deviousness and corruption, were looking for ways to remove him. His personal popularity had long since faded and would-be opposition politicians were raising their heads. These pressures led to a stunning announcement in April 1990 – Mobutu ended the one-party state and called for a National Sovereign Conference.

Democracy was not yet at hand. Mobutu suppressed student riots with violence and did all he could to impede the Conference, but it managed to establish a new regime under opposition leader Etienne Tshikeledi. Mobutu undermined that by bribery and intrigue, and finally suspended it, an act that cost him all foreign aid. By now, he was spending most of his time in the lavish palace he had built in his remote birthplace, Gbadolite (its vast halls were lined with Italian marble and filled with French antiques), making himself less accessible and virtually irrelevant. The end came as a result of the genocide in neighbouring Rwanda. Mass movements of refugees into eastern Zaire produced a major revolt led by the unknown Laurent Kabila. As rebel forces advanced in 1996, Mobutu's army fell apart. It had been trained to protect Mobutu's regime against its own population, rather than for national defence. Its highly paid officers stole the salaries of their men and inflated the size of the army to collect even more. A quartet of generals ran defence where their most notable achievement had been to sell Zaire's fleet of Mirage jet fighters. The unpaid soldiers lived by extortion or stealing from the public. The army simply collapsed when faced with serious military opposition. In May 1997, Kabila's forces entered the capital and Mobutu fled into exile, where he died in September. He had succeeded in ruining a country with enormous wealth and potential.

Jean-Bedel Bokassa

(1966–79)

'The international leaders respected me because
I was an Emperor.'

Bokassa, the Emperor of a poor landlocked central African state, is the only tyrant to have been put on trial for cannibalism. France installed Bokassa, maintained him in power, even after he had become an embarrassing megalomaniac, and subsidized his grandiose coronation, but finally threw him out when he became notorious for slaughtering schoolchildren. He eventually returned from exile, was tried and imprisoned but released under the terms of an amnesty.

Jean-Bedel Bokassa was born in 1921 in French Equatorial Africa, the son of a village chief (whom Bokassa later claimed was a king). He grew up in a poor and neglected country that had been devastated by slave raiding, contained over 80 ethnic groups, and was subject to an unusually harsh colonial regime. This undesirable posting attracted administrators who brutally suppressed revolts and allowed private companies to exploit the country's natural resources. Uncooperative native inhabitants were subject to flogging, torture or murder. After Bokassa's father was beaten to death for a minor violation, his wife committed suicide, leaving 12 children, including the six-year-old Jean-Bedel, to be raised by grandparents. When he was 18, Bokassa joined the army, fighting for the Free French during World War II, then with the French forces in Indochina. He was a highly decorated soldier, receiving the Croix de Guerre twice, as well as the Legion d'honneur. He was demobilized in 1961, and sent home to build a national army.

Bokassa returned to his native country, which had become the independent Central African Republic in August 1960. Political activity centred on the dominant party, the Movement for the Social Evolution of Black Africa founded by a dynamic defrocked priest Barthélemy Boganda. When Boganda was killed in a plane crash, his Interior Minister and relative David Dacko took over the party, becoming the nation's first President under independence. Dacko's ambitions outran his abilities. He abolished rival political parties, but never established firm central control. Instead, despite incessant purges and reforms, corruption drained the country's resources and stirred widespread resentment. Dacko entrusted the army to his cousin Bokassa, an experienced military man. Bokassa led the forces that overthrew the Dacko regime on 1 January 1966. He became President and head of the sole political party.

At first, Bokassa ruled as a populist, closing down the corrupt national assembly, cleaning up the civil service and improving the economy, but he soon showed his true character. He purged anyone who disagreed with him and affixed his name to hospitals, schools, and roads as well as the university and military academy. His only serious rival, Lieutenant-Colonel Alexandre Banza, who had organized the 1966 coup, was executed in 1969. By then, most politicians of the previous regime had been brutally killed. Bokassa frequently ordered tortures and beatings, and often supervised them in person. However, he ruled with the carrot as well as the stick. Rapid rotations of government posts allowed many of his followers to exploit public wealth, but they never knew how long they would stay in office or what their fate might be. As often as not, they would be dismissed for corruption, but subsequently restored.

For Bokassa, foreign relations, ideology and religion were closely connected. In 1969, he leaned toward Marxism, but when he decided there was little to be gained from it, he suddenly converted to Islam, taking the name Saladin as part of a rapprochement with Libya's leader, Muammar al-Qaddafi. That brought no particular advantages either, so Bokassa reverted to Christianity, and even visited the Vatican in July 1970. He later claimed that Pope Paul VI had baptized him in a special ceremony in a private chapel because of secret services he had rendered the Catholic church. On this occasion, according to Bokassa, the Pope named him the Thirteenth Apostle of the Holy Mother Church.

By 1972, when he made himself President for Life, Bokassa held the ministries of Defence, Justice, Home Affairs, Agriculture, Health and Aviation. He showed a real interest in justice by ordaining punishment for thieves in 1972: for a first offence, loss of one ear; for the second, the other ear; for the third, a hand. Bokassa presided over the amputations, which were carried out in public. In September 1976, he dissolved the government, replaced it with Central African Revolutionary Council and two months later, at the Party Congress, announced that Central Africa had become a monarchy.

His coronation took place on 4 December 1977 in the Jean-Bedel Bokassa Sports Palace on Bokassa Avenue adjacent to the Bokassa University, attended by 3500 guests, but none of the heads of state he had invited. Even his fellow Emperors, Hirohito and the Shah of Iran, declined. France lent him the money for the extravaganza, which cost $30 million, equivalent to 20 per cent of the national income. Bokassa sat on a golden throne in the shape of a ten foot (3m) high Napoleonic eagle, and like that Emperor, seized the diamond-encrusted crown and placed it on his own head. He rode in an imperial carriage pulled by eight white horses and escorted by mounted guards in Napoleonic costumes. His guests had 24,000 bottles of French champagne at their disposal.

Bokassa was close to the French President Valéry Giscard d'Estaing, whom he later claimed to have supplied with women and granted free run of the country for hunting. More persistent rumours maintained that his gifts included the diamonds that ensured French support despite the Emperor's increasingly erratic behaviour. Giscard's friendship apparently embraced the royal family, for Bokassa later accused him of adultery with the Empress Catherine. There was a practical side to the relationship, however, as Bokassa supplied France with the uranium it needed for its extensive nuclear programme.

Bokassa was the Empire's leading businessman. He contracted for ivory with a Spanish company that slaughtered 5000 elephants a year, giving the Emperor 33 per cent of the profits. Similar arrangements covered the trade in diamonds and timber. Bokassa also owned airlines, shops, apartments, small manufacturing plants and a restaurant.

He was also an extravagant builder. Among his public works was a motorway that ran 50 miles (80 km) to his country palace, a compound of villas, guest-houses, farms and barracks, decorated with real or bogus French antiques and displaying the arms and mottoes of the Empire on its walls. Here Bokassa met with the all-powerful Imperial Council and enforced a strict etiquette modelled on that of the Shah of Iran. He built other villas for his numerous foreign girlfriends, particularly a Romanian ballerina who used her villa to preside jointly with him over trials of opponents of the regime. They would decide whether the firing squad or the crocodiles should kill them, or whether they should be left simply to rot in jail. David Dacko maintained that human flesh was served there. The Romanian outranked the Tunisian, Gabonese, Belgian, Libyan and various other women – several of them reputed to be gifts from friendly governments – whom Bokassa maintained in separate villas, awaiting his pleasure.

Education led to Bokassa's downfall. After a visit to China, where he was impressed by the skill and discipline of the students, he was deeply disappointed in the poor performance of his own. Discipline was obviously the answer, so from 1 October 1978, all elementary and secondary schoolchildren were required to wear uniforms designed by Bokassa himself. They were made by a company he owned and could only be bought in his shops. When the students ignored the order and the secondary schools started to turn them away, they responded with riots that soon took on a political edge, referring ominously to the Shah of Iran who had just been removed from power. Bokassa sent in troops, whom he led in person. Some 100 students were massacred. University students were next. Dozens of them were taken to one of the most sinister of Bokassa's prisons, where the leader supposedly watched their torture and execution. Some of the bodies were found in his refrigerator, prompting rumours that he had eaten them. All this, and the publicity it generated, proved too much even for Bokassa's French supporters.

On 20 September 1979, his former friend Giscard d'Estaing sent in French troops who packed Bokassa off to exile in the Ivory Coast. He eventually moved to France where he lived in the only one of his villas he could still occupy (the rest had been seized by the Central African government). He was tried *in absentia* for murder, cannibalism and fraud and sentenced to death. Part of the evidence against him was discovered by French legionnaires who searched the villa of the Romanian ballerina. When they found dozens of bodies in a giant freezer, they drew the obvious conclusion that the Emperor had preserved them for his cuisine.

In 1986, Bokassa voluntarily returned to Bangui, for reasons that were never clear, was promptly arrested, tried again (ironically in the stadium where he had been crowned) and again condemned to die. The charges relating to cannibalism were dropped, but those of stealing public money, concealing children's bodies and murder stuck. In 1988, his sentence was reduced to life imprisonment, and in 1993 quashed altogether as he was released in a general amnesty. Bokassa died in 1996.

Muammar
al-Qaddafi
(1969–)

'This is genuine democracy, but realistically the strong always rule.'

Muammar al-Qaddafi was born in a Bedouin tent in 1940 or 1942. He belonged to an insignificant tribe in a country then under Italian rule. Mussolini's regime had unified the country and smashed its most vital organization, the Moslem Senussi brotherhoods, but their leader, Idris, became King of independent Libya in 1951. Libya was a backwater until oil was discovered there in 1969. Wealth brought public works and modernization, but also corruption. There was no political activity. Libya was much influenced by Egypt, which provided teachers and skilled workers and unceasing nationalist, anti-western propaganda by its leader Gamal Abdel Nasser.

Qaddafi was the first member of his family to attend school. He was a quiet and serious student who slept in the mosque. In secondary school he memorized and recited Nasser's speeches. When he started giving speeches of his own and leading demonstrations, he was expelled, but found another school where he organized supporters who agreed to abstain from alcohol, gambling and women. Qaddafi was a puritan, inspired by Nasser and Islam but without an ideology of his own.

In 1963, Qaddafi entered the Military Academy where he was a mediocre and disruptive student. He devoted his energies to planning the revolution he believed Libya needed. He gathered meticulous information and recruited cadets into cells that became the nucleus of a Free Officers Movement (imitating Nasser). In 1966 he went to England for further training. He resolved that the injustice and moral decay he saw there would have no place in Libya. By 1969, he was ready to move against the corrupt pro-western royal government.

Qaddafi's forces took control on 1 September 1969 in a bloodless coup. Their first broadcast justified the take-over but did not reveal their names. Nasser, delighted but mystified, responded by sending intelligence officers to help the new regime consolidate its power. Qaddafi's closest associates formed the Revolutionary Command Council whose decisions, according to the constitution that it issued in December, could not be questioned. By mid-1970 the press and trade unions were under RCC control. Dissidents faced special People's Courts. Qaddafi purged the army and promoted himself to Colonel. He banned alcohol and nightclubs, expelled 30,000 Italians and converted the cathedral in Tripoli into a mosque.

Qaddafi next moved against the western oil companies. He met little opposition since the Americans favoured his anti-Communism and supplied him with arms. He cleverly set the companies against each other and by 1973 was in control of enormous revenue. Qaddafi was devoted to Arab unity and to the Palestinian cause. The other Arab leaders, however, found him ignorant and capricious and rejected his attempts to unite any of them with Libya. His trip to Egypt in 1973 to spread his doctrines failed when he told a women's group what was in store for them under his puritanical regime, and Egyptian President Anwar Sadat was horrified when he suggested the Egyptians should torpedo the British ocean liner *Queen Elizabeth 2*. Qaddafi's travels were ultimately unproductive, but he did provide significant support to the Palestinians and to terrorist groups like the Irish IRA and the Basque ETA.

At first, Qaddafi's dictatorship imitated Nasser's. Its sole party was the Arab Socialist Union, recruited in 1971 from elements loyal to the revolution. All party decisions had to be countersigned by the RCC which could dissolve any party organization. Membership in any other party or in non-government trade unions was a capital offence. At the party's founding congress, Qaddafi proclaimed politics based on the Koran, maintaining that Allah had ordained consultation but not democracy.

Qaddafi actually gave a great deal of thought to the problems of democracy. The results appeared in the three-volume *Green Book*, published in 1975 and enshrined as official doctrine ever since. In his 'Solution of the Problem of Democracy' he concluded that all political systems were fraudulent because they denied the people direct participation in government. True democracy was only possible through people's congresses, starting at the local level. Likewise, the 'free' press only reflected the opinions of its owners – a truly democratic press could only issue from a people's committee. Qaddafi's Bedouin background influenced his vision of a society based on the family, tribe and nation. The *Green Book* promulgated the Third Universal Theory, neither Communist nor capitalist.

In 1973, Qaddafi announced his plans to replace existing laws with the Islamic *sharia*, arm the people to defend the revolution, bring government back to the people, and clear the universities of foreign influence. By 1975, the basic structure of 'Direct Democracy' was in place. The population assembled four times a year in Basic People's Congresses in towns, villages and workplaces. They elected People's Committees, whose heads formed a national committee that supervised the secretaries of the ruling General People's Congress. Oil and defence were not subject to this control. Qaddafi, who gave the orders, held no official position or title in the renamed Socialist People's Libyan Arab *Jamahiriya* (a novel term meaning 'state of the masses').

As oil money poured in, politics became irrelevant. The government had no need of taxation and could provide universal benefits. The standard of living increased as everyone had education and health care, houses (they could own only one), fresh water and cars. At the same time, the regime took over private trade and turned companies over to their workers, in accordance with its favourite slogan, 'Partners not wage-earners'. With so much money, there was little incentive to work. Libyans staffed the police and government offices, but foreigners did virtually everything else – they were wage-earners, not partners, and had no claim on the regime's munificence.

Libya was officially a socialist state. It formed close ties with the Soviet bloc and took advice from East German intelligence agents. Secret arrest and torture accompanied a revival of capital punishment as Qaddafi moved against rioting students, dissidents, corruption and potential rivals in the army. In 1977, officers accused of planning a coup were executed. Others succumbed to blackmail. Qaddafi had previously allowed a certain amount of corruption but now he denounced and punished it. To balance the army he created Revolutionary Committees who received special training and were led by members of Qaddafi's own tribe. The greatest danger, however, came from the Senussi networks and the radical Moslem Brotherhood. Qaddafi ordered the religious establishment to avoid politics and pointedly mentioned his admiration for the secularist Kemal Ataturk, the founder of the first Turkish republic. He never hesitated to destroy mosques and even the main Senussi pilgrimage shrine in a campaign that culminated in the arrest and disappearance of the Grand Mufti of Tripoli in 1980. After that, there was no more opposition at home.

Qaddafi pursued opponents who had taken refuge abroad. He sent hit men against them and smuggled weapons into Libya's People's Bureaux (as its embassies were renamed). One incident made international headlines when shots from the London People's Bureau killed a young female police officer. Qaddafi never followed the rules of diplomacy but moved unpredictably against unfriendly states. By the 1980s he was the biggest financier of international terrorism. He tried to persuade the Syrians to bomb Israel and plotted to assassinate King Hussein of Jordan. Because he considered Libya the natural capital of Africa, he opened his borders to Africans and tried to cajole or subvert their governments. His greatest efforts were directed towards neighbouring Chad, which he almost succeeded in occupying. He never hesitated to attack, at least verbally, fellow Arabs whom he considered insufficiently radical. Qaddafi wanted Libya to be a great power. He imported huge quantities of weapons from the USSR, tried to buy an atomic bomb and started a nuclear programme of his own. He also embarked on one of the world's greatest engineering projects, an artificial river that brought fresh water from aquifers beneath the Sahara 1000 miles (1600 km) to the thirsty cities of the coast. The costs were enormous, but the project was a success.

Qaddafi's ambitions received a major setback when Ronald Reagan became President of the United States. Reagan closed down trade with Libya and in 1986 bombed Tripoli and Benghazi in retaliation for an explosion in Berlin that had killed US servicemen. Two years later, a US civilian airliner exploded above the town of Lockerbie in Scotland, killing all on board. When the blame fell on Libya, the UN joined the US in imposing sanctions that shut down international trade with Tripoli. Finally in 1999, Qaddafi turned the Lockerbie suspects over to an international court and in 2003 accepted responsibility for the crime and offered compensation. Sanctions were removed and Qaddafi's reputation improved when he willingly gave up his programme to build weapons of mass destruction and turned the weapons and records over to international inspectors.

In 2006 Qaddafi still ruled a country where opposition was forbidden and surveillance universal. He was opening Libya to the West, but keeping it under firm personal control.

Idi Amin

(1971–9)

'*In any country there must be people who have to die. They are the sacrifices any nation has to make to achieve law and order.*'

Idi Amin's sense of showmanship often deluded foreigners into thinking that he was merely a colourful buffoon. His innumerable victims and their families knew better as they lived through a decade when torture or death might strike anyone, anywhere. Amin's flamboyant brutality attracted the world's attention, but left Uganda, the Pearl of Africa, a devastated and bankrupt wreck. Stories that he was a cannibal, who kept the heads of his victims in his refrigerator and brought them out for discussions, or that he fed his enemies to crocodiles, may not be true.

Idi Amin Dada, born around 1925 in the remote West Nile district of northern Uganda, then a British protectorate, grew up in rural poverty. His parents both belonged to minor tribes collectively called Nubians. He was a Moslem because his father (who deserted the family) had converted to Islam. He was raised by his mother, who was reputed to be a sorceress. In 1946, Amin joined the King's African Rifles as an assistant cook and rose rapidly through the ranks. In the 1950s he fought the Mau Mau rebels in Kenya, and in 1959 was granted the rank of *Effendi*, reserved for Africans who were potential leaders. After he was commissioned as Lieutenant in 1961 (a rare distinction for a native African), he started to demonstrate sadistic tendencies. He tortured, beat and killed nomads who had been stealing cattle and on one notorious occasion, to force the members of a fractious tribe to reveal their hidden weapons, he lined them up against a table and threatened to cut off their members. By then, the six-foot four-inch, 300-pound Amin was an outstanding swimmer and army boxing champion.

Amin supported Uganda's leading politician Milton Obote who rewarded him when he became Prime Minister upon independence in 1962. He received paratroop training in Israel, and by 1964 was Deputy Commander of Uganda's expanding army. That year Obote sent Amin with $350,000 to help rebels in the Congo. In 1966, Parliament protested that Obote and Amin had stolen the funds. This led to a crisis. Amin's forces arrested five offending ministers. Obote suspended the constitution, gave Amin full command of the army and air force and launched him against his partner, the king of the powerful Baganda tribe, who was the country's President. Obote, with Amin as his right-hand man, eliminated the Baganda from the army, replacing them with his fellow tribesmen.

Relations between the two deteriorated as the self-proclaimed President sought to curb the military Commander's growing powers. In January 1971, Obote ordered an account of defence spending, then made the mistake of leaving for a Commonwealth conference. No sooner was Obote out of the country than Amin moved, executing a successful coup. People rejoiced to see the politicians fall, especially as Amin promised conciliation and free elections, and released political prisoners. Foreigners, too, were pleased as they had perceived Obote's increasing move to the left as dangerous. Even the Israelis welcomed the rise of their old friend.

Within weeks, Amin ended all political activity and dismissed the officials of Obote's regime. He abolished the parliament, ruled by decree and announced that the military regime would remain in power for at least five years. This was overwhelmingly a personal dictatorship, without any clear policy or ideology, run by a man of the people, a soldier who, unlike most African leaders, was neither an intellectual nor a politician. Amin promoted himself to General and lifted the state of emergency. For a short time, the domestic situation seemed to improve, but Uganda soon faced a huge budget deficit, some inherited from Obote, much owing to Amin's lavish spending on the military. To ensure the army's loyalty, Amin enrolled masses of his fellow Nubians and used them to massacre 4–5000 of Obote's recruits. The army doubled in size. To balance the budget, Amin simply printed more money. His foreign policy changed dramatically in 1972 when Israel refused his request for increased aid and jet fighters. He turned to Colonel Qaddafi of Libya, who responded generously. Amin, who had supposedly promised to convert overwhelmingly Christian Uganda to Islam, expelled Israelis from the country, denounced Zionism and praised Hitler. However, he never erected a statue of the *Führer*, as he had proposed, nor did he complete the great mosque overlooking the capital, funds for which were stolen.

As the economy deteriorated, Amin sought a scapegoat. He found it in Uganda's enterprising Asians, most of them long-established immigrants from the Indian subcontinent who controlled the nation's commerce and industry and dominated the professions. Claiming the authority of a dream sent by God, Amin blamed them for sabotaging the national economy. In August 1972, he gave them three months to leave, taking only what they could carry. Everything else they owned was distributed as loot to Amin's cronies in the army. Amin was carrying out his determination to make Uganda a 'black man's country'. The exodus of some 70,000 Asians, which earned him widespread contempt (although it boosted his popularity at home), irreparably damaged the Ugandan economy. After the expulsions, exports were handled by the government, which used its hard currency earnings to buy Scotch whisky and luxury goods for the pampered army.

In 1972, exiles mounted an attack from Tanzania. It was easily repelled but served as an excuse for savage repression. Amin ran a military regime where soldiers occupied high posts, civil officials were subject to military discipline and military tribunals operated outside the legal system. Military barracks were the bases of power throughout the country. Amin directed a campaign of mass slaughter against rival tribes and followers of Obote. His new security services, the Public Safety Unit and the State Research Bureau, identified and tortured suspects, while the Presidential Guard became his favourite death squad. These frightening organizations employed some 18,000 agents. Their victims included politicians, cabinet ministers, Supreme Court judges, Christian clergy (foreign missionaries were fortunate only to be expelled), professionals of all kinds, journalists, and the occasional foreigner. A pair of shoes left by the side of the road was often the only hint that someone had been taken away, never to return. Others were shot in public before large crowds. So many bodies were thrown into the Nile that a major dam risked becoming clogged.

'Giving the VIP treatment' meant murder; 'giving tea' was whipping and dismemberment. Amin is supposed to have been responsible for 300,000 deaths during his years in power.

Amin reached the pinnacle of success in 1975, when he headed the Organization of African Unity. He promoted himself to Field Marshal, awarded himself the Victoria Cross and became President for Life. During celebrations, he forced four resident British businessmen to serve as his bearers, carry him on a litter, then kneel before him to pledge their loyalty. The image, which symbolized the humiliation of Uganda's former rulers, was transmitted throughout the world. The next year, when Britain broke diplomatic relations with Uganda, Amin adopted his grandest title: His Excellency President for Life, Field Marshal Al Hadji Doctor Idi Amin, VC, DSO, MC, Lord of All the Beasts of the Earth and Fishes of the Sea, and Conqueror of the British Empire in Africa in General and Uganda in Particular. The same year, Uganda joined the UN Commission on Human Rights.

Amin's first real setback came in June 1976 when terrorists hijacked an Air France flight from Tel Aviv to Uganda's Entebbe airport. Amin welcomed the pro-Palestinian hijackers, but was thoroughly humiliated when Israeli forces rescued the hostages and destroyed Amin's air force. He retaliated by killing one elderly female passenger who had been taken to the local hospital, but he took out his frustration on his own officers and officials, slaughtering 200 whom he accused of negligence. From that point, his fortunes declined rapidly.

Opposition to Amin grew in confidence as exiles attacked, troops mutinied and the threat of armed coups increased. Amin's close associates often fell victim to his growing suspicions. At the same time, the economy deteriorated even further when the price of coffee, a major export, collapsed, and Libya started to reduce its aid. Amin, who had lavished the country's wealth on his enormous army, thought he could deflect attention from domestic problems by annexing the northern province of Tanzania. Instead, his forces, who were more interested in looting than fighting, rapidly fell back before a counter-attack, despite the support of a Libyan contingent. On 11 April 1979, as the Tanzanians took the Ugandan capital, Kampala, Amin fled with four wives, several mistresses and two dozen of his children. After a brief stay in Libya, he found permanent asylum in Saudi Arabia. The Saudis gave him a house, servants, cars and drivers and a monthly subsidy that enabled him to live in comfort, if not luxury. Except for a brief episode when he tried to return to Uganda in 1989, he lived quietly in Jeddah, passing his time at the gymnasium, swimming pool and shops, and avoiding political activity and interviews. He died there in 2003, after Uganda's new President threatened to arrest him if he returned to the country alive.

Augusto Pinochet

(1973–86)

'Power must be vested in the armed forces, since only they have the organization and the means to fight Marxism.'

Augusto Pinochet saved Chile from Communism and set it on the path to economic success. He also ran a regime that killed thousands. Pinochet replaced a threatened Communist dictatorship with a real military one, bringing material prosperity while violently suppressing freedom. He reluctantly laid the foundation for democracy and surrendered power. Thereafter, he faced incessant legal problems.

Chile had long been polarized between conservatives and reformers. Socialists had the upper hand until World War II, after which liberal Christian Democrats dominated, following many socialist programmes. When conservatives and liberals split in 1970, Salvador Allende, a popular and eloquent Marxist, won the election with 36 per cent of the vote. He pledged to rule democratically, but brought in ideologues whose policies caused crippling shortages and explosive inflation. Hostility between left and right paralyzed the government, while strikes and Allende's efforts to create a popular militia increased the fury of the opposition. The military had traditionally stood outside politics, but now seemed the country's only hope for stability. Urged on by politicians and the press, leaders of the navy and air force planned a coup. They called on General Pinochet to join them.

Augusto Pinochet, born in 1915, was a devout Catholic who entered the Military Academy in 1932. He gradually rose through the ranks. When the pro-US government outlawed Communism in 1948, Captain Pinochet was put in charge of a camp for political prisoners, then sent to suppress a Communist miners' strike. He became convinced that Communism was a destructive force. Pinochet was a competent enough officer to be promoted, but not so outstanding as to attract unwanted attention from his highly competitive colleagues. In 1971, Allende appointed him Commander of the garrison of the capital, Santiago, then chose him to accompany the Communist Cuban leader, Fidel Castro, during his long tour of Chile. In 1973, when opposition was intense and army loyalty dubious, Allende named him army Commander. A fortnight later, Pinochet joined the coup against him.

On 11 September 1973, the army attacked the presidential palace. Allende shot himself, and troops swept through working-class districts and the universities rooting out Communists. A junta of four generals proclaimed a state of siege that banned political parties, closed the Congress and instituted censorship. They started to bring people in for interrogation. By the end of the year, the junta had purged the universities and taken over the trade unions. They claimed they would rule only as long as necessary, then restore democracy. The officers, however, tended to believe that leftists were traitors who deserved punishment, and continued resistance from armed youth groups stirred them to further anger. Pinochet himself envisioned a complete break with the new social and economic order that would give Chile a thorough moral cleansing.

The junta had collective authority but Pinochet started manoeuvring for supreme control immediately. He intimidated the others by his command of facts and made sure his allies occupied key positions. By June 1974 he had persuaded his colleagues to grant themselves unlimited terms in office, with Pinochet as Supreme Commander. He was free to remake Chile as he liked.

Pinochet drank only herbal tea, worked 12 hours a day, and avoided corruption, although he did allow family members to become rich. A simple soldier with a country accent, he never trusted intellectuals. He could be generous, charming and witty, but also furious and vengeful. He had supreme self-confidence, believing that his strength came from God.

Pinochet planned a state where the Commander held supreme power. The regime's bulwark was the National Directorate of Intelligence (DINA), created in 1974 to exterminate Marxism. Responsible only to the President, it eventually had 4000 agents and informers. Its Director ate breakfast with Pinochet every day. DINA built prisons and camps and employed psychological pressure, torture and murder. Together with the army, it interrogated 45,000 people. About 1500 were killed and thousands more sent to the camps. It had a far reach. In 1975 DINA joined the intelligence services of the Southern Cone countries and Brazil in Operation Condor, directed against exiles and potential opposition leaders. Its most notorious achievement was the assassination of one of Allende's high officials in the centre of Washington DC, an event that caused such a scandal that DINA was shut down. However, the National Information Centre that replaced it was not very different.

The army was firmly on the dictator's side: hardliners were promoted and independent-minded officers held back. The government employed educated technocrats in high positions, but kept them in line by having a military officer as nominal second in command in each ministry. These men, however, were constantly rotated back to the barracks, as Pinochet did not want to encourage any potential rivals. Officers ran the universities and governed provinces. Below them, Pinochet personally named all 323 municipal mayors, hoping to create a professional apolitical government. He remodelled the education system to produce a new generation free of poisonous ideology. But his suppression of politics stifled debate and created a stultifying atmosphere in higher education.

Pinochet had no problems with the judicial system. He gave judges lavish benefits, and most of the legal profession, who had bad memories of Allende, were anxious to keep their jobs. For some years, military tribunals also exercised considerable extra-legal power. Laws had to be published to be valid but Pinochet ensured that very few had access to the publication, so he could legislate virtually as he pleased.

Pinochet revitalized the economy of a state burdened with a bloated bureaucracy and nationalized industries it could not manage. Aided by economists from the University of Chicago, he gave free rein to experts who devalued the currency, sold off state-run businesses and stuck to free-market principles. Although this caused a severe downturn, the programme attracted universal attention, foreign investment began to pour in (it had dwindled away under Allende) and prosperity returned. The economy plunged again in 1982 when the price of copper, Chile's main export, collapsed, while the increasing foreign debt became unsustainable. Pinochet turned from the 'Chicago Boys' to pragmatists who introduced a programme of public works, and then appointed Hernan Buchi, who held an MBA from Columbia, as Minister of the Economy. Carefully controlled reforms produced such expansion that Chile became a model for Latin America.

In 1977, the UN had condemned Chile for human rights abuses. Pinochet responded by holding a referendum that gave him 70 per cent approval. He then outlined his plans for the promised transition to democracy. It would take a long time. The new constitution gave Pinochet an eight-year term, after which he and the other generals would choose a candidate to be approved in a referendum. If the people voted against the proposed candidate there would be an election. When this was approved in 1980, Pinochet took the title of President and moved into the restored presidential palace.

Economic problems led to the first massive demonstration against the government in 1983. Pinochet liberated the press. Politics revived, with leaders of the suppressed parties demanding democracy. Even worse, the previously friendly US government started to demand change. The Communists hoped 1986 would be a decisive year, but their attack on Pinochet's motorcade led to universal revulsion, and the far left had to yield to centrist politicians.

Pinochet's constitution demanded a plebiscite in 1988. To the dismay of his generals, he decided to run for President himself. Political activity was legalized, the united opposition forces campaigned effectively, and the US decided that it was time for Pinochet to go. To Pinochet's astonishment the vote went against him by a large margin. Pinochet, who accepted the verdict, drew a comparison with the death of Christ, noting that an earlier plebiscite had chosen Barabbas. He had been betrayed by his own conviction that he was indispensable, and by his subordinates' fear of revealing the true political situation. When elections duly followed, the winning Christian Democrats assumed the power that Pinochet peacefully relinquished.

Pinochet was still commander of the army, a post he used to intimidate succeeding Presidents until he finally retired in 1998. Meanwhile the atrocities his regime had committed came to light and serious questions were raised about 2000 people who had been killed or had disappeared during his time in office. Pinochet thought he was safe. As a Senator, he had immunity from prosecution for life but when he went to London for a routine medical operation in October 1998, a Spanish judge issued a warrant for his arrest. The previously friendly British cooperated with the demand for extradition. His poor health, however, allowed Pinochet to return to Chile where the Supreme Court revoked his immunity and placed him under house arrest. In 2006, he was still fighting legal battles, even though he had passed his 90th birthday.

Pol Pot

(1975–9)

'Only several thousand Kampucheans might have died due to some mistakes in implementing our policy of providing an affluent life for the people.'

Dreams of a Communist utopia inspired Pol Pot to kill more than a million Cambodians. Mao, Stalin and Hitler had more victims, but Pol Pot, without a war, destroyed a greater proportion of his population than anyone in history. His three years in power so devastated the country that, nearly 30 years later, it is still recovering. He led such a clandestine existence that few reliable details of his history are known and virtually nothing about his private life.

Pol Pot's real name was Saloth Sar. He was born in 1925 in French Indochina, to a landowning family with connections to the royal court. When Sar was nine, he went to live with his relatives in Phnom Penh, then a sleepy backwater. He spent a year in a Buddhist monastery then entered a French Catholic school. This was a time of rising nationalism, stirred by the fall of France to the Germans in 1940 and Japanese occupation, which proclaimed Cambodia's independence in 1945. After the French returned, they promised elections and a constitution, policies agreeable to the new King Norodom Sihanouk.

Saloth Sar, who never passed his school examinations, seemed to be an agreeable mediocrity. His life took a major turn in 1949, when he went to France to study radio electronics. There, he found enormous enthusiasm for Communism among the young, encouraged by France's powerful Stalinist party. Thanks to his association with radical Cambodian students, and inspired by a summer of voluntary labour in Yugoslavia, Sar joined the Party. By then, Cambodia was in turmoil. When a liberal party edged closer to dominance, Sihanouk seized dictatorial powers. Sar's first published article denounced the monarchy.

In 1953, Sar returned home to be inducted into the Indochinese Communist Party and begin clandestine work. Later that year, France granted independence, but Cambodia was to have a constitutional government. Parties rose and campaigned, only to see Sihanouk abdicate as King, form his own movement and win a crushing victory. Political life came to an end. Saloth Sar took a position teaching French at a private college in Phnom Penh, where he was very popular with the students. He also worked as a Party activist, organizing its growing membership. Since most of the recruits came from urban intellectuals and workers, his role in the capital was important.

After the leader of the Party mysteriously disappeared in 1962, Saloth Sar became secretary of the Central Committee, and left to organize insurrection in the countryside. The public period of his life ended. From now, he was Pol or 'Brother Number One'. Few, even in the Party, knew his real identity.

For the next seven years, Sar was in constant danger. His only respites came in 1965 when he walked to Hanoi and in 1966 when he visited China at the height of the Cultural Revolution, whose destructive lessons he absorbed. In Cambodia, Sar met only fellow believers who would formulate ever more utopian plans for the Revolution. Their ideals reflected the agrarian Communism of Mao Zedong at a time of US intervention in Indochina. The spreading war disrupted Cambodia's economy and increased opposition to the government. Sar's fortunes were at a low ebb in 1969 when Sihanouk took the side of the Americans. US bombing of eastern Cambodia claimed tens of thousands of lives and antagonized the rural population, making them a fertile recruiting ground for the Communist fighting forces, the Khmer Rouge.

In 1970, General Lon Nol, supported by the US, seized power in Phnom Penh. Sihanouk set up a government in exile in the countryside, allying himself with the Communists while Vietnam and China forged the Khmer Rouge into an organized force of 100,000 by 1972. As the Americans pulled back from Vietnam, the Khmer Rouge advanced. Continued US bombing added to the misery, driving the peasants into the cities. In the areas they controlled, the Khmer Rouge set up Party schools, recruiting leaders from poor peasants and workers. They collectivized the land, suppressed religion and traditional culture, indoctrinated the young, and obliged everyone to work, wearing the traditional black cotton pyjamas of the peasantry. By the end of 1973, they controlled 60 per cent of the country. A year later, the capital was isolated.

On 17 April 1975, the silent, young black-clad Khmer Rouge marched into Phnom Penh, home of the hated capitalists who had not joined the revolution. The Party decided the fate of the urban 'new people'. Within 24 hours, they were ordered to evacuate: everyone – young, old, weak or sick – was forcibly dispersed into the countryside where they could pose no threat. Thousands died along the way. Foreigners were expelled, embassies were closed, and money, markets, schools, newspapers, religion and private property were all prohibited.

A week later, a triumphant Sar entered an empty Phnom Penh. Cambodia was at 'Year Zero', to be reconstructed as the Khmer Rouge liked. For the moment, the Party ruled behind the scenes, with Sihanouk as nominal head of state. In January 1976, Democratic Kampuchea was proclaimed and elections called for a National Assembly. No 'new people' could vote. The Party chose the candidates, and the assembly was dissolved after they were named. They included an unknown 'rubber worker', Pol Pot, as Prime Minister.

The new regime maintained intense secrecy. No one outside the inner circle knew who the leaders were, or that the mysterious *Angkar*, the organization that gave orders, was actually the Communist Party. Pol Pot moved constantly and hardly ever appeared in public. He was planning a new society. Rice production was to be its centrepiece. Pol Pot, who knew nothing of economics or government, envisaged a self-sufficient agrarian state whose rice surplus would pay for development. Taking his cue from China's Cultural Revolution, he demanded a tripling of rice production, not from advanced methods but by revolutionary zeal. A million of the despised 'new people' were sent off to remote provinces to convert forest into rice paddy. The regime did not regret the loss of the tens of thousands who died, noting that: 'Keeping you is no gain; losing you is no loss.'

The population was subject to merciless discipline. Traditions, culture and families were destroyed. Everyone lived in agricultural collectives and ate in communal dining halls. Their lives were supervised and they were subject to endless political indoctrination. There was no formal education. Death was the punishment for slacking, complaining, expressing religious beliefs or grief over loss of relatives, taking food for personal consumption, or having sexual relations. Many more died from overwork, malnutrition or starvation. Employees of the former regime, policemen, priests, bourgeois and intellectuals (recognizable because they wore glasses) were killed. The Khmer Rouge regime was responsible for the deaths of at least 1.5 million people, out of a population of seven million.

In Phnom Penh, the notorious interrogation centre of Tuol Sleng tortured 'anti-Party elements' until they confessed. Of the 15,000 who entered, only seven left alive. There were 20 similar establishments throughout the country. 'Evidence' from these 'confessions' convinced Pol Pot that there were dangerous hidden 'microbes' within the Party itself. This led to a Stalinist purge that destroyed the party intelligentsia and some 100,000 followers and their families. The killings ended only with the collapse of the regime.

Democratic Kampuchea enjoyed the support of China, which Pol Pot visited triumphantly in September 1977. For the first time, he appeared in public as Prime Minister and secretary of the Cambodian Communist Party, whose existence was only now revealed. Some recognized, to their surprise, that he was Saloth Sar. He soon sank back into anonymity. Photographs of him were never published, he had no biography, and there were no statues or images. For Pol Pot secrecy meant security.

In 1977, the Khmer Rouge started to face growing hostility from their powerful neighbour Vietnam. A chronic border dispute grew worse as the regime slaughtered resident Vietnamese and began incursions across the border. The Vietnamese responded in massive force in December 1978. When they took Phnom Penh in January, Pol Pot fled to the remote Thai borderland where he carried on a guerrilla war. The Vietnamese installed a puppet People's Republic of Kampuchea and *in absentia* condemned Pol Pot to death for genocide. For political reasons, however, China and the United States continued to recognize the murderous Khmer Rouge, allowing them to retain Cambodia's seat in the United Nations.

The depleted Khmer Rouge tried to rebuild their guerilla forces and enlist recruits to whom Pol Pot gave study sessions. Pol Pot was their military commander until 1985, then remained head of the Communist Party for another 12 years. By then, his followers were deserting and he suffered a stroke in 1995. He still had enough energy, however, to have his defence minister and long-time associate Song Sen murdered, along with his wife and children, in 1997. That was the last straw. A 'people's tribunal' sentenced him to life imprisonment for the murder. He died under arrest in April 1998. A month later, the last bastion of the Khmer Rouge fell to government forces.

Ayatollah Khomeini

(1979–89)

'In the world there is no democracy better than
our democracy. Such a thing has never before
been seen.'

Ayatollah Khomeini was a learned theologian who believed that only a wise Islamic Jurist could bring justice to a deeply divided Iran. He opposed foreign influence and became a bitter critic of the reigning monarch, Reza Shah, whom his followers overturned in 1979. In power, Khomeini replaced a dictatorship disguised as a monarchy with one lurking behind the façade of republican government. He established a unique regime based on Islam that long survived him.

Ruhollah Khomeini took his name from the poor village of Khomein where he was born in 1902. He was a devout, disciplined student who had memorized the Koran by the age of six. He grew up in a traditional country whose lackadaisical dynasty ruled in its own interests, leaving the extensive Shiite religious establishment to provide education, law, justice and social services. By 1918, Ruhollah left home to enter a system where religious students learnt by attaching themselves to a teacher who subsidized their education. At that time, the clergy was split between modernizers willing to accept growing western influence, and traditionalists who adhered closely to the word of the Koran. Khomeini found a traditionalist who had settled in the minor town of Qom, attracted by local merchants who wanted to enhance the town's reputation. His studies were progressing when the new dictatorial regime of Reza Shah began an assault on the power of the clergy by introducing foreign law codes and secular education. This turned into active persecution that stirred widespread resentment and resistance.

During these years Khomeini became known as an austere mystic and writer who strongly opposed western-influenced nationalism, which he saw as anti-Islamic. By the 1930s his studies had earned him the title of *Hojat al-Islam* and his wife's dowry enabled him to buy a bus and start a successful business. With the money that generated, he could make the pilgrimage to Mecca and attract a growing body of students. He started to give radio broadcasts and write pamphlets denouncing corruption and anti-clerical government policies. Khomeini broke with Iran's religious leader, the Grand Ayatollah, who supported the traditional policy of keeping religion separate from politics. His writings attacked the government of the new Shah, a modernizer firmly aligned with the West. By 1958, Khomeini's reputation was so well established that he could hope to become one of the country's 12 ayatollahs, but the Shah, who saw him as a troublemaker, blocked the appointment. Khomeini went into seclusion, abandoned his mystical style and stopped writing poetry. He adopted popular language, and took the radical position that only the clergy could save Iran from the corrupting influence of the West. He emerged as the Shah's leading religious opponent.

The Shah's programme of modernization, backed by huge oil revenues, was winning considerable support. The public was not much moved by Khomeini until he added a new element: that the Shah was in the pay of foreigners, especially the United States and Israel. This resounded with Iranian nationalists, long hostile to foreign interference and domination. After an especially violent denunciation of the Shah, Khomeini was arrested. He was marked out as a leading opponent but soon released.

In 1964, when the government passed a bill to give US military personnel immunity and to borrow $200 million from the Americans, Khomeini's attacks led to his forced exile, first to Turkey, whose secularism he detested, then to Iraq, where he took up residence in the Shiite holy city of Najaf. His protests gained force in 1975 when the border with Iran was opened and pilgrims flocked to hear Khomeini, bringing his speeches back in print and on audio cassettes. By now he had evolved a coherent doctrine of *velayat i-faqih*, or rule by the Jurist – that is, only a pious man learned in the religious law could provide justice. He published his ideas in *Islamic Government*.

Meanwhile, the Shah was making drastic changes that infuriated religious Moslems. Land reforms reduced the clergy's revenues, women were given the rights to vote and divorce, and a policy of co-education was introduced. These changes were interpreted by conservative Moslems as encouraging moral corruption. The Shah's growing megalomania worsened matters. He identified increasingly with the rulers of ancient Iran and even changed the calendar to count from their dynasty. Khomeini spoke out and the regime's virulent attack on him in the press stirred a violent reaction. Riots in Qom were followed by larger demonstrations elsewhere, often coinciding with religious celebrations that the Shah could not suppress. Young men uprooted from the villages by the Shah's policies of large-scale mechanized agriculture provided a core of support. Other religious leaders, although they disagreed with much of Khomeini's doctrine, supported him in defence of Islam, which the Shah seemed to be attacking.

The Shah had the biggest army in the region, a huge income and an effective secret service but he had lost touch with the people. Khomeini organized the secret Council of the Islamic Revolution, which allowed others to take the ostensible lead in opposition. His vast network of sympathetic clergy dominated the religious establishment and created a parallel, underground government that could put demonstrators into the streets at short notice. The Shah, abandoned by US President Jimmy Carter, made major concessions but crossed a fatal line when his troops fired on a demonstration in Tehran in September 1978. The next month Khomeini moved to France where for the first time he had a western audience. He told them exactly what they wanted to hear about his love of democracy. Strikes, guerrilla attacks and mass demonstrations finally forced the Shah into exile in January 1979. Khomeini returned to Iran in triumph a fortnight later.

At first, Khomeini took no office but appointed a Prime Minister while he organized the Islamic Republican Party. He called for a referendum to vote for or against an Islamic republic (no alternative was offered). It won a huge majority on 1 April 1979. A largely clerical constituent assembly drew up a new Islamic constitution that vested supreme power in the Jurist – Khomeini – for the term of his life. The Jurist, responsible only to God, commanded the armed forces, could dismiss the President and veto laws, and appointed half the council of Guardians that vetted all legislation to ensure that it conformed to Islam. The constitution provided for a President, a

Prime Minister and a parliament to run the business of government. In this complex system, the democratic elements were overwhelmed by the Jurist's power. Khomeini lived in a simple compound in the suburbs, devoting himself to theology, while the Prime Minister nominally governed, overshadowed by Khomeini's Revolutionary Council. This organization gained supremacy through new elements: the Komitehs, vigilante groups who ran neighbourhoods; the Revolutionary Tribunals who could execute opponents; and the Revolutionary Guards, the party's militia. By the end of the year, Khomeini's men were all-powerful, and a sympathetic President was elected.

Executions began in April 1979. The Shah's Prime Minister and leading generals were shot openly. Following international protests, the firing squads operated secretly. About 1250 were killed in the first year of Khomeini's regime. Khomeini had no trouble with the media, which were muzzled, then suppressed or nationalized. Unauthorized demonstrations were banned. Opposition still came from the extreme left who assassinated the President, Prime Minister, party chairman and numerous politicians during the summer of 1981. Khomeini responded with force: thousands were executed and 30–50,000 imprisoned and often tortured. During this time, the Americans could do nothing, as armed activists had occupied their embassy in Tehran in November 1979 and held its employees hostage for over a year. The foreign presence in Iran shrank drastically as contracts were cancelled, workers expelled and companies nationalized. This was a serious blow for the Shah's middle class, though they suffered perhaps less than religious minorities like the Bahais, who were actively persecuted.

Khomeini's regime enforced Islam. In 1982, Khomeini decreed that all laws passed by the Shah were annulled unless they conformed with Islamic *Sharia* law. *Sharia* enforced public morality. Consumption of alcohol was banned, and women had to wear a veil. Music disappeared from the radio and cinemas were closed. Kissing in public could earn 100 lashes and stoning was restored as the penalty for adultery.

In 1980, Saddam Hussein attacked Iran, thinking he could profit from the country's political chaos. The eight-year long war caused widespread devastation and loss of life but accomplished nothing. Meanwhile, Khomeini had been spreading revolution, especially in Lebanon where his Party of God kidnapped his enemies and killed 241 US marines in a bomb attack. When the Iran-Iraq war, which had exhausted the country, finally ended, Khomeini allowed some relaxation: chess, previously forbidden as a royalist entertainment, was allowed, as was western music, but Khomeini himself never deviated from the strict Islamic path. Parliament passed many bills only to see them vetoed by the Guardians. Khomeini, however, occasionally intervened in the interests of social welfare. He regained intentional notoriety in February 1989 when he issued a death sentence against Salman Rushdie, who had published a novel considered offensive to Islam. This act cancelled most of the gains Khomeini had made in foreign relations. It was his last major public pronouncement. He died in June 1989, mourned by the greatest crowds in Iranian history. The political system he instituted survives.

Saddam
Hussein

Saddam's ability and family connections enabled him to rise in Iraq's revolutionary governments. As Vice-President, he improved social welfare and literacy. As President, he introduced a totalitarian system modelled on Stalin's and surrounded himself with sycophants who could never reveal any unpleasant truths. Ignorance and bravado led him into two wars he could not win. The second destroyed his regime and put him on trial for crimes against his people.

Saddam Hussein grew up in poverty in Tikrit in central Iraq where he was born in 1937. He was raised by his stepfather who reputedly treated him badly and kept him from school. In 1947, Saddam went to live with his uncle Khairullah and went to primary school where his intelligence and photographic memory made up for his late start. In Khairullah's house in Baghdad he met his cousin Ahmad Hassan al-Bakr, and had his first exposure to politics. Khairullah was a member of the Ba'ath party that advocated a united secular Arab nation. When Saddam joined the party in 1957, his first job was to organize gangs to beat or intimidate the party's enemies.

A violent revolution led by Abd al-Karim Qassem overturned the corrupt Iraqi monarchy in 1958. After initially cooperating, the Ba'athists and Qassem became bitter enemies. After Qassem massacred insurgent Ba'athists, the party tried to assassinate him. Saddam was condemned to death for his part in the failed attempt. He managed to escape to Syria, and later Egypt where he completed his studies and was impressed by the power of Gamal Abdel Nasser's dictatorship. Saddam returned to Iraq in 1963 when the Ba'ath overthrew Qassem, but a further coup by anti-Ba'athists led to his arrest in 1964 for plotting against the President. After he escaped in 1966, Saddam helped reunite the Ba'ath party, which had been split by quarrelling factions, led demonstrations and joined a military plot to restore the Ba'athists under his friend and patron al-Bakr, who took power in July 1968.

The new regime was an unnatural alliance between the Ba'ath and the military, with neither side trusting the other. Al-Bakr put Saddam, a skilled in-fighter, in charge of the party's security services. Within a month two powerful colonels lost their positions and al-Bakr took control of the Revolutionary Command Council and the armed forces. Saddam was his second in command, with responsibility for internal security. Since the regime had seized power in a coup and had no base of popular support, it moved to crush opposition and re-educate the public. Saddam led the first purges of non-Ba'athists in the autumn of 1968. The party publicly executed Jews as its militia patrolled the streets, broke into houses and carried off their victims. Saddam sent agents to the villages to recruit members, favouring Sunnis, especially those from Tikrit. As a result, the Ba'ath leadership passed from middle-class intellectuals to uneducated but deeply loyal tribesmen. Within a year, 60 per cent of the leadership was from Tikrit. The army, which posed the greatest potential threat, was next to be subdued. Saddam established a system of political commissars to supervise the officers. A strong paramilitary organization, recruited mainly from the Tikrit area, provided a counterbalance to the national army

The al-Bakr government introduced social benefits, and improved health care and opportunities for women. Saddam, who visited all parts of the country, was the popular face of the regime, but remained deferential to his superiors. He carefully prepared and conducted the long negotiations that led to nationalization of Iraq's oil in 1972. The enormous revenues freed the government from dependence on its own people and allowed it to expand public works, welfare, the civil service and the military at the same time.

By 1973, Iraq was firmly under the control of the Ba'ath party. Al-Bakr ruled surrounded by officers from Tikrit and Saddam virtually ran the country through his network of secret services and informants, which crushed opposition before it could arise. The standard of living improved. In 1977, Saddam's literacy campaign was so successful that he received an award from the United Nations. He encouraged women to enter the workforce, with a hidden agenda to weaken family structures and increase the power of the state. Not for nothing had he studied the career of Stalin.

In July 1979 President al-Bakr retired and Saddam assumed full power. He immediately called a special party meeting where, with great sadness, he denounced people in the room as 'conspirators'. Sixty-six were led off for imprisonment or execution. The purge affected the whole party, regardless of rank or closeness to Saddam. Iraq became a totalitarian state ruled by Saddam and staffed by Ba'athists. Iraqis were induced to love Saddam as well as fear him. He gave numerous speeches, wrote hundreds of articles and appeared everywhere. He wanted his people to see themselves as the powerful heirs of the glorious ancient Mesopotamian civilizations. Khairullah, now Minister of Defence, presided over a military buildup that included plans for chemical and nuclear weapons.

Saddam ran a personal dictatorship where children were taught that the party and state were their father and mother. Party membership was essential for employment in the bureaucracy, trade unions, education or army. Full membership, which took ten years, was for the committed. The penalty for leaving the party was death; after 1996, insulting the President, party or government also invited capital punishment. But the Ba'ath was really a conduit for Saddam's orders. In reality, a small clique of Tikritis ran the country. They were totally loyal because they knew their fate was bound up with Saddam's. They agreed with anything he said, exposing him to a tyrant's most pernicious problem, the inability to obtain accurate and disinterested information. Ignorance of real situations, especially those involving foreign powers, proved deadly for Saddam.

The army was completely politicized, with promotion gained by loyalty rather than competence. It was not allowed within 150 kilometres of Baghdad. The elite corps was the Republican Guard. Saddam supervised their training, and provided them with the most modern weapons, which he issued as required. The popular militia provided further security against coups. But the regime's greatest protection came from the complex web of secret services that penetrated the government and army.

Saddam himself took no chances. He had several palaces and few knew where he might be at any given time. He wore bulletproof clothing and had eight doubles to stand in for him on public occasions or to sit in the duplicate motorcades that concealed his true movements.

In 1980, Saddam was preparing for the summit of Non-Aligned Nations in Baghdad, where the Cuban leader Fidel Castro would hand leadership over to him. The summit was cancelled when Iraq attacked Iran. Saddam personally directed the operations that initially pushed deep into Iran. The campaign, however, soon felt the effects of incompetent leadership as Saddam wanted to keep casualties low and failed to coordinate air and ground attacks. His subordinates were afraid to make any decision that might contradict him – Saddam never hesitated to shoot officers who disagreed with him or failed. By 1982 he had lost 100,000 men and exhausted his reserves. The Soviet Union and his fellow Arabs rescued him as he posed as the defender of the Arab world against its traditional Persian enemies. When Iraq's Kurds took advantage of the situation to revolt, Saddam bombarded them with poison gas, destroyed thousands of villages and displaced half a million people. Finally, in 1988, Iran requested a cease-fire. The war ended by restoring the *status quo* and accomplished nothing.

The war left Iraq impoverished, but it still had a huge military and government apparatus to support. Badly needing new sources of revenue, Saddam cast his eyes on Kuwait. He demanded that the Kuwaitis cut back their oil production and cancel the $8 billion debt that Iraq owed. When they refused and the US ambassador equivocated, Saddam struck. He overran the country in a few hours in August 1990, never suspecting that his bluff would be called – his advisers had kept western press reports from him because their analyses contradicted Saddam's. When the USSR failed to back him and other Arab states ranged themselves in opposition, he was in a helpless position. The Americans attacked in January 1991 and Iraq surrendered in March. President George Bush kept Saddam in power on the grounds that removing him would only bring instability. That allowed Saddam to crush Shiite opposition, but he could not touch the Kurds, now protected by the Americans. For the next decade, his regime held on, although the country suffered from desperate shortages caused by economic sanctions.

Saddam maintained the same impenetrable security and ruthless control until he ran up against western determination to end his programme for building weapons of mass destruction. He denied having them, but nevertheless ejected UN-appointed weapons inspectors. His intransigence led to invasion by the United States and its allies in March 2003. Saddam escaped but was finally pulled out of his underground hiding place in December 2003, still claiming to be President of Iraq. His statues fell, his regime disappeared, and Iraq sank into chaos barely controlled by the foreign occupiers. Saddam had denied having chemical or nuclear weapons. Ironically and uniquely, he was telling the truth. In 2005, he was put on trial for war crimes, a process that promised to last a long time.

Slobodan Milosevic

(1989–2000)

Many tyrants have committed war crimes, but Slobodan Milosevic was the first to be put on trial for them. He was a grey *apparatchik* who would never have attracted international attention had he not exploited the disintegration of Yugoslavia by advocating a ferocious Serbian nationalism. His devastating campaign of 'ethnic cleansing' finally attracted a military response from the West. He ultimately had to face an international tribunal, but died in prison before he could be brought to justice.

Slobodan Milosevic was born in 1941 in a town east of Belgrade a few months after the Nazis had seized control of Yugoslavia during World War II. His mother was a schoolteacher and a Communist, his father a defrocked priest. Both later committed suicide. Slobodan grew up in a country wrecked by the war but filled with enthusiasm for President Tito's Communist reconstruction. A dull, serious student, he did well in school. His classmates thought he would make a good bureaucrat or stationmaster. He joined the Communist Party in 1959, and studied law at Belgrade University, where he became deputy leader of the school's Party branch and head of its ideology committee. He gained a reputation for diligence and efficiency. In law school, Slobodan became friends with Ivan Stambolic, a rising Communist and critical influence in his life.

After graduating near the top of his class in 1964, Milosevic married Mira Markovic, his girlfriend since childhood, and took a job with the Party in Belgrade. By 1968, he was head of the city's Information Department, where he learnt about propaganda and control of the press. Stambolic made him director of a state energy company in 1970 then president of the biggest state bank in 1975. In this post he frequently travelled to the United States, where he shopped but otherwise showed no interest in the country or its society. He acquired the ability to charm and convince. For Yugoslavs he was an orthodox Communist, while westerners saw him as a reforming liberal. All the while, he assiduously cultivated Stambolic. For 35 years, Tito had held the country together as a federation where unity overcame nationalism. When he died in 1980, a rotating presidency took over, run by the heads of the six republics (Slovenia, Croatia, Bosnia, Serbia, Montenegro and Macedonia) and Serbia's two autonomous regions (Kosovo and Vojvodina).

In 1982, Stambolic became head of the Communist Party in Belgrade, capital of both Serbia and Yugoslavia. He brought Milosevic with him as a member of the Party's Executive Committee, the first step to political power; and when Stambolic was put in charge of the Serbian Party, Milosevic filled his old position in Belgrade. In 1985, Stambolic became President of Serbia and Milosevic overcame liberal opposition to succeed him as Party chief. Within a few months, he began playing the nationalist card. Leading intellectuals were claiming that Serbia had been shortchanged by Tito and criticized conditions in Kosovo where Serbs, they maintained, were being persecuted by the majority Albanian population. Milosevic saw that exploiting nationalist sentiment could lead to supreme power. He made his first move in 1987 in Pristina, capital of Kosovo, when he told the local Serbs, 'No one will ever dare to beat you again.' In this, he violated two established principles: Communists should not criticize their peers, nor take sides in ethnic disputes. That day marked both the beginning of the end for Yugoslavia and the rise of Milosevic, whose words resonated throughout Serbia. The last obstacle was Stambolic. As tensions rose in Kosovo, Serbia's press, run by a Milosevic ally, stirred nationalist frenzy against those like Stambolic who advocated moderation. Stambolic resigned as President in September 1987 and Milosevic succeeded him in February. Stambolic, Milosevic's close friend and patron, was found murdered in 2000, allegedly by Milosevic's secret police.

As President, Milosevic turned his attention to Kosovo where he was determined to enforce Serbian control. In March 1988, he deposed the local Party leadership, arresting the principal Albanian with whom he might have established a dialogue, then violently suppressed a miners' strike. He also took over the Party in Montenegro and Vojvodina, giving him four out of eight votes in the collective presidency and paralyzing the nation's politics. Yugoslavia disintegrated. Slovenia and Croatia walked out of the 1990 Party Congress, elected their own governments and in 1991 withdrew from the Federation. Milosevic produced a new Serbian constitution that provided for a directly elected President. He won the election in December 1990.

Milosevic realized that he could not rule Yugoslavia. Instead he decided to build a powerful Serbia that would include all Serbs living in the other republics. To that end, he launched a war against Croatia, destroying frontier cities, occupying territory and supporting the large block of Serbs in the Krajina region. The biggest problem was Bosnia, which declared its independence in March 1992. It had a hopelessly mixed population of Serbs, Croatians and Moslems but Milosevic wanted to dominate it. Rather than sending in the army, he operated behind the scenes by organizing and supplying paramilitary units who embarked on a programme of 'ethnic cleansing', which involved expelling or killing Moslems and establishing concentration camps. Hundreds of thousands fled as the Serbs occupied 70 per cent of the country and mercilessly shelled its capital Sarajevo. The violence culminated in the massacre of 6000 men and boys in the Moslem enclave of Srebrenica in July 1995. The Bosnian war turned the West against the Serbs. The UN imposed an economic blockade, the costs of the wars led to hyperinflation, and the Serbian economy faced collapse. Despite constant demonstrations against his policies, and erratic attempts to achieve stability – most notably choosing a rich American Yugoslav as Prime Minister – Milosevic was re-elected in 1992, with the help of vote rigging. He realized it was time to make peace – the situation was growing desperate. By 1995 NATO was backing the Moslems and Croats who pushed the Serbs out of Krajina and much of Bosnia. Milosevic ditched the Bosnian Serbs and went to Dayton in Ohio for discussions that produced an agreement to divide Bosnia among the three communities. He was praised abroad as a peacemaker, but the Serbs saw the agreement as a defeat.

On his return, Milosevic purged many of his close associates, arranged his re-election as head of the Party and tried to rig the municipal elections, an attempt that provoked massive noisy demonstrations, with Belgrade in virtual revolt. Milosevic, who started to smoke and drink heavily, came to rely more on his wife Mira, who had formed her own political party. He finally had to concede defeat and see the first non-Communist mayor since 1945 assume office in Belgrade. But he exploited divisions in the opposition and became President of Yugoslavia in 1997. In all this, he demonstrated his political skills of intrigue and manoeuvring, encouraging chaos and conflict to enhance his own power. Yet he had no sense of strategy, no clear long-term goals other than staying in power. He ran foreign policy, taking no advice and making all decisions himself. Problems in Kosovo revealed his fatal misunderstanding of the broader issues.

During the winter of 1997, the separatist Kosovo Liberation Army began a rebellion that escalated into civil war. Serbian police shot KLA suspects, the KLA drove Serbs from their homes and by the next summer controlled 40 per cent of the region. Milosevic responded with an offensive that resulted in some 800,000 refugees and the death of at least 10,000 – Kosovo was being cleansed of its Albanian majority. Milosevic, who ran the operation single-handedly, was convinced that threats from the West in response were bluffs, but they were not. The bombing of Serbia by NATO forces began in March 1999 and continued until June when Milosevic finally backed down after desperate shortages led to anti-government riots. The Albanians returned and Kosovo gained autonomy but this time no one praised Milosevic as a peacemaker.

Believing he still had popular support, Milosevic ran for re-election in 2000. When it seemed the opposition had won, he tried to rig the results. His efforts provoked mass demonstrations that brought his opponent, Vojislav Kostunica, to power in October. Milosevic's political career was at an end but his troubles had just begun.

In 1999, the UN Special Tribunal for Yugoslavia indicted Milosevic for crimes against humanity for his treatment of the Kosovo Albanians. The Serbian government had no intention of agreeing to his extradition. They wanted him tried at home, to avoid the risk of angry protests from nationalists opposed to foreign justice. The Tribunal feared that a local court would only try Milosevic's lesser offences, but it had no power to force a sovereign government to surrender one of its own citizens. However, when the United States threatened to cut off $100 million of financial aid, Milosevic was brought to the Tribunal headquarters in The Hague in 2001. Charges of genocide in Bosnia and war crimes in Croatia were added. The trial began in 2002 with Milosevic representing himself and refusing to recognize the court's jurisdiction. He obfuscated, delayed the proceedings and threatened to indict NATO for criminal bombing of Serbia. As the trial dragged on inconclusively, Milosevic's health deteriorated. He was found dead in his cell in March 2006.

Index